DIVIDED SOCIETY

CONTEMPORARY IRISH STUDIES

Series Editor Peter Shirlow (The Queen's University of Belfast)

Also available

James Anderson and James Goodman (eds)
Dis/Agreeing Ireland:
Contexts, Obstacles, Hopes

Denis O'Hearn
Inside the Celtic Tiger:
Irish Economic Change and the Asian Model

Peter Shirlow and Mark McGovern (eds)
Who are 'the People'?:
Unionism, Protestantism and Loyalism in Northern Ireland

Gerry Smyth
Decolonisation and Criticism:
The Construction of Irish Literature

Gerry Smyth
The Novel and the Nation:
Studies in the New Irish Fiction

DIVIDED SOCIETY

Ethnic Minorities and Racism in Northern Ireland

Edited by
Paul Hainsworth

Pluto Press

LONDON · STERLING, VIRGINIA

First published 1998 by Pluto Press
345 Archway Road, London N6 5AA
and 22883 Quicksilver Drive, Sterling, VA 20166-2012, USA

Copyright © Paul Hainsworth 1998

The right of the individual contributors to be identified as the authors
of this work has been asserted by them in accordance with the
Copyright, Designs and Patents Act 1988.

British Library Cataloguing in Publication Data
A catalogue record for this book is available from the British Library

ISBN 0 7453 1196 2 hbk

Library of Congress Cataloging in Publication Data
Divided society : ethnic minorities and racism in Northern Ireland/
    edited by Paul Hainsworth.
        p.   cm. — (Contemporary Irish studies)
    Includes index.
    ISBN 0–7453–1196–2 (hardcover)
    1. Northern Ireland—Ethnic relations. 2. Northern Ireland—
Social conditions—1969–   3. Northern Ireland—Race relations.
4. Ethnic groups—Northern Ireland. 5. Minorities—Northern
Ireland. 6. Racism—Northern Ireland. I. Hainsworth, Paul, 1950–
.   II. Series.
DA990.U46D59   1998
305.8'009416—dc21   98–24921
                                                                    CIP

Designed and produced for Pluto Press by
Chase Production Services, Chadlington, OX7 3LN
Typeset by Stanford DTP Services, Northampton
Printed in the EC by Athenaeum Press, Gateshead

Contents

List of Tables

Foreword

Glyn Ford

Within three years of being elected to the European Parliament in 1984, I found myself precipitated into the office of Chair of the first Committee of Inquiry into the Rise of Fascism and Racism in Europe. The Committee was set up primarily in reaction to the success of the French Front National in Dreux in 1983 and the subsequent election to the European Parliament of their leader Jean-Marie Le Pen and nine other MEPs. This was the first harbinger of a very nasty political spring, with further victories for the extreme right in local, regional, national and European elections across Europe – notably in Austria, Belgium, Germany and Italy. As we entered the 1990s, it became abundantly clear that the extreme right and racism were not merely a passing fancy but very much a feature of European politics. Moreover, election results are not the sole measure of the success of racism and extreme right phenomena, as is demonstrated in the pages which follow. Across Europe, for instance, the number of racially motivated crimes has soared and legal and illegal immigrants live in fear. In 1992, I was appointed Rapporteur for a second Committee of Inquiry on Racism and Xenophobia, which produced 77 recommendations for action. In the spring of 1997, a European Union-wide survey undertaken by Eurobarometer showed that 33 per cent of those interviewed openly described themselves as 'racist'.[1]

This book graphically illustrates the problem of racism in Northern Ireland, an area much neglected in the past; partly due to a denial that racism even exists there and partly because of the masking of racism within religious sectarianism. That said, several common factors serve to feed the growth of racism across Europe today: feelings of insecurity, unemployment, fear of the future and loss of faith in the public authorities and the workings of the political establishment. Such feelings provide fertile breeding ground for the racist menace. Education, legislation and employment are three vital factors, if we are to guarantee racism will be driven back into the political margins where it belongs.

Education. We now find ourselves with the first post-war generation which has no living relatives who lived through the horror of the 1930s–40s. As a result, the forgetting has begun. We need to ensure through education that the testimony of the evil of racism is preserved and remains intact, to ensure that future generations are inoculated to help prevent the mistakes of the past from being repeated. On the plus side, we need to illustrate how countries across Europe and the lives of citizens and residents are enriched by the diversity of the different cultures within them.

Legislation. This is important to lay down clearly and help police the limits of intolerance. In this area, the UK leads with the 1976 Race Relations Act which, despite its weakness, remains in advance of other domestic legislation across the European Union. Legislation must be at the forefront in the battle against racism; as is illustrated so poignantly in this book, Northern Ireland has trailed behind here and, as a result, ethnic communities have suffered.

Employment. A European job creation strategy is crucial to help counter sentiments which feed on racism and to undercut the extreme right-wing slogan which, in the Jean-Marie Le Pen version, intones: 'Three million immigrants, three million unemployed, three million immigrants too many', with other national variants substituting appropriate numerical totals. These echo dangerously the slogan of the Austrian Nazi Party in the 1930s: 'One million Jews, one million unemployed, one million Jews too many.'

Governments are always ready to declare their intentions to improve the lot of immigrants and minorities and to fight against racism and xenophobia, yet we have witnessed a simultaneous introduction of repressive measures against these groups. The rhetoric and policies of some mainstream politicians merely reflects the extent to which the centre of political gravity has shifted, often due to the electoral success of the extreme right. Nevertheless, there have been countervailing moves against racism at the European level, particularly in the last two or three years. The setting up of a Council of Ministers Consultative Committee to look at the problem of racism and xenophobia, the 1997 European Year Against Racism and the subsquent establishment of the European Union monitoring observatory in Vienna in 1998 are three which spring to mind. Current attempts by the Council of Ministers Consultative Committee to draw up a Code of Practice on racism and on co-operation with racist parties are to be also welcomed. The European Union recognises that the prime responsibility for combating racism and xenophobia lies with member states but with an important role for regional or local authorities. However, as anyone who has worked in the field knows, there are clear transnational elements and a need for Europe-wide responses to complement and support action already underway in the member states. With the ratification of the Amsterdam Treaty, European Union institutions and legislation will be able to be used to introduce a variety of measures which will begin to address such problems as the need for a race relations directive, outlawing Holocaust denial and working against racism on the Internet.

The contributors to this book examine in detail a number of different areas relating to ethnic minorities in Northern Ireland, recounting at times individual experiences of racism. Europe is faced with a challenge and an overwhelming responsibility to work collectively to eliminate the spectre of racism which continues to plague the continent. Our future lies with a Europe in which we pull together, not against each other, and where all residents have the same rights and duties; where we celebrate our differences rather than trying to eradicate them.

Glyn Ford, MEP
March 1998

Note

1   This opinion poll was carried out between 26 March and 29 April 1997 in the 15 member states at the request of the Employment, Industrial Relations and Social Affairs Directorate (DGV) of the European Commission and was commissioned as part of the European Year Against Racism.

Acknowledgements

Editors rely upon the goodwill and expertise of individuals who are both willing and qualified to read and referee material. This editor is no exception and would like to thank the following for their contributions: Karl Atkin, Greg Benton, Vidya Borooah, Michael Chan, Brian Fitzpatrick, Pauline Ginnety, Derek Hawes, Mary McMahon, Farhat Mansoor, Martin O'Brien, Bill Rolston and Patrick Yu. As well as these individuals, several of the authors also read and commented upon other chapters in the book and I would like to acknowledge their extra inputs. A particular debt of gratitude is due to Glyn Ford, MEP, for his supportive foreword and positive, longstanding work against racism and xenophobia. At Pluto Press, Roger Van Zwanenberg has been a patient, understanding and helpful publisher and Robert Webb and Lisa Jolliffe have provided useful and friendly editorial and marketing advice. Peter Shirlow has been a further source of assistance and encouragement as editor of the Pluto Press Contemporary Irish Studies Series. Tom Fraser and Henry Patterson have also given consistent professional and workplace backing to the editor. In the final stages of shaping the manuscript into a presentable format, Debbie Mitchell and Mary Williamson contributed enormously. Thanks go to Tracey Day for her editorial work on the manuscript. Finally, I would like to acknowledge financial support from the Political Studies Association of Ireland, the Law Research Unit (University of Ulster) and the Research Office (University of Ulster).

Paul Hainsworth
Belfast
March 1998

Notes on Contributors

Mark Bell graduated in 1995 with a BA (Hons) in Government and Law at the University of Ulster. He went on to take up a scholarship at the European University Institute (Florence) and will soon complete his doctorate on the European Union and anti-discrimination policies.

Brice Dickson is a Professor of Law at the University of Ulster. Active in civil liberty campaigns in Northern Ireland since 1981, he is also the editor of *Civil Liberties in Northern Ireland: The Committee on the Administration of Justice Handbook* (3rd edition, 1997). Amongst his numerous publications are books on *The Legal System of Northern Ireland* (3rd edition, 1993) and *Human Rights and the European Convention* (co-editor, 1995).

Hastings Donnan is Professor of Social Anthropology at the Queen's University of Belfast. He is the author of *Marriage among Muslims: Preference and choice in northern Pakistan* (1988) and co-author of *Economy and culture in Pakistan: Migrants and cities in a Muslim society* (1991) and *Islam, globalization and postmodernity* (1994). In 1993, he was appointed editor of *Man: The Journal of the Royal Anthropological Institute*.

Liz Fawcett is Lecturer in Media Studies at the University of Ulster. Prior to this, she was BBC Northern Ireland's education correspondent and produced and presented documentaries on racism/racial discrimination in Northern Ireland. She completed her PhD in 1997 and has published widely on issues on the media, society and politics in Northern Ireland.

Paul Hainsworth is Senior Lecturer in Politics at the University of Ulster. Amongst his publications are *The Extreme Right in Europe and the USA* (editor, 1992) and *The Politics of the Extreme Right* (editor, 1998, forthcoming). He has published widely on European politics, including on Northern Ireland, and is an editor of the journal *Regional and Federal Studies*.

Greg Irwin is a Social Researcher in community relations and social policy issues. He is co-author, with Margaret McKay, of *Political Co-operation in Local Government in Northern Ireland* (1995), and also co-authored, with Seamus Dunn, *Ethnic Minorities in Northern Ireland* (1997). More recently, he has worked with Area Development Management Ltd/Combat Poverty Agency on the Peace and Reconciliation programme in the border counties of the Republic of Ireland, and is currently researching cross-border homelessness with the Simon Community.

Carolyn Mason is Assistant Director of Nursing at the Eastern Health and Social Services Board (Northern Ireland) and Lecturer in Nursing at the Queen's University of Belfast. Formerly a qualified staff nurse and a health visitor, she is the author of numerous articles on health matters. Amongst her recent publications is *Achieving Quality in Community Health Care Nursing* (editor, 1997). Her PhD in Social Anthropology contrasted health provision and take-up in Jamaica and Northern Ireland.

Eleanor McKnight is Co-ordinator, Capacity Building Project with the Northern Ireland Council for Ethnic Minorities. Previously, she worked as Race Relations Adviser and Co-ordinator for the Chinese Welfare Association (Northern Ireland). She has a Postgraduate Diploma in Community Education and, as a trainer and campaigner, has been at the forefront of anti-racism, advocacy work and racial discrimination monitoring in Northern Ireland, also publishing on these themes.

Robbie McVeigh is a researcher with the West Belfast Economic Forum. Formerly a researcher with the centre for Research and Documentation (Belfast), and with the Committee on the Administration of Justice, he has published widely on racism, ethnic minorities, justice and rights. His PhD thesis examined comparatively racism and sectarianism in Tottenham and West Belfast. Amongst his publications is *The Racialization of Irishness: Racism and anti-racism in Ireland* (1997).

Paul Noonan is the Director of the Belfast Travellers' Education and Development Group. Prior to this, he was Co-ordinator for the Northern Ireland Council for Travelling People and also a community worker with the Navan Travellers' Committee. In addition, he has advised government on Travellers' issues and is an executive member of the Northern Ireland Council for Ethnic Minorities. Amongst his publications is *Travelling People in West Belfast* (1994).

Mairead O'Brien is completing a PhD in the Department of Sociology, Queen's University of Belfast. Her fieldwork has focused upon Pakistanis employed in business and professions in Belfast and Craigavon. Also, she is researching the relationship between class and ethnicity.

David Warm is Senior Lecturer in Social Research Methods at the University of Ulster. He has published work on cross-community links and on integrated education in Northern Ireland. His extensive empirical work on Northern Ireland's Jewish community has led to the construction of the Jewish Oral History Project.

Anna Manwah Watson is Director of the Chinese Welfare Association (Northern Ireland). Prior to this, she worked at Barnardos on the Chinese Lay Health Project. Since leaving Hong Kong in 1974, she has worked as an interpreter, social worker and voluntary sector worker. Her dissertation on *The Chinese Community in Northern Ireland* (1991) was accredited at the University of Ulster.

Ciarán White is Lecturer in Law at the University of Ulster. He is Chair of the racism sub-group of the Committee on the Administration of Justice and has researched and published on the impact of law on ethnic minorities in Northern Ireland. Amongst his publications is *Law for Northern Ireland Social Workers* (editor, 1995).

Introduction: Ethnic Minorities and Racism in a Divided Society

Paul Hainsworth

A voluminous body of literature exists on the history, politics and society of Northern Ireland. Much, too, has been written and published globally on ethnicity and racism. This book brings together both of these themes in order to focus upon a greatly neglected area of study and attention: Northern Ireland's smaller ethnic minority communities and their concerns within contemporary society. As a recent survey pointed out (Irwin and Dunn 1997:25): 'The paucity of literature on Northern Ireland's ethnic groups is a lost opportunity to increase awareness amongst the wider population of the existence and experiences of ethnic minorities in the Province, and of their specific and individual cultures and values.' An even more recent report (Mann-Kler 1997:13) underlined this assessment: 'One of the most important effects of the lack of written evidence on the experiences of ethnic minorities in Northern Ireland has been the denial of the existence of racism here.' An initial purpose of this volume, therefore, is to help redress the vacuum identified by the above authors.

A more specific aim of the book is to counter the suggestion that racism is not a problem in Northern Ireland. This particular assertion has been coupled sometimes with the contention that, since there are relatively few persons from ethnic minority communities living in Northern Ireland, the charge of racism is not warranted. As contributors below suggest, this kind of distorted, numbers game logic tends unfortunately to blame the victims rather than the perpetrators of racism. Moreover, as Cant and Kelly (1995:10) explain, the numbers argument is a pessimistic one 'in so far as it suggests that there can be no harmony in a multiracial society'. Moreover, it is a distraction from recognising and attending to the concerns of ethnic minority communities – including countering racism. The same authors warn against racist denialism in Scotland in words which are equally applicable to Northern Ireland: 'The lesson for organisations and for all white people in Scotland is that it is important to listen to what people from black and minority ethnic communities have to say about

1

their own experiences. They make it clear that racism is something which they find in all parts of their everyday lives' (Cant and Kelly 1995:22). Racism, of course, may be targeted against individuals (for instance, in the form of personal attacks, abuse or graffiti) or might be institutional, whereby the unintentional or other outcome of practices or decisions results in discrimination against members of ethnic minority groups. Anthias and Yuval-Davis (1992:12–13) define racism as 'a discourse and practice of inferiorising ethnic groups' – with questions of power and racist effect seen as central to racism. As Husband (1991) also explains, power (notably the control of resources) and prejudice are at the heart of racism. Again, the Committee on the Administration of Justice (CAJ) in Northern Ireland has construed racism as an attitude, action or institution which subordinates a person or group because of colour, 'race' or ethnic difference (CAJ 1992a:1). Northern Ireland, then, does not escape this broad picture and there is a growing body of evidence (see below) to substantiate allegations of racism herein.

Racism is a widespread global phenomenon, but it is exhibited and experienced in distinct contexts and settings. A further key purpose – suggested by the title above – is, therefore, to assess the specificity of racism in Northern Ireland. In this respect, McVeigh's opening chapter situates racism and examines the process by which it has been produced and reproduced in Northern Ireland. He examines the ways in which social relations between the minority and majority ethnic communities have been racialised and explores the intersection of 'race' and other social processes – notably the question of how racism is structured by sectarianism. Elsewhere, Brewer (1992) notes the parallels between racism and sectarianism – without seeking to equate the two phenomena. Both processes, for instance, sponsor discrimination, inequalities, conflictual social relations and individual abuses. Consequently, some voices have interpreted racism and sectarianism as both emanating from the same politics of 'difference' in Northern Ireland (see Chapter 2).

McVeigh again (Chapter 1) highlights how ethnic minorities in Northern Ireland have lived, worked and struggled for equality in a society marked by considerable conflict, division and sectarianism. Inevitably, this has impacted upon ethnic minorities and in various ways. First, several contributors below point to the deterrent effect of sectarian violence and 'the troubles'. Donnan and O'Brien, for instance, contend – in Chapter 10 – that the sectarian nature of politics in Northern Ireland has served to reinforce the outsider feelings of ethnic minorities. Warm (Chapter 11), in part, attributes the numerical decline of the Jewish community to this factor while Irwin (Chapter 9) points to the similarly deterrent effect of violence following the signing of the 1985 Anglo-Irish Agreement. Undoubtedly, too, the nature of politics in Northern Ireland has dissuaded individuals from ethnic minorities from becoming politically engaged for fear of being seen to take sides. As Hainsworth illustrates (Chapter 2), political parties have only recently begun to relate to broad ethnic minority concerns and individuals from ethnic minority communities have even won political party praise for 'keeping their heads down' and 'not bothering anyone' – suggesting an unfortunate view of a would-be passive citizenry expectation for ethnic minority persons.

A further consequence of 'the troubles' has been the tendency to neglect, ignore or minimise ethnic minority problems – such as individual or institutional racism – as the preoccupation with traditional socio-political matters has left scant room for other agendas. In this context, the 1995 screening of *The Hidden Troubles* (*East*, BBC2) was aptly named, with the programme dealing with racist attacks and discrimination in Northern Ireland. However, the concentration on violence here, whilst important and illustrative of the need for better policing of racially motivated crime, was arguably at the expense of underplaying the widespread institutional racism in Northern Ireland. Mann-Kler's (1997) report on racism and exclusion in Northern Ireland provides much evidence of institutional racism and neglect – such as restricted access to health and social services, accommodation problems for Travellers and general absence of mainstreaming of ethnic minority needs in the public sector. Moreover, some of the most glaring examples of neglect include the non-existence of race relations legislation in Northern Ireland for so many years until 1997 (see Chapter 4), the widespread refusal to recognise Traveller culture (see Chapter 8) and cultural insensitivity in public service provision. As regards the last point, Mason (Chapter 5) – presenting an overview of the gap between the rhetoric of health policy and the reality of ethnic minority provision – suggests that the official, well-intentioned attempt to help overcome sectarianised divisions, by providing one standard of health service for all, may have actually worked against the pluralistic requirements (including those of ethnic minorities) within Northern Ireland society. This *de facto* marginalisation is perceived by Fawcett (Chapter 6), too, who argues that the primary focus of media attention in Northern Ireland – again 'the troubles' – has served to put ethnic minorities further down the line.

While 'the troubles', sectarianism and the traditional stuff of Northern Ireland socio-political debate is perhaps bound to dominate various structures and spheres – politics, policing, media, public services and so on – it is important not to lose sight of the growing diversity of society in Northern Ireland. As a recent editorial in the Cultural Traditions Journal, *Causeway* (1998), summed up:

There is a myth that society in the North consists of two monolithic communities – Protestant/unionist and Catholic/nationalist. One of the aims of *Causeway* has been to shatter this misconception, to demonstrate through the lives and experiences of those who live here that there is a much more diverse culture than any casual glance at a newspaper or a TV bulletin would lead you to believe ... Within Northern Ireland, there are many sizeable minorities, people who contribute to our culture in many surprising ways yet lie outside the concept of a two-tradition society.

Noonan (Chapter 8), in fact – assessing anti-Traveller sentiment – categorises sedentarism (defined as a specific form of racism which pathologises and represses nomadism) as a much more hegemonic and telling phenomenon than sectarianism, although the latter is still seen as a process which interacts with and structures anti-Traveller racism. McVeigh (Chapter 1), too, warns against treating Northern Ireland as 'a society marked by a fundamental sectarian bifurcation in which everyone has to be seen as Protestant or Catholic without exception'. The same author even suggests that the process of '[n]egotiating equality for minority ethnic groups teaches broader lessons about how to create a society which is capable of managing and celebrating differences'. Mann-Kler (1977:90) also underlines this approach:

Dealing with difference is difficult in any society, but it is an even greater challenge in Northern Ireland which has been so identified with divisions. Part of creating a peaceful, democratic and inclusive Northern Ireland must be the ability to recognise and celebrate differences without creating diversion.

What various observers, below and elsewhere, are suggesting, then, is that ethnic minority concerns have become part of a burgeoning agenda which values cultural pluralism and celebrates diversity in Northern Ireland. That they have become so is largely the result of ethnic minority communities and their representative organisations working together and with civil liberties bodies, the voluntary sector and other concerned organisations and individuals, at regional, national and international levels. As contributors below point out, a product of this process was the securing of race relations legislation and the struggle to achieve this helped to secure constructive alliances which included the Travellers and ensured that this group were 'named' in the legislation. The inclusion of Travellers helps confirm their status as an ethnic minority group. This is not the place to embark upon a discussion of the Travellers and ethnicity but, nevertheless, it is worth noting David Mason's qualifications on ethnicity: 'Although there is no single, universally accepted definition of ethnicity ... most academic commentators and policy makers would stress some sort of cultural distinctiveness as the mark of an ethnic group' (Mason 1995:12). Hargreaves (1995:27) also suggests that 'the core of ethnicity lies in a sense of group belonging', while Anthias and Yuval-Davis (1992:8) see ethnicity as involving sharing the conditions of existence within a group. Other commentators too (see, for instance, the contributions in Hutchinson and Smith 1996) point to familiar enough components which characterise ethnic groups: such as common ancestry, shared memories, cultural traits, boundaries, sense of difference and some element of solidarity, community, consciousness or belonging. As White (Chapter 4) and Noonan (Chapter 8) illustrate, Travellers in (Northern) Ireland exhibit all the above characteristics as an ethnic group, and will enjoy the protection of the race relations legislation.

Whilst the Race Relations (Northern Ireland) Order 1997 (assessed in Chapter 4) will have its limitations – some of which are raised in the Commission for Racial Equality's Second Review of the Race Relations Act (CRE 1992) and others of which pertain to the specific nature and practice of direct rule and local government weakness in Northern Ireland – it is undoubtedly a step in the right direction and testifies to the strength of civil society and the effectiveness of lobbying, campaigning and speaking out for its introduction. As Dickson and Bell (Chapter 3) explain, 'sound appreciation of international developments in the area of minority rights' has helped the cause of ethnic minorities in Northern Ireland. The same authors point, however, to 'an endless stream of solemn declarations and determined resolutions [from the European Union], but a failure to proceed beyond the rhetoric into the realm of substantive policy actions'. Only relatively recently has the European Union (EU) turned to the issue of racial discrimination. It should be noted, therefore, that the introduction of the Race Relations (Northern Ireland) Order 1997 – in the EU's first designated European Year Against Racism – coincided with the European Union's Amsterdam Treaty, which incorporated a potentially useful anti-discrimination clause, for which ethnic minority groups in Northern Ireland and elsewhere had been lobbying. Coincidentally, these developments were followed by the Labour government's proposal to incorporate the European Convention on Human Rights into UK law, thereby providing further advance in adopting protective legislation (see Chapter 3).

Many of the next steps are flagged up by contributors below. They include the reform of the Race Relations Order/Act to make it more effective (see CRE 1992) – with Northern Ireland possibly playing a vanguard role here. The strengthening and mainstreaming of the Policy Appraisal and Fair Treatment (PAFT) guidelines is a priority identified by many organisations and individuals (see, for instance, McCrudden 1996; 1998). Introduced in 1993, PAFT guidelines (discussed in several chapters below) are intended to provide equality proofing yardsticks for government policy and practice. But critics have pointed to difficulties in evaluating the effectiveness of the guidelines in improving public service provision for groups such as ethnic minorities. As the Committee on the Administration of Justice's Maggie Beirne (1998) has contended: 'If government really implement PAFT, the nature of the decision making process would change beyond recognition.' The target here is to succeed in getting government to put PAFT on a statutory basis. A recent government White Paper, *Partnerships for Equality*, in fact, points out that: 'One of the most radical proposals in the White Paper envisages statutory obligations to promote equality of opportunity throughout the public sector, superseding the current PAFT guidelines' (Secretary of State for Northern Ireland 1998:49). However, there are still concerns to be addressed, for the White Paper actually proposes to replace PAFT by a new statutory obligation upon public authorities to promote equality of opportunity for those groups – such as ethnic minorities – covered by PAFT guidelines. This proposal can be seen as a retreat from the idea of promoting strong, participatory and anticipatory (with equality impact assessments) mechanisms at the core of decision making – as recommended by *inter alia* the official Standing Advisory Commission on Human Rights (SACHR 1997a), McCrudden (1998) and McCormack (1998). Moreover, the historic Good Friday Agreement (1998) went further than the White Paper, supporting 'arrangements for policy appraisal, including an assessment of impact on relevant categories, public consultation, public access to information and services, monitoring and timetables' (quoted in McCormack 1998).

Both the Agreement and the White Paper also float the proposal of a single equality commission for Northern Ireland, created by merging the Fair Employment Commission, the Equal Opportunities Commission, the Disability Council and the 1997 Commission for Racial Equality (Northern Ireland). Whilst the stated intention of government is not to downgrade the work of any of these bodies, but rather to promote equality of opportunity in a broad sense, there may exist genuine anxieties that race relations machinery will be overshadowed before it has time to 'settle in' and make an impact. With government proposals still (in principle, at least) at the consultative stage here, there is obviously much 'to play for': what is crucial is that anti-racist, anti-discriminatory progress is consolidated not weakened by any new structures and developments.

A further goal of anti-racism in Northern Ireland is to ensure that appropriate codes of conduct are drawn up by public bodies, private companies and political parties. Monitoring will be an important part of this process and the new Commission for Racial Equality (CRE) (Northern Ireland) (and/or Equality Commission) will have a key role here – although the workings of this body will also merit monitoring. Monitoring on a wider scale will be enhanced by the setting up, in 1997–98, of the body highlighted by Glyn Ford (see Foreword), the European Monitoring Centre for Racism and Xenophobia in Vienna. A key task of this body will be to provide a pan-European structure for co-operation and networking amongst anti-racist bodies. Anti-racist practice, training and awareness will, of course, be a major concern of ethnic minority organisations and other bodies (such as those providing public duties and services) in Northern Ireland. Complying with the new race relations legislation and working it will be important too.

A further need is to provide reliable figures on the size of Northern Ireland's ethnic minority population in order to identify relevant needs and develop strategies for monitoring them. Therefore, an ethnic minority question in the next census (2001) remains an imperative. Reliable statistics on unemployment are needed, too, to avoid relying on unsubstantiated or misleading generalisations. For instance, when introducing the race relations legislation in the Houses of Parliament, Northern Ireland Minister Baroness Denton (House of Lords 1997:62) first supported the inclusion of Travellers and then proclaimed that employment 'is not a current problem' for ethnic minorities in Northern Ireland. This went against much evidence pointing to a very high unemployment rate amongst Travellers (see Noonan, Chapter 8; Irwin and Dunn 1997; Mann-Kler 1997). The provision of reliable official data needs to be complemented by further research into ethnic minorities in Northern Ireland. For instance, contributors below point to the emergence of assertive (and often well educated) second-generation ethnic minorities currently negotiating their identities in Northern Ireland and beyond. Again, Irwin (Chapter 9) and Donnan and O'Brien (Chapter 10), in particular, point to ethnic minority communities such as the Indian and Pakistani populations as by no means monolithic entities. Ideally, therefore, culturally sensitive research can help to illustrate the diversities within Northern Ireland's ethnic minority communities and enhance understanding of them.

This book is structured to facilitate an understanding of ethnic minority communities in Northern Ireland and their main concerns. Part I focuses upon key issues and Part II provides case studies of ethnic minority communities. Four of these studies cover the largest ethnic minority groups in Northern Ireland, namely Chinese, Traveller, Pakistani and Indian communities. Watson and McKnight (Chapter 7), for instance, portray Northern Ireland's largest (small) ethnic minority community, the Chinese – a relatively young and growing population with historic links to the Hong Kong New Territories and currently facing problems of language (interpreting and translating) institutional racism and intermittent violence. Noonan's assessment of Travellers (Chapter 8) points also to experiences of racism, including widespread refusal to recognise Traveller ethnicity, nomadism and lifestyles. In contrast, Irwin presents a study of the Indian community, showing it to be more integrated within Northern Ireland society and even suspicious, in part, of the merits of race relations legislation. Donnan and O'Brien (Chapter 10), too, point to a Pakistani community in Northern Ireland coming to terms with defining and expressing its own identity (or identities) – 'too western to be Pakistani and too different to be western'. The Jewish community is included as a case study here, in part, to invite comparisons with Jewish diasporic communities elsewhere, but also to take advantage of a unique and rich data source, the Jewish Oral History Project in Northern Ireland (constructed by author David Warm). Moreover, as Harold Ross (1998:32) suggests – writing recently about his Belfast Jewish community – 'the time is getting close when a more concise record will need to be made ... The steady erosion of members by immigration and the inevitability of an ageing community have hastened the process of decline ....' Chapter 11, therefore, makes a timely and important contribution to understanding the Jewish community in Northern Ireland.

Chapters by Fawcett and Donnan and O'Brien below particularly complement Warm's approach by drawing upon exclusive sets of interviews which record the voices of ethnic minorities in Northern Ireland and add to the emerging body of data in this respect. Fawcett's contribution records, too, the views of media elites responsible for reproducing a discourse which assists in marginalising, stereotyping and problematising ethnic minorities, especially Travellers. Drawing notably upon the theoretical work of van Dick, Fawcett assesses how the printed news media contributes towards a process which neglects and denies cultural diversity in Northern Ireland.

The relatively young and growing ethnic minority communities discussed below testify to the cultural diversity within Northern Ireland. This diversity enriches society and militates against reducing all identities to representations of the two main traditions in Northern Ireland. In short, there are other voices to be heard and other stories to be told. However, the experiences of ethnic minorities in Northern Ireland have included marginalisation, racism and inequitable treatment. Difference must not be an excuse for reproducing these phenomena and it is important, therefore, that in the future, mechanisms and processes introduced to reverse these deficits are not sidelined, bypassed or downgraded. As David Mason (1995:12) suggests (referring specifically to Britain but equally applicable to Northern Ireland): 'The final outcome will depend both on the political will of the powerful and on the way ordinary people of all ethnic groups, respond to the challenges of the future.' The challenge, then, is to aspire to a peaceful and inclusive Northern Ireland in which ethnic minority persons are in a position to participate as equal citizens.

PART I

ISSUES

1 'There's no Racism Because There's no Black People Here': Racism and Anti-racism in Northern Ireland

Robbie McVeigh

In 1993, the former Manchester United and Northern Ireland soccer star George Best gave a speech at the Northern Ireland Football Writers' Dinner. Previously, the world-renowned African-Brazilian soccer player Pelé had been generous enough to suggest that Best was the greatest player of all time. Best's reported response to this modesty was to say that Pelé 'wasn't bad for a nigger' (*Belfast Telegraph*, 24 May 1993). Examples like this illustrate all too clearly the existence of racist ideas in Northern Ireland and among people from Northern Ireland. They supplement the testimony of minority ethnic people in Northern Ireland who have identified serious problems with racism (Mann-Kler 1997). Despite this, there is little quantitative analysis of the experience of racism by minority ethnic people in Northern Ireland. Indeed, there are few anecdotal or personal accounts – a major challenge for local historians is the historiography of Northern Ireland's minority ethnic populations. (In this respect, the Jewish Oral History Project is an important model for other communities – see Chapter 11). Given this silence around minority ethnic people and racism, the account of how racism forced one Black migrant, Carl Ford, out of Northern Ireland is particularly illuminating:

Initially I assumed that with all the problems that Northern Ireland has there wouldn't be room for racism as such – but I was proven wrong. My experiences stemmed from the fact that I was Black and there weren't many Black people around. I saw very few there. My experiences were that I'd be out in the street, going shopping, going about my own business and people would shout verbal abuse – 'you black this', 'you black that', 'go home nigger'. I'd be at a bus stop and a bus load of people would go by and every single head would turn and if there was a traffic jam I'd spend the duration of that traffic

11

jam being scrutinised. Or I'd be on my way home from work and the bus would be jam-packed – people would be standing and I'd have a spare seat beside me ... I went to Boots once and there were people at the counter. I said 'Excuse me' and stretched my arm to pick up a particular item and the person that was in front of me turned and took a deep, sharp breath and went bright red – It was that type of experience made me make up my mind to leave ... (Ford 1991)

Carl Ford's encounter with widespread 'hate stares' – which do not simply say, 'you are different' but also 'you do not belong here' – is characteristic of African and Asian experience in Northern Ireland. This kind of testimony immediately repudiates the commonsense notion that, 'there's no racism in Northern Ireland because people are too busy being sectarian'. It does not, however, necessarily help us greatly in understanding where expressions of racism come from and how they relate to sectarian division. Racism is not a 'natural' thing which permeates every society – rather, it is a socially constructed phenomenon. It exists in particular societies because there are reasons for its existence. We need to examine and understand these reasons if we wish to understand and challenge the expression of racism in a particular society. From this point of departure, my analysis 'situates' racism in Northern Ireland.

I have argued elsewhere in terms of the *specificity* of Irish racism (McVeigh 1992a; 1996a). There are aspects of Irishness which encourage the development and reproduction of racism. Here I want to focus on the question of the specificity of Northern Irish racism. This is to ask a question which is deceptively simple: *why* is there racism in Northern Ireland? This encourages us to examine a series of questions which are the subject matter of this chapter. First, we need to look at the question of why racism in Northern Ireland is so commonly and routinely denied. Then, we need to examine the particular characteristics of Northern Ireland which produce and reproduce racism. We also need to look at the ways in which social relations between the minority and majority ethnic communities in Northern Ireland have become racialised. In particular, we need to explore the question of how racism is structured by sectarianism as a dominating feature of Six Counties society. Finally, we need to look at the development of anti-racism in Northern Ireland and review the particular ways in which racism has been challenged within existing ideological and political discourse.

Denying Racism in Northern Ireland

When I first started researching racism in Ireland several years ago at Queen's University, the comment I heard most often was: 'There isn't any problem with racism in Northern Ireland because there aren't any Black people.' This response often came from people within the University where there is quite clearly a minority ethnic population. The implication was that this was not a 'real' community because it involved students rather than permanent migrants. But these ideas are equally common in communities across Northern Ireland. I remember having one conversation in particular. I got the routine response – 'there are no Black people in Ireland'. Five minutes later, we went out to get a taxi and there was a Black person waiting for a taxi. I assumed that this person was a visitor to the area, but thought that this proved a point nevertheless. 'There' I said, 'you do see Black people in Ireland.' 'Oh', he said, 'that's Jane, she lives in number 25 – she baby-sits for us sometimes.' This is an anecdotal illustration of the way in which a commonsense ideological construction – the proposition that there are no minority ethnic people in Ireland – can exist fairly comfortably alongside 'facts' which clearly contradict the proposition. The idea that people of colour in Northern Ireland do not experience racism has also dovetailed neatly with the idea that Travellers in Northern Ireland *cannot* experience racism. While it has rarely been supported by research or analysis, there has long been a widespread commonsense belief that anti-Traveller prejudice can be explained in terms of some paradigm other than racism. More recently, however, the overwhelming evidence in support of the idea that Travellers belong to an ethnic group experiencing systematic racism has begun to gain acceptance (McVeigh 1992b; McDonagh and McVeigh 1996b). In the Race Relations (Northern Ireland) Order which was implemented on 4 August 1997, the British government named Travellers as an ethnic group to be protected by anti-racist legislation. This marked the end of the equivocation around Travellers and racism by central government but it seems likely that Traveller ethnicity will continue to be contested at other levels given the persuasiveness of anti-Traveller racism.

The real question to be asked about racism in Northern Ireland is not *whether*, but *why?* This deceptively simple starting point raises a whole series of related questions. Where does this racism come from? Why does it persist? How do we begin to challenge it? It bears emphasis that the proposition that there is no racism in Northern Ireland because there are no minority ethnic people here is unsound for *two* basic reasons. It is wrong simply because, as this volume clearly illustrates, there *is* a minority ethnic population. There are substantial numbers of minority ethnic people – people of South Asian, Chinese, African and Middle Eastern origin as well as Travellers and Jews. It is also unsound because it is not a requirement of racism that there be minority ethnic people in a given society for racism to exist. There can be racist jokes, for example, in an environment in which there are no minority ethnic people. The notion that there needs to be minority ethnic people before there is racism is dangerous because it inevitably suggests that the presence of Black people in a given society *causes* racism. This kind of analysis feeds directly into racist – and in some cases genocidal – practice because it suggests that the way to get rid of racism is to remove existing minority ethnic people from a society and keep others out.

There are minority ethnic people in Northern Ireland and they experience systematic racism. It is not the absence of racism but rather the relative absence of discussion of racism which makes Ireland different from most European countries. This sense of difference is sometimes what people mean when they say that racism is not a problem in Ireland – they really mean that racism here is *different* from racism in Britain or the US or South Africa. This, of course, is palpably true. They may also be suggesting that racism is not a problem in Northern Ireland because it *is not a problem for white people*. Put cynically, this confirms that the uprisings in Black areas of Britain or the US mark the point at which the consequences of racism impact directly on the lives of most white people. Racism is 'not a problem' when minority ethnic people are being discriminated against or harassed or even murdered, but it is a problem when anger about living in a racist society spills over into confrontation with that society. This has not happened in Northern Ireland, but the absence of uprisings or 'race riots' is a function of the size of the minority ethnic communities rather than the intensity of racism here. The popular construction of Northern Ireland as a society 'free' of racism is itself an example of racism. Challenging the widespread denial of the existence of racism in Northern Ireland is itself a key part of the struggle against racism.

The Racialisation of Irishness

There are a number of different dimensions to Irishness, north and south, which encourage the 'racialisation of Irishness' (McVeigh 1996a). Broadly, these can be dichotomised in terms of *historical legacy* and *contemporary location*. The attention to historical legacy recognises the specific location of Ireland in terms of the wider colonial expansion which first gave rise to racism. Of particular importance, obviously, was the relationship of Ireland to British imperialism and its attendant racism. This history is still manifest in a whole range of ways in Northern Ireland. You have to look no further than some of the streets in Belfast which have most characterised *sectarian* conflict – Bombay Street, Kashmir Road, and so on – to see the intimacy of this connection. It is evident in the apocryphal stories about the non-vernacular architecture of Dungannon police barracks being explained by the fact that its plans were mixed up with those of a hill fort in India or the fact that the City Hall in Belfast is identical to one in Durban, South

Africa. The iconography on the statues around the City Hall further makes clear the relatedness of subjects of Empire from around the world. The peoples of Bombay and Belfast, Derry and Durban were bound together by their supposed role within the great chain of being that was the British Empire. This historical nexus has long influenced the ideas of everybody in the north of Ireland.

The Irish diaspora also took place in the context of British imperial expansion and established Irish blocs in each of the settler colonial formations created by British colonialism in North America, Australasia and Africa. Protestants and Catholics from the north of Ireland played a key role in this migration. These Irish settler blocs in turn created interfaces between Irish people and other colonised and indigenous people – Native Americans and African-Americans in the US, Chinese and Aboriginal Australians in Australia, and so on. While this history is rarely explored in popular constructions of the relationship between northern Irish identity and emigration in venues like the Ulster American Folk Park in County Tyrone, there is no doubting the deep impact it had in terms of Irishness and its attitudes towards people of colour.

The contemporary location of Ireland, north and south, draws on the colonial legacy but also encourages different and newer reasons for racialisation. For example, Irishness may still be influenced by Britishness but it also learns from other European and North American sources. The position of Northern Ireland inside the United Kingdom and the European Union involves it immediately in two packages of racist nationality, immigration and refugee policy. Northern Ireland is inside a United Kingdom committed to prevent 'swamping' from non-white cultures and inside the 'Fortress Europe' being built by the European Union to exclude the peoples of the Majority World. This gives its citizens a new structural relationship with other colonised peoples and potential 'immigrants' which is immediately racialised. Likewise, the empowerment of Irish emigrant blocs in countries of settlement like the US and Australia makes them capable of new racisms which are impossible in Ireland itself. The remarkable number of American presidents with roots in the north of Ireland is an historical example of this but the process also continues in more contemporary forms. For example, many young people from the north of Ireland migrate to the US to work and find themselves in much more frequent contact with people of colour. In this situation most of them are directly empowered because they are both white and Irish. Many of them link into Irish-American racism – an identity that can be consciously Irish and racist. If and when they return 'home', they can bring a new, more actively racist, consciousness with them. In combination, these processes lead to a specific racialisation of Irishness – they mean that racism has become part of Irish identity. It is not simply

something that a few nasty individuals do but part of what it is to be
Irish.

Racism and 'Minority Ethnic People'

Although my analysis will touch on the issue of anti-Irish racism, I am
concerned principally with racism and minority ethnic people. This
means in effect the racism experienced by three key groups: 'people
of colour', Jewish people, and Travellers (recognising of course that
these are not mutually exclusive). There is no consensus – either
within or without these communities – about how to name generically
Northern Ireland's minority ethnic communities. Even without the
inclusion of Jewish and Traveller people, the use of the term 'Black'
as a generic has been disputed (CAJ 1992a:27–8). I adopt the term
'people of colour' advisedly, recognising that it does not enjoy common
usage. (It is worth noting, however, that the term 'people of colour' –
which has enjoyed popularity among minority ethnic groups in the US –
could, if desired, incorporate Jewish and Traveller people who have
themselves been racialised in terms of colour in Ireland. The 'yellow'
Jew was an early anti-Semitic stereotype – likewise the 'yellow Tinker'
or *an Bacach Bui* has been a continual theme in Traveller stereotyping.) It is unarguable, however, that a number of communities are
distinguished by *ethnicity* from the two *majority* ethnic blocs – white
British/Protestant/unionist/loyalist and white Irish/ Catholic/nationalist/
republican. While 'whiteness' may rarely seem to be a defining feature
of either of these blocs, it is clearly a sub-text to both identities.
Witness Willougby de Broke, in a speech at Dromore, County Down
during the 'home rule' crisis in 1912, making the link between unionism,
'race' and Empire:

> The Unionists of England were going to help Unionists over here,
> not only by making speeches. Peaceable methods would be tried first,
> but if the last resort was forced on them by the Radical government,
> the latter would find that they had not only Orangemen against them,
> but that *every white man in the British Empire* would be giving support,
> either moral or active, to one of the most loyal populations that ever
> fought under the Union Jack. (cited in Hepburn 1980:74,
> my emphasis)

Later, in explaining why he was going to take his seat at Stormont
despite the nationalist abstention policy, T.J. Campbell was to argue:
'They had no representative at Westminster or Dublin. Were [Northern
Irish Catholics] to be *the only community of white ones* with no representation anywhere?' (cited in O'Clery 1987:105, my emphasis). So,

both dominant cultural and political traditions in Northern Ireland are underpinned by notions of their own whiteness, however little this seems to impinge on their everyday consciousness. In truth, the absence of discussion of whiteness is in itself a function of hegemony. The assumed identity between whiteness and 'Northern Irishness' is so 'commonsense' that it rarely needs articulation. The debate which opened up in Britain around notions of 'Black Britishness' has hardly begun in Northern Ireland. Of course, the majority unionist and nationalist blocs are in turn profoundly divided on religious and ethnic lines. This is a significant point. In this sense, racism in Northern Ireland can be seen as a *dual majority problem* – inverting one of the classical explanations for sectarian conflict (Jackson and McHardy 1995). By this I mean that minority ethnic groups experience racism in a particular way precisely because the *white majority* ethnic bloc in the north of Ireland is deeply divided. Minority ethnic people find themselves struggling for equality against a backdrop of widespread sectarian division and conflict. This division sometimes makes it uniquely difficult for people of colour to build anti-racist alliances – identity with 'one side' may involve further marginalisation from the other. It is also particularly difficult to negotiate a place for minority ethnic identity in a situation in which there is no consensus around white identity.

'People of colour' in Northern Ireland have their origins, mostly, in the 'Black Commonwealth' – that is, their families have come from countries which were British colonies – and are relatively recent migrants to Northern Ireland. They are predominantly, but by no means exclusively, of South Asian and Chinese origin. The Irish Jewish community is long-established in the north of Ireland (see Chapter 11). In addition, the Irish Traveller community is present in – *and indigenous to* – both parts of Ireland. Since Travellers are a nomadic people, at one level the notion of 'coming from' either Northern Ireland or southern Ireland is inappropriate; but certainly a number of extended families have been particularly associated with the north of Ireland since well before the partition of the island.

Demography and the Minority Ethnic Population in Northern Ireland

Establishing a demographic profile of minority ethnic people in Northern Ireland is not an easy exercise (MCRC 1994; Irwin 1996; McVeigh 1997a). In 1991, for the first time, the UK census asked an 'ethnic' question as well as one in terms of 'country of origin'. The Northern Irish census, however, did not ask an ethnicity question. The consequence of this absence is that only first-generation minority ethnic migrants are recorded even indirectly; second- and third-generation people who are Black British and Black Irish are ignored. Jewish people are recorded as a religious category but not as an ethnic category, so this obviously excludes people who see themselves as ethnically Jewish but do not practise in a religious sense. Travellers are not recorded at all as a discrete category. Travellers were the subject of a Traveller-specific 'census' which only recorded information on Travellers on sites – which suggests that there are 1115 Travellers in Northern Ireland (DOE 1993). This figure ignores the substantial numbers of Travellers in housing and the more nomadic Traveller population (sometimes identified as 'Traders'). So, official statistics are inherently problematic and seriously underestimate the size of the minority ethnic community. A more reasonable estimate is that there are around 20,000 minority ethnic people in Northern Ireland constituting some 1.5 per cent of the population (McVeigh 1997a).

As far as any predictions can be made on these figures, the indications are that the minority ethnic population will grow. The Jewish community in Northern Ireland is the only minority ethnic community with declining numbers (see Chapter 11). Marger has suggested that there will be little increase in the 'Black' population in the Six Counties, arguing that 'restrictive immigration policies and concentration in specific economic roles – would seem to preclude more than minimal population growth in the foreseeable future' (1989:207). This ignores, however, three crucial aspects relevant to the location of the Six Counties within the United Kingdom. First, of course, there will be some migration from Hong Kong in the aftermath of British withdrawal in 1997. The size of this migration is still unclear but no doubt some Hong Kong people, especially those from the New Territories, will join friends and family in Northern Ireland. Second, although as Marger points out, the 'ethnic' restaurant business may have reached saturation point, other areas of minority ethnic business remain almost completely undeveloped in Northern Ireland. Consequently, minority ethnic – especially South Asian – expansion in the business sector in Northern Ireland remains a distinct possibility. Third, Black people are increasingly employed in sectors of the economy which require regional fluidity among staff and there is an increasing penetration of British-based transnational capital into Northern Ireland. Thus, more Black people will be based in Northern Ireland – at least temporarily – because they work for the BBC, Boots, Sainsbury's, and so on. There is no evidence of the recent increase in the numbers of refugees in the south of Ireland being replicated in the north but this development illustrates how quickly the dynamics of ethnic identity can change in contemporary Europe. As the numbers of southern Irish people of colour increases, this will, no doubt, have some impact in the north. All of these developments are likely to lead to an increase in the minority ethnic population in Northern Ireland. In addition to this, the existing minority ethnic population starts from a fertile base – more younger people and fewer older people than the majority population – hence, even without further migration, numbers will increase.

So, there is a growing minority ethnic population in Northern Ireland and this population experiences a growing amount of racism. This racism needs to be challenged. In order to do this, this racism also needs to be situated and explained. As we have already seen, anti-racism without analysis can end up being racist and damaging the communities it aspires to protect. Therefore, we need to look at the specific connection between racism as experienced by minority ethnic people and sectarianism in Northern Ireland. There are a number of different dimensions to the way in which religion and sectarianism structure racism in Northern Ireland. Principal among these are: (1) religious imperialism, (2) the sectarianisation of racism, (3) the connection between loyalist and fascist and racist groups, and (4) the relationship between anti-Irish racism and sectarianism.

Racism and Religious Imperialism

In terms of religious imperialism, there is no doubt that attitudes towards the 'heathen' in the colonies informed racism in Ireland. While most Irish churches have repudiated the overt racism of their past mission, they still invest a great deal of time and effort in missionary work. This work has tended to be laden with racist assumptions and practices. For example, Irish Catholicism manifested elements of anti-Black racism in a specifically religious phenomenon. This is illustrated by the ubiquitous collections for 'Black Babies' which, until recently, were a feature of Irish Church missionary appeals. These necessarily conditioned Irish Catholic people to regard Black people in a particular way – passive, helpless, to be saved by the proselytising ambitions of the Church. Thus, even if the Catholic Church in Ireland was not implicated in the process of Western military and political imperialism and its accompanying racist ideology, it certainly was implicated in a specifically Catholic Western religious imperialism. Catholicism also carried with it an inherent anti-Semitism which became manifest in anti-Jewish boycotts and violence at different times in Irish history (Hyman 1972).

In contrast, Irish Protestant churches tended towards a more Calvinist pro-Semitism – at least in terms of their theological approach to Jewish people. Their practice was, however, less salutary in terms of racism and the colonial process. The relationship of the Protestant bloc in Ireland to Western imperialism – particularly, of course, to British imperialism – was even less ambiguous than that of the Catholic Church. Although Presbyterian radicalism ensured that Belfast would not benefit from the slave trade, subsequent developments within the

Protestant bloc secured general support for, and involvement in, the process of British imperialism in Asia and Africa. This sometimes encouraged a more thoroughgoing racism and toleration of racism amongst Irish unionists. For example, it is doubtful whether a racist of the ilk of Enoch Powell would ever be given a political home by Irish nationalists. Nor indeed would it be acceptable for an Irish nationalist representative to sit with a group of racists and fascists in the Group of the European Right in the European Parliament, as did the Ulster Unionist Party MEP John Taylor.

Racism and Sectarianism

Sectarianism pervades life in Northern Ireland. Not surprisingly, it also structures the way in which racism is reproduced and experienced. The old story about the question of whether someone is a Protestant Jew or a Catholic Jew has assumed the status of the most venerable of sectarian clichés. But this kind of sectarianisation is also part of people's real experience – the same question has recently been reworked in terms of the Muslim community (see Chapter 10). This kind of sectariani-sation often affects people of colour in the north. Witness Carl Ford whose experience of racism in Northern Ireland was cited earlier: 'The analogy that I used to describe myself there was you've got two football teams ... and each person on the pitch is taking shots at one goalie – in Northern Ireland I was that goalie' (Ford 1991). While he uses soccer as an analogy, it has also been one of the sites for racist abuse. Some of the reason for this is simply the aping of the racist abuse of Black sportspeople which is common in British soccer but in Northern Ireland this phenomenon is simultaneously sectarianised. In a perverse contradiction, Linfield soccer club, whose identity is closely linked to loyalist sectarianism, have had their Black players racially abused by opposing fans. Likewise, Black players at Cliftonville, whose association is more Catholic and nationalist, have suffered serious verbal harassment (*Irish News*, 2 March 1995).

In Northern Ireland, anti-Traveller racism cannot be abstracted from sectarianism any more than 'imported' racisms can. As Butler argues:

> In the author's experience in Derry and Tyrone, there is indeed a sectarian aspect involved, in that the Travellers are at least nominally viewed as 'Catholics' and their 'brogue' defines them as Irish. It is sometimes said that the 'South' should deal with its own problem and not export it 'up North' while some of the naked sectarian prejudice that is present in our settled society is from time to time aimed at the Traveller population. This sectarian factor is present and may be seen to be reflected in the voting patterns at local

council meetings when the 'itinerant problem' is raised. (Butler 1985:20)

This has meant that, over the last 30 years, Travellers in the north have stopped visiting some 'Protestant' areas which were historically Traveller sites, including Larne, Portadown, and areas of Belfast (Butler 1985:11–12). No doubt this has had the consequence of focusing anti-Traveller prejudice in Catholic areas while it remains relatively unfocused in Protestant areas. In this sense, sedentary Catholics tend to attack Travellers as a specific and pathological ethnic group, Protestants tend to regard them as a manifestation of the most degenerate aspects of Catholicism and Irishness. In other words, 'Catholic' anti-Traveller prejudice is classically racist while 'Protestant' anti-Traveller sentiment also carries a sectarian dimension. Whatever these differences, the reality is that there is often little welcome from either settled community. As Butler recognises:

While the sectarian factor is present and is a cause for concern, I would immediately point out that it is in no way cut and dried. 'Unionists' have helped Travellers and some will take the more positive of attitudes towards the problems that arise while some 'Nationalists' are seen to be just as bigoted and biased against Travellers as it is possible to be. (Butler 1985:20)

It bears emphasis that minority ethnic people have never been simply passive observers of this kind of sectarianisation. At times this has meant that minority ethnic people have played a part in sectarian conflict. Boyd records how in the 'Lady's Day Riots' of 15 August 1872:

One of the leaders of the eviction gangs was George Henry Thompson, a negro who lived among the Protestants of Shankill Road. Andrew Doherty, a member of the Royal Irish Constabulary, first saw Thompson on Saturday morning, leading a mob of about 2000 people towards the home of a widow named Donaghy. Constable Doherty was to see Thompson several times that day and on every occasion he was driving Catholic families from their homes. When he led the attack on the widow's house, Thompson was shouting, like a man demented, about papists and Fenians ... That morning, Thompson's followers drove more than twenty Catholic families from their homes ... For several weeks after these incidents the negro kept under cover, but Constable Doherty saw him in Ligoneil at the beginning of September and immediately put him under arrest. Thompson was eventually charged with being the leader of a riotous mob and was sentenced to two years in prison,

with hard labour, at the County Antrim Assizes of 1873. (Boyd
1969:96–7)

Despite examples like this, however, most minority ethnic people have
tried to find a place for themselves distinct from the traditional sectarian
blocs. They have often intervened in ways which emphasise the
difference of minority ethnic communities from the two majority
ethnic blocs while simultaneously marking their specific place and right
to have a role within the society. For example, at the outbreak of the
current phase of 'the troubles', the *Irish News* (25 August 1969) carried
a headline which read, 'Jewish Councillor offers services as
Ombudsman'. The story reported how:

A Jewish town Councillor last night offered his services to the
Northern Ireland Government as an ombudsman. Councillor Sam
Daly of Newtownabbey U.D.C. who describes himself as the 'only
Jewish Councillor in Northern Ireland' said he would be the ideal
choice to adjudicate between Protestant and Catholic. Mr. Daly said
he had already made approaches to Stormont on the matter.

This kind of approach still informs the struggle for minority ethnic
people to forge a distinctive place for themselves in Northern Ireland
alongside the dominant sectarian blocs. In essence, this involves the
recognition that Northern Ireland is and has long been a multi-ethnic,
multicultural society, rather than one permanently and exclusively
dichotomised on Protestant/Catholic lines.

Racism and Fascism

There has long been an overlap between the British right and conservative forces in the north of Ireland. The institutional link between
the British Conservative Party and the Ulster Unionist Party was one
example of this. These links sometimes coalesce indirectly around
racism. For example, after his banishment from Conservative politics,
Enoch Powell was not recruited by the Ulster Unionists *because* of his
views on race and racism. Neither, however, did the fact that he was
such an important icon for the racist right *prevent* them from offering
him a political home. Likewise, when he was an MEP, John Taylor –
the current Ulster Unionist Party deputy leader – saw no great problem
with being associated with European fascists and racists in the Group
of the European Right led by Jean-Marie Le Pen. It seems likely that
this choice was made less in terms of convinced racism than populist
right-wing views; nevertheless, the alliance with fascist and racist
parties was made in the face of widespread concern about the rise in
racism and fascism across Europe.

This overlap with organised racism still surfaces in different ways which are, once again, connected to sectarianism. *Ulster* – magazine of the Ulster Defence Association (UDA) – captured this racism/sectarianism nexus succinctly in a song entitled 'The Pope's a Darkie'. This kind of racism has also been evident in the overlap between loyalism and British racist and fascist groups. In particular, soccer clubs like Linfield (the name often appears as LinNField on graffiti) and Crusaders have a section of supporters who carry fascist and racist iconography and have links with Nazi groups like Combat 18 (*News Letter*, 6 March 1996; *News Letter*, 11 March 1997). These links are primarily with British fascist groups but local interest in racist organisations also extends elsewhere. In 1995, the *Irish News* interviewed Dr Edward Fields, the editor of a North American racist publication with subscribers in Belfast, who 'sang the praises of white Belfast': 'It was clean and very nice, very safe. It was amazing to see people walking the streets all night long. When I was there I saw only one black. It's a lovely place to live!' (18 November 1995).

At a more structured level, however, the process has been largely one-way in that racist and fascist groups have targeted Northern Ireland for recruiting 'political soldiers' without any developed response. Every now and then, there is evidence of British racist and fascist groups trying to mobilise support in Northern Ireland around racism (*Sunday Life*, 29 January 1995). While the 'Third Position' element of the National Front (NF) has argued that 'the British revolution starts in Ulster', this attention has not always been reciprocated. Although NF iconography certainly has some appeal to loyalist youth, this has remained largely unfocused. Indeed, the loyalist Progressive Unionist Party has done some of the most important anti-racist and multicultural work of any political party in the north (see Chapter 2). The NF presence in East Belfast ended abruptly when the UDA characterised them as 'tossers and perverts' after they found that the NF locally was selling the work of Colonel Ghaddaffi (*Searchlight* 1989:168:3). The UDA was also reputed to take a certain pleasure in sending one of its minority ethnic members on delegations to meet with racist British groups. Despite the belief that Northern Ireland holds enormous potential for British fascism, there is no simple way to graft British racism onto Northern Irish sectarianism. This does not mean, however, that the two do not influence and reinforce each other. The danger of a mobilisation of populist, right-wing racism remains.

Sectarianism and Anti-Irish Racism

The overlap between Northern Irish sectarianism and British racism brings us full circle and raises difficult conceptual questions. Sectarianism is connected to British racism; British racism has a specifically anti-Irish dimension to it; is sectarianism therefore really racism? But anti-Irish racism can attach to unionists as much as nationalists; is anti-Irish racism really sectarianism? There are no simple answers to these questions. They do, however, point up some of the complexity of the connection. What is clear is that there are similarities between racism and sectarianism. Moreover, they overlap at points. This was brought home recently with the tragic death of a young person of colour in the aftermath of the Drumcree standoff around Orange marches in Portadown:

> Sectarian hatred caused by the siege of Drumcree has led to the death of an 11-year-old Portadown boy, his mother said last night. Darren Murray, from Garvaghy Park, died in Belfast's Royal Victoria Hospital yesterday, two days after he was knocked down by a van on Corcrain Road in Portadown. He had been running towards loyalists who had gathered at an interface area and were shouting taunts. Darren, a dark-featured Catholic, was often the subject of abuse. 'They shouted nigger, Fenian nigger ... he hopped off his bike and ran across the road. He never looked and the van just hit him. The crowd cheered when he was hit. They shouted "Yeah, Up the UVF, Up the UVF" his 14-year-old sister Maria said'. (*Irish News*, 11 October 1996)

For different reasons, many actors – including the British government and minority ethnic communities in Northern Ireland – would prefer to separate racism and sectarianism, analytically and practically. It is more and more difficult to do this, however, as the conceptual distinction between anti-Irish racism and sectarianism becomes increasingly blurred (McVeigh 1998). The Race Relations Order (Northern Ireland) 1997 will lend further impetus to the necessity of addressing the sectarianism/racism nexus. The British Race Relations Act (1976) now clearly protects Irish people in Britain, with some 5 per cent of the work of the Commission for Racial Equality (CRE) being taken up with Irish cases (CRE 1997; Hickman and Walter 1997). This carries with it the strong implication that almost identical legislation will cover Irish people in Northern Ireland where sectarianism is often unambiguously anti-Irish in content. Thus, the issue of the racism/sectarianism interface is going to increasingly structure the development of racism and anti-racism in Northern Ireland (McVeigh 1998).

Is Irish Racism Different, North and South?

We have already seen that there is a specificity to Irish racism. But this begs a further question in terms of the comparison of the two state formations in Ireland. There are obvious differences in emphasis between north and south. Moreover, states play a crucial role in the reproduction of racism. Given this, it is possible to argue that it is more appropriate to examine 'Northern Ireland racism' and 'Republic of Ireland racism' as two essentially separate entities.

Certainly, racism in the north continues to be structured by sectarianism in a way that racism in the south does not. Rather obviously in terms of the power blocs within both states, racism in the north tends to be 'Protestant' while racism in the south tends to be 'Catholic'. Ultimately, however, the commonality between racism in the two states is much more significant than these differences. It would be erroneous to construct divorced 'Northern Ireland' and 'Republic of Ireland' racisms as if these were separated discourses. For example, the *Irish News* (4 November 1997) recently recorded how:

A West Belfast man yesterday hit out at 'racist' Garda officers who demanded to see his passport while on a bus to Dublin. David Carlin said police by-passed all of the passengers on board and questioned him and a Chinese woman at the back of the bus ... 'They asked her for her passport, but she was searching for it and couldn't find it. They then turned and asked me for my passport and I told them they weren't getting it. I said to them that if they had asked everyone else on the bus for their passports I would have done the same. When I asked why they had picked on me and the Chinese girl, they said it was the law.' Mr Carlin, a civil servant, said he was born and bred in West Belfast and was subjected to 'blatant racism'.

This example is a timely, if unfortunate, reminder of *continued commonality* within the Irish social formation and the continued necessity for transborder political analysis in Ireland. Racism in the north of Ireland has more in common with racism in the south than it does with racism in Britain, despite the importance of the state within the construction of racism. Although racism is not identical either side of the border, Irish racism has an all-Ireland specificity which separates it from other racisms.

Irish racism cannot be explained simply in terms of the development of racism elsewhere. Thus, it is not the same as the imperial conceit which structured the way in which white British people 'made sense' of post-war Black migration to Britain. Neither is it rooted in the colonial theft and slavery which underpins white identity in North America. Irish racism has its basis in the strength of community in Ireland. This strength developed in a rural setting but has been reworked in an urban environment. In the north especially, it has been reinforced by the process of sectarian conflict and social closure. Within the 'security' of supposedly homogeneous community, any outsiders have been problematic. Travellers, Jewish people and, more recently, people of colour have threatened such notions of community.

Of course, there is nothing uniquely Irish about this but it is a defining characteristic of Irish racism which raises significant questions about the relationship between racism and notions of 'community'. In this sense, the existence of racism in Ireland can play an important role in problematising the notion of community in other racialised situations. This suggests that a polity which repudiates racism and defends equality and human rights should focus less on 'community development' and more on the task of creating a society which recognises, cherishes and, where necessary, arbitrates between, very different and sometimes conflicting identities. Such an approach places less of an emphasis on 'community' and more on 'society', less on homogeneity and more on heterogeneity. This project involves much more than ethnic difference since it also includes differences based on class, gender and sexuality. Nevertheless, it should be at the core of any attempt to address racism in a way which recognises the integrity of both the right to *equality* and the right to *difference*. It should underpin anti-racism in the Northern Ireland context.

The Development of Anti-racism in Northern Ireland

Not surprisingly, it was minority ethnic groups themselves that first began to challenge racism in Northern Ireland. As soon as minority ethnic community associations developed they recognised that racism was one of the issues which they had to address. As we have already seen, these interventions were often low-key and carefully worded. They rarely characterised themselves as anti-racist and were more likely to talk in terms of the contribution of minority ethnic groups to society. There were also local white and settled people willing to challenge different manifestations of racism. The earliest examples of this involved Travellers. Almost from the inception of the state, unionist politicians at Stormont were keen to make political capital out of attacking Travellers. Travellers were defended by different politicians including Cahir Healy and the redoubtable Sheila Murnaghan. These challenges to racism were never couched in terms of racism or anti-racism but they did begin to recognise Travellers' right to difference, albeit in a way that was in itself stereotyping of Travellers. In 1956, in the face of moves to introduce anti-Traveller legislation, Healy argued: 'Does the Minister not realise that these people are the only picturesque features of Northern Ireland ... and that if they disappear the Ulster Tourist Development Association will lack one of its chief assets' (Commons Debates (NI) 1956:2041–2).

By the 1960s the debate had shifted slightly as those supportive of Travellers' rights moved away from simply resisting anti-Traveller measures and towards advocating action in support of Travellers. In 1965, for example, Murnaghan asked 'what steps the Minister of Development was taking to provide sites for itinerants evicted by local authorities from sites they customarily occupy' – a question which remains depressingly familiar in the 1990s: 'I just want to ask the Minister whether the Government are prepared to accept responsibility for a particular category of society which is part of our system whether or not he approves of it' (Commons Debates (NI) 1965:1016). A supplementary question in this debate made an interesting comparison with the situation of African-Americans in the US illustrating the movement towards making sense of Traveller disadvantage in terms of racism:

Might I ask the right hon. Gentleman to realise that we are not living down in Dallas and that these poor unfortunate people are members of the human family for whom we have responsibilities? Does he not believe that the local authorities have a moral obligation not only to provide for these people's temporary well-being but to look after their future well-being? Is not that obligation being terribly violated day by day by the refusal to give them the facilities which are represented in this question? (Commons Debates (NI) 1965:1016)

To some extent, this kind of recognition of difference took a step backwards as settled people began to intervene more actively in 'support' of Travellers. In parallel with the rest of Ireland, the Travellers' Support Movement in Northern Ireland first developed as an expressly assimilationist movement through itinerant settlement committees – Travellers would be 'helped' by becoming absorbed into the settled community (see Chapter 8). Travellers and settled activists uncomfortable with the assimilationist tone of early practice began to develop an analysis of Traveller oppression which explained Traveller disadvantage in terms of ethnicity and racism. Groups like the Northern Ireland Council for Travelling People and the Belfast Travellers' Support Group started to popularise the use of racism when explaining anti-Traveller prejudice and discrimination. This was the first time that racism had been used in a sustained way in the Northern Ireland context.

It is not insignificant, however, that among the first anti-racist groups in the north were the Anti-Nazi League – a British-based coalition against racism – and SHARP – Skinheads against Racial Prejudice – a local chapter of a North American anti-racist group. It has been fairly typical of anti-racist organisations in Northern Ireland that their practice is informed – indeed, sometimes directly caused – by anti-racism elsewhere. In this sense, and with the notable exception of Travellers, *majority* ethnic anti-racism was rarely organic to Northern Ireland. Skinheads became anti-racist because progressive Skins in the US were anti-racist; Trotskyite groups set up anti-racist organisations because their 'sister' organisations were doing the same in Britain; social workers became anti-racist because social work practice in Britain demanded that they take racism seriously; and so on. There was often nothing wrong in these developments and they gave anti-racist work a new impetus. They did, however, carry with them the danger of simply importing anti-racist practice wholesale. Even when this had been successful elsewhere, there was no guarantee of its efficacy or appropriateness in the Northern Ireland context. Worst of all, this could often be anti-racism without local minority ethnic involvement. In other words, white people rarely stopped to ask whether local minority ethnic people – who were, after all, the targets of racism in Northern Ireland – wanted all this anti-racist work in the forms it took. If they had asked, they might have found that the last thing which many minority ethnic people wanted was anti-fascist and anti-racist marches which alerted proto-racists and fascists to the fact that they had a vulnerable minority ethnic population in their midst. If white and settled anti-racist practice is to avoid becoming itself racist, it must be rooted in the analysis and demands of the minority ethnic population it aims (or claims) to protect.

Anti-racism and the Campaign for Legislation

As the Travellers' Support Movement began to use a more sustained analysis of racism in Ireland and the way that it affected one particular minority ethnic group, this development dovetailed with the concerns of others working in areas touching the lives of people of colour in Northern Ireland. This produced an alliance of interests working through the Committee on the Administration of Justice (CAJ) – a Belfast-based human rights and civil liberties group. The CAJ, in alliance with minority ethnic organisations, took a lead role in demanding effective anti-racist legislation for Northern Ireland. The campaign for effective legislation was given definitive expression in a groundbreaking conference on *Racism in Northern Ireland* and the subsequent conference report (CAJ 1992a).

While groups were often wary of addressing the same agendas as, say, the Black British community, the campaign for anti-racist legislation had the backing of all the main minority ethnic organisations. This campaign had three key demands – distinct anti-racist legislation, a distinct anti-racist body (a Commission for Racial Equality, Northern Ireland) and the inclusion of Travellers as a named ethnic group protected by any legislation. The CAJ alliance also exerted effective international pressure on the British government through the United Nations International Convention on the Elimination of All Forms of Racial Discrimination and its constituent committee, the Committee on the Elimination of Racial Discrimination (CERD). The absence of British NGOs at the CERD in 1993 left the way clear for a focus of discussion on the absence of legislation in Northern Ireland. This proved highly embarrassing for the British Home Office which had not anticipated any concern with Northern Ireland.

The campaign for anti-racist legislation culminated in the publication of a draft Race Relations Order for Northern Ireland in July 1996. The success of this campaign was remarkable for a number of reasons. First, there was little institutional backing for the demand. Other than the British CRE, few influential organisations or political parties were pushing the demand for legislation. (Although few were actively opposing it either.) There certainly were concerns in government about the implications of anti-racist legislation for Northern Ireland but these were informed more by concerns about 'read-across' into other areas of law than equivocation on the moral imperative to protect Northern Ireland citizens from racism. In particular, government was concerned about the implications of protecting Travellers in Northern Ireland while they further attacked their rights in Britain through interventions like the Criminal Justice Act. Alongside this were concerns about new remedies for sectarian discrimination. The CRE had long admired the powers of the Northern Ireland-specific Fair Employment Act and Fair Employment Commission (FEC). The remit of the FEC, however, was limited to political and religious discrimination in employment. The 1976 Race Relations Act (RRA), while more limited in powers and sanctions, has a wider reference – its covers housing and education specifically as well as other goods and services (see Chapter 4). These are areas where there is still institutionalised discrimination in Northern Ireland. Of course, this discrimination sometimes happens with good reason and popular support – for example, the sectarian ghettoisation of housing probably enjoys the support of both sectarian blocs. Nevertheless, if Protestants and Catholics are ethnic groups, and if the RRA applied in Northern Ireland, then housing policy would be institutionally racist under the Act. It remains unclear how important these different read-across implications will prove to be.

Out of the campaigns and alliances around legislation came the development in 1994 of NICEM (the Northern Ireland Council for Ethnic Minorities). NICEM was the first body rooted in the different minority ethnic organisations to take a strategic cross-ethnic alliance. It suggested that the 'initial idea for NICEM developed from the linkage and working relationship between the Chinese, Indian and the Travelling communities, which together with the Committee on the

Administration of Justice, have been to the fore in campaigning for the introduction of effective Race Relations legislation in Northern Ireland since 1991' (NICEM 1996a). NICEM defines itself as, 'a voluntary sector, membership-based, umbrella organisation representative of ethnic minority groups and their support organisations in Northern Ireland'. Its mission statement says: 'NICEM is committed to combating racial discrimination in Northern Ireland, campaigning to have effective Race Relations legislation to outlaw racial discrimination and also effective social policy to eradicate institutional racism in Northern Ireland' (NICEM 1996a). So, the setting up of NICEM represents an important step forward as a representative alliance of minority ethnic groups in Northern Ireland with racism a central concern in their work. The alliance between the Travellers' Support Movement and other anti-racist groups has been particularly strong in Northern Ireland. As we have seen, the Travellers' Support Movement took a lead in setting the agenda *vis-à-vis* racism. In other situations the Traveller experience has often been left out of anti-racism. For instance, in Britain political solidarity around racism has been strong between the sedentary Irish population and other minority ethnic groups, but the specific experience of Irish Travellers (and 'Gypsies') is often missing from this anti-racist alliance. Whatever the many limitations of anti-racism in Northern Ireland, the strength of the political and analytical alliance between anti-racists, Travellers and other minority ethnic people is something to be cherished and developed.

Racism, Anti-racism and Future Developments

It seems likely, then, that anti-racism in Northern Ireland is about to enter a second phase. The advent of NICEM marked an important historical step forward for minority ethnic groups in general and anti-racism in particular. It is to be hoped that the racism they address remains as ill-focused as it has been historically. While racist harassment and discrimination remain serious problems, the key problem is more one that is captured by the notion of 'parity of esteem' which has been much abused within the majority ethnic population but rarely applied towards minorities. This means, of course, recognising the equal rights of minority ethnic people within Northern Irish society but it also means recognising and celebrating the specific contribution which they make to that society.

New developments will probably broadly mirror similar earlier developments in Britain and elsewhere. There will be a movement away from the campaign for an effective legislative framework against racism towards more specific demands for equality in a whole range of service provision. Likewise, it seems likely that the focus will turn from the broad concerns of the whole minority ethnic community towards addressing the specific needs of different groups of community members – women, young people, and so on. These changes of political focus are likely to be accompanied by changes in the politics of identity. As the present first-generation migrant leadership is succeeded by more and more second- and third-generation people, there will be developments around newer, ever more complex identities. Younger people of colour have to come to terms with their own relationship to the traditional identity question in the north of Ireland of being Irish or British or Northern Irish. But they also have to decide how this connects with their minority ethnic identity – do they become 'Black Irish' or 'Black Northern Irish' or 'Black British' or something else instead (see Chapter 10)? Irish Travellers and Jewish people face similar decisions. This process has hardly begun for most of the minority ethnic communities but it will involve a different emphasis in terms of the role that racism plays in structuring each of these identities.

The empowering of the minority ethnic community will also entail anti-racism being more directed and controlled by minority ethnic people. There is a specific need in the Travellers' Support Movement for Traveller involvement and control but this is mirrored in terms of broader anti-racist work and interventions. We are likely to see minority ethnic people taking control of minority ethnic organisations and setting the agenda in terms of the struggle against racism.

Conclusion

Despite the routine denial, there is racism in Northern Ireland and it is a 'problem' – for both white people and people of colour. Addressing the question of *why* is there racism suggests that there are particular characteristics of society in Northern Ireland which produce and reproduce racism. These include an historical legacy of racialised relationships with other colonised peoples as well as a contemporary relationship to racism in Britain and Europe alongside a deep-seated 'indigenous' anti-Traveller racism. When we look at the ways in which social relations between the minority and majority ethnic communities in Northern Ireland have become racialised, it becomes clear that racism is structured by sectarianism as a dominating feature of Six Counties society. In other words, racism in Northern Ireland has a certain specificity. On the one hand, the contrast between systematic staring in Northern Ireland and systematic racist violence in other parts of Europe might appear relatively positive; on the other, the isolation and social exclusion associated with racism in Northern Ireland can sometimes make the experience even more unbearable than situations in which there are larger minority ethnic communities. Awareness of this specificity must in turn inform approaches to anti-racism. The aspirations of minority ethnic communities in Northern Ireland are not necessarily the same as those of communities of colour in the south of Ireland or Britain or the rest of Europe.

Over the past 30 years, it has become increasingly difficult to represent Northern Ireland as a society marked by a fundamental sectarian bifurcation in which everyone has to be seen as Protestant or Catholic without exception. While this transformation has been most obviously marked by the ubiquity of Chinese and Indian restaurants and take-aways, it has involved a much more complex ethnicisation of Northern Irish society. As newer migrants have supplemented the older Jewish and Traveller populations, Northern Ireland has become a society with a host of different minority ethnic groups – a multicultural and increasingly *intercultural* society. More than Northern Irish eating habits have changed: from the increasing numbers of minority ethnic business people to the growing awareness of cultural diversity in schools, Northern Ireland itself has been transformed in a way that is significant and beneficial for everyone. If more racism has been the downside of this transformation; more anti-racism has been the reverse. The development of a stronger anti-racist culture has important benefits for majority as well as minority ethnic communities. It also has wider ramifications in terms of other social divisions in Northern Ireland. Negotiating equality for minority ethnic groups teaches broader lessons about how to create a society which is capable of both managing and celebrating difference.

2 Politics, Racism and Ethnicity in Northern Ireland

Paul Hainsworth

In this chapter some of the political dimensions of racism and ethnic minority issues are explored. First, some initial observations situate racism and ethnic minorities in Northern Ireland in the context of traditional 'orange and green' politics. Second, the birth of race relations legislation in Northern Ireland in 1997 is portrayed as largely the result of effective, focused lobbying and mobilisation from ethnic minority groups, civil liberties bodies and voluntary organisations, rather than as an initiative from locally or nationally based political parties. In fact, it is argued here that when the campaign for such protective machinery was waged vigorously by the former collectivities, only then did the body politic begin to explore and take up ethnic minority demands in any significant fashion. Furthermore, the process of responding to ethnic minority concerns has been uneven: some political parties in Northern Ireland moved noticeably quicker than others, some have still to develop their policy perspectives in this sphere. Crucially, too, the main parties of government in the United Kingdom – Conservative and Labour – came round very slowly to the idea that race relations legislation was essential if citizens in Northern Ireland were not to be permanently deprived of the basic, protective rights enjoyed elsewhere in the UK. This chapter first examines political party perspectives on race relations, racism and ethnic minorities in Northern Ireland, looking principally at the recent manifesto and other relevant party sources; this is followed by an examination of the politics of Travellers to illustrate how parties have responded to the concerns and presence of this particular ethnic minority community. What is evident here is that political party representatives have paid considerable, intermittent attention to Travelling People but, often, the end result has not been positive for this community, as some politicians have contributed to a racist discourse which negatively stereotypes Travellers and fails to acknowledge the validity of their lifestyles. Also, there has been some political opposition to defining the Travellers as an ethnic group and to including them in the remit of the Race Relations (Northern Ireland) Order 1997.

Context

Until quite recently, concern for bringing in race relations legislation for Northern Ireland and for formulating policies on ethnic minority issues has not featured too conspicuously on the agendas of political parties and other sections of society. Preoccupation with traditional communal politics and divisions has tended to leave little space for 'other' agendas (or the agendas of 'others'). An editorial (entitled 'We must cherish our minorities') in the (nationalist) *Irish News* (11 May 1996) expressed the view that: 'So blinkered have the rest of us become by our grim sectarian vision, that we have closed our eyes to the plight of our neighbours who trace their roots to other parts of the world.' Eoin Ó Broin (1997:54), also, has suggested that the politics of Northern Ireland 'allows public representatives, opinion makers, policy developers and sections of the general public to ignore the other fault-lines along which discrimination and exclusion takes place beyond the pale of mainstream politics'. In an important and timely research report on families, racism and exclusion in Northern Ireland, Deepa Mann-Kler (1997:5) specifically dates the advent of public debate surrounding ethnic minorities: 'It was only since the ceasefires in 1994, that matters concerned with ethnic minorities have been deliberated in the wider public arena in Northern Ireland.'

The same author also elaborates upon another by-product of the politics of Northern Ireland, explaining how ethnic minority persons have been reluctant to approach the Royal Ulster Constabulary (RUC) force to report incidents of racial harassment, because 'the troubles' were perceived to be the police's main, overriding concern. Thus in the words of one ethnic minority youth: 'They're more dealing with the troubles than anything else. If you had a problem they would deal with it, but probably wouldn't pay as much attention to it as if it was Catholic or Protestant' (Mann-Kler 1997:79–83). Lack of confidence in the police is a theme picked up by Irwin and Dunn's research study, *Ethnic Minorities in Northern Ireland* (1997:116–17), with the Chinese community identified as being dissatisfied with the failure of the police to prevent recent crimes against them. In response to such criticisms, the RUC did begin – in the mid-1990s – to adopt a more conscious policy towards ethnic minorities, including monitoring of attacks, deployment of Harassment Support Officers and liaison with ethnic minority organisations. The Police Authority for Northern Ireland (PANI), via a 1995 community consultation exercise, also accepted the necessity of placing more constructive focus on ethnic minority and race relations matters: 'There can be little doubt that a police service must have an anti-discrimination ethos if it is to gain credibility with ethnic minority groups. Race relations must, therefore, be given a high priority within the RUC and should be an integral part of the planning process in developing future policing strategies' (PANI 1995:5.5.19).

What emerges then – certainly up until recent times – is a context in which traditional and sectarian politics and reflexes have tended to crowd out significant discussion, let alone prioritisation, of ethnic minority issues and grievances. Additionally, though, ethnic minority individuals and communities themselves may not have been too anxious to push their cause vociferously, possibly not wishing to draw attention to their minority presence. Another relevant factor perhaps is the fact that ethnic minority representative organisations were hitherto at a developmental and embryonic stage in advocacy, lobbying and organisational matters. In the 1990s, however, change was in evidence. Of note here was the work of the Committee on the Administration of Justice (CAJ), the Belfast-based civil liberties organisation, which began to focus upon race relations and anti-racism, including a key 1991 conference on these themes. The event drew together ethnic minority bodies and individuals, civil libertarians, voluntary sector representatives, academics and others. At the same time, ethnic minority organisations and spokespersons were becoming increasingly more professional and outspoken in defence of their rights and cause. One result of these developments was the creation, in 1994, of the Northern Ireland Council for Ethnic Minorities (NICEM), which provided co-ordination, leadership, energy and expertise – plus an awareness of cross-border, 'across the water' and international dimensions to anti-racist campaigning. Other bodies, too, such as the Chinese Welfare Association (CWA), the Northern Ireland Council for Travelling People (NICTP), the Standing Advisory Commission for Human Rights (SACHR), the Multi-Cultural Resource Centre (MCRC) (Belfast) and the Northern Ireland Council for Ethnic Equality (NICEE) kept up the momentum for change and race relations legislation. Networking and lobbying have been crucial and the CAJ, CWA, NICTP and NICEM have known how to work together to exploit international mechanisms, notably embarrassing the British government before the United Nations Committee on the Elimination of Racial Discrimination (CERD) (see Chapter 3).

In 1993, CERD had strongly criticised the British government for failing to extend race relations legislation to Northern Ireland. The Home Office's 104-page-long report to the Committee only briefly touched on racism in Northern Ireland, yet much of the discussion had turned around continued British failure in this respect. According to CAJ spokesman Martin O'Brien: 'Given the comments by the committee, the government must now act quickly to introduce strong and effective legislation if it is to comply with the terms of the convention (that is, the International Convention on the Elimination of All Forms of Racial Discrimination)' (*Irish News*, 11 August 1993). By 1994, following its own consultative paper (*Race Relations in Northern Ireland*) (CCRU 1992) and exercise (1992–93), although the Conservative government seemed to be won over on the need for some form of race relations legislation nothing concrete emerged, leading therefore to further condemnation by CERD in 1996. In the same year, NICEM's co-ordinator, Patrick Yu, told an anti-racist seminar at Queen's University Belfast: 'We have been lobbying and fighting for legislation for the last six years ... Northern Ireland badly needs race relations legislation' (*Irish News*, 7 March 1996). Eventually, in 1996, draft legislation was put forward and the following year, the Race Relations (Northern Ireland) Order 1997 was laid before Parliament and became law (see Chapter 4) – 32 years after the 1965 Race Relations Act.

The importance of international lobbying and putting pressure on the British government can be seen from Northern Ireland Office (NIO) minister Baroness Denton's speech to the House of Lords, when introducing the Race Relations Order. After first explaining that such legislation had not been deemed necessary hitherto, Denton conceded that 'Great Britain, however, has obligations not only to its own citizens but internationally through its ratification of the UN International Convention on the Elimination of All Forms of Racial Discrimination.' Moreover, as regards the inclusion of Travellers, the minister admitted: 'Their inclusion was the subject of considerable lobbying during the early consultation period ... [and] ... In the response to the proposal for a draft order there was great urging that the legislation should make clear the status of the Irish traveller community as a separate ethnic group.' Significantly, too, Denton paid tribute to 'the work of community groups in making quite certain that their members have been able to work with us in bringing the legislation forward' (House of Lords 1997:623–33).

The belated extension of race relations legislation to Northern Ireland constituted a political volte-face on the part of government. Previously, the longstanding official line had been that the ethnic minority population was too small to warrant such a measure and that racism was not a problem in Northern Ireland. Neither of these claims was rooted in any research, census enumeration or serious investigation – as authors in this volume illustrate. Alternatively, advocates of protective legislation had argued that ethnic minority persons were being classified as *de facto* second-class citizens through the absence of legislation. Moreover, correlating the size of ethnic minority populations with instances of racism is a dubious and victim-blaming exercise. They needed protection precisely because they were (estimated to be) small in number and vulnerable as such. As the Equal Opportunities Commission for Northern Ireland (EOCNI) pointed out, in a submission to the 1992–93 consultative exercise, 'the mere fact that the group potentially adversely affected is small cannot be a justification for continuing to deny protection against discrimination on grounds of race' (EOCNI 1993:2). The Northern Ireland Committee of the Irish Congress of Trade Unions (NIC/ICTU) made a similar point in its submission to the exercise: 'The rights of ethnic minorities are important, and the elimination of discrimination against them is a matter of principle not to be determined simply by the size of the problem' (NIC/ICTU 1993:1).

What is apparent from the above brief account is that groups and organisations within civil society were in the vanguard role of lobbying for race relations legislation in Northern Ireland. Political parties featured here in a secondary, back-up or peripheral role, or not at all. Sometimes, in fact, their interventions brought negative, dissenting voices into the debate to extend the legislation to Northern Ireland and, as already intimated, the Traveller population faced particular opposition to their specific inclusion. Significantly, out of 57 submissions to the 1992–93 consultative exercise, only one of these came from a political party of note – namely the Social Democratic and Labour Party (SDLP) – although two others were provided by the South Belfast Constituency Labour Party and a trio of Ulster Unionist councillors from Craigavon district. The rest largely emanated from ethnic minority bodies, voluntary sector organisations, statutory agencies, the 'social partners' and concerned individuals. The consultative exercise was moreover an important process in mobilising opinion (as Baroness Denton acknowledged above) and paved the way to the official decision to proceed with race relations. It was not, perhaps, that the political parties were disinterested in the campaign to bring in race relations machinery – this would be too reductionist an analysis and would ignore the contributions made by some political parties or individuals therein – but the main running (especially initially) unquestionably was done elsewhere. However, once ethnic minority issues and concerns began to command more attention, in the mid-1990s, then most political parties in Northern Ireland proceeded to reflect this in their electoral manifestos, policy documents, press releases and literature. I turn now to an examination of the responses of political parties to ethnic minority issues, focusing especially upon the race relations legislation, the 1996 Forum and 1997 Westminster elections. Also, I refer to material drawn from replies to a brief questionnaire sent (by the author) to candidates contesting the Westminster election. The questionnaire simply asked about personal and party attitudes to race relations and ethnic minorities.

Political Parties

An examination of party political manifestos and other relevant material reveals that the parties had different views and approaches on ethnic minority issues and concerns. Most parties active in Northern Ireland welcomed or supported the new race relations legislation. Some (notably the Alliance Party and the SDLP among the larger parties) concluded that the legislation did not go far enough and, consequently, they made criticisms which reflected the analysis of bodies such as NICEM. Other parties though (notably the Democratic Unionist Party (DUP) and the Ulster Unionist Party (UUP)) thought that the legislation went too far by including Travellers therein.

The 1997 manifesto of Northern Ireland's principal unionist party, the UUP, put forward the Union as offering to 'everyone the best prospect for peace and fair play because it links us to a genuinely plural, liberal democratic state capable of accommodating social, cultural and religious diversity'. The UUP supported the incorporation of the International Covenant on Civil and Political Rights (ICPPR) and the standards and procedures of the Organization for Security and Co-operation in Europe (OSCE) and the Council of Europe's Convention on Minority Rights as 'a possible role model for the group rights of all the minorities in Northern Ireland' (UUP 1997:2). In a manifesto sub-section on fair employment and equal opportunities, the UUP suggested that: 'As a modern, pluralist party, we support equality in employment. We believe that, in trying to achieve fairness and equality, it is essential that the highest value is placed on equality of opportunity irrespective of race, gender or creed.' However, this did not mean support for any 'so-called positive discrimination'. In fact, the UUP called for a total restructuring of the various agencies and tribunals currently servicing fair employment matters – the Labour Relations Agency (LRA), Fair Employment Commission (FEC), Equal Opportunities Commission (EOC) and 'the Race Relations Commission' (UUP 1997:6). Indeed, a UUP statement on *Race Relations in Northern Ireland* (March 1993) had expressed scepticism of 'excessive monitoring practices' and about bringing in any *new* race relations legislation, beyond simply extending existing British provisions to Northern Ireland. The onset of race relations legislation in 1996–97 clearly was seen by the UUP as an opportunity to criticise fair employment legislation and monitoring practices. This was demonstrated *in extremis* by UUP Member of Parliament William Ross, during the House of Commons debate on introducing the Race Relations Order: 'To be perfectly honest, I think it is nonsense, like a great deal of the legislation relating to minorities that has passed through this house' (House of Commons 1997:10). An alternative conjugation of this particular argument had been put forward by Owen Bowcott ('Bias and bigotry', *Guardian*, 22 September 1993) and is worth quoting at length:

> It is a strange anomaly: in Northern Ireland where successive governments have battled against bigotry and prejudice, racial discrimination remains quite legitimate. A quarter of a century of sectarian violence has spawned an elaborate framework of acts, quangos and tribunals designed to prevent discrimination on the grounds of religion. The Province even has its own Equal Opportunities Commission to ensure that women and men are fairly treated in the workplace. But when Belfast's landlords refuse to rent flats to ethnic Chinese students or employers select local white applicants with less experience than Asian graduates there is no redress.

Ross's comments during the Commons debate revealed him to be out of sympathy with the legislation for several other reasons (House of Commons 1997:10). First, he opposed the anti-discriminatory intent of legislation applying to property sales: '... should the seller not be free to sell his property for whatever price he likes to whomever he likes? ... I do not see why an individual should not discriminate over that if he wants to ... The disposal of property is a basic human right.' Second, he questioned the need for the legislation: 'I wonder whether there is a real problem of discrimination, or whether it is more imagined than anything else.' The basis of this particular assertion was Ross's observation that his few Indian and Pakistani constituents 'give no trouble to anybody, live their lives and do their own thing ... Nobody bothers about them. They are accepted as part of the scenery and I am not aware that they suffer any discrimination.' A similar, summary verdict was given for the Chinese community: 'As far as I know, they have no problems with the local population.'

Not dissimilar views were expressed by the leader of the small Ulster Independence Movement, Ken Kerr, who denied the existence of racism in Northern Ireland and therefore described the proposed race relations legislation as 'an insult to the people of Ulster' (Letters, *Belfast Telegraph*, 4 May 1996). All this seemed to fly in the face of a growing body of evidence, which suggested that Northern Ireland's ethnic minorities were in some need of protective legislation. As McVeigh points out in Chapter 1, this practice of denialism was part of the problem and reality which confronted ethnic minorities. Moreover, Ross's depiction of ethnic minorities as 'giving no trouble' served to conjure up a would-be idealisation of them as passive communities. Unsurprisingly, the Ulster Unionist Party MP was taken to task for his analysis. For instance, Labour MP Michael Connarty contended: 'I have not heard such talk for 30 years ... The saddest comment came when people from an ethnic minority were praised for being quiet and not causing trouble ... They deserve protection from discrimination not so that they can be quiet but so that they can speak up and demand their rights' (House of Commons 1997:20–1). Within Northern Ireland, too, the Democratic Left's spokesperson on ethnic minorities and racism called the speech by Ross 'appalling' (*Sunday Life*, 9 February 1997) and the Alliance Party was critical of the comments on race relations. A further problem with the legislation, according to Ross, was the inclusion of Travellers – and this is discussed below.

The Democratic Unionist Party was also against the inclusion of Travellers in the Race Relations Order, but not against the legislation itself – in fact, a DUP annual conference resolution welcomed it. However, the DUP manifestos for the Forum and Westminster elections (albeit short) had nothing to say about ethnic minority issues. The same applied to Sinn Féin, although a 1996 policy document revealed the party to be not unsympathetic to Travellers' concerns: 'Sinn Féin condemns all racist attacks on and intimidation of Travellers, people of colour and gay and bisexual people ... Recognition of ethnic differences and racism awareness, including awareness of anti-Irish racism, anti-Traveller discrimination and racism against people of colour, should be incorporated in the primary school curriculum' (Sinn Féin 1996:16).

In contrast to the DUP and SF, the SDLP had quite a lot to say about race relations in its 1997 Westminster manifesto, *Real Leadership, Real Peace*. At least a whole page of the 20-page document was devoted to this theme – with other fleeting references too, such as support for securing equality of opportunity and representation 'regardless of wealth, ability, gender, age, faith, sexual orientation or race' (SDLP 1997:11). The SDLP expressed support for ethnic minorities and welcomed race relations legislation, including the provision for the Irish Traveller community, whose nomadic lifestyle was seen to be a 'fundamental freedom to be vigorously defended'. Moreover, the party went beyond egalitarian flourishes and legislation welcoming gestures to support a raft of measures – a development which demonstrated an appreciation of ethnic minority demands. These measures included calls for proper funding to underwrite race relations legislation, on-site amenity provision for Travellers, a question on ethnicity to be inserted in the next census, tougher machinery against racial violence and harassment, adequate resourcing of ethnic minority needs in public service provision and government backing urged for a European Union (EU) monitoring centre against racism. In addition, like a number of other organisations in Northern Ireland, the SDLP was critical of the ineffectiveness of the government's Policy Appraisal and Fair Treatment (PAFT) guidelines, notably the failure here to do justice to ethnic minorities (SDLP 1997:14). Some of these concerns had been raised in a pioneering resolution to the SDLP's 1993 conference and further resolutions on race relations were put forward at subsequent party conferences. Also, as already noted, the SDLP had presented a submission to the 1992–93 consultative exercise, criticising the absence of race relations legislation, calling for Travellers to be included, urging the government to not simply extend an unreformed Race Relations Act to Northern Ireland and – true to the party's European vocation – supporting the inclusion of a racial discrimination clause in the EU's statutes. With the above developments from 1993–97, the SDLP had come some considerable way to articulating an ethnic minority policy perspective.

The SDLP's concerns and reservations over race relations were shared by the Alliance Party, which also had a declared policy of supporting ethnic minorities. Party literature had to some extent been translated into ethnic minority languages and 1994 Euro-election candidate and spokesperson Mary Clark-Glass was a particularly prominent anti-racist campaigner – culminating in her appointment as a commissioner on the new (1997) Commission for Racial Equality (Northern Ireland) (CRENI). The Alliance Party's 1997 Westminster election manifesto, *Agenda for Change*, put forward the idea of a Ministry for Community Relations to promote good community relations. In the tradition of a centrist, anti-sectarian party, the Alliance Party was against 'dividing the community into two mutually exclusive camps' and in favour of 'building a single but diverse community with a pluralist ethos'. In a specific manifesto section on 'Anti-Discrimination Legislation', there was support for race relations legislation: 'Alliance welcomes the introduction of Race Relations legislation to Northern Ireland, albeit some 20 years after the corresponding legislation was introduced in Great Britain ... Alliance has consistently supported effective legislation to ensure equality of opportunity and to counter discrimination on grounds of religion, political belief, gender, race, disability and age' (Alliance Party 1997:11). However, like the SDLP, the Alliance Party felt that the legislation did not go far enough, for instance in the provisions relating to local authorities. NICEM and other ethnic minority organisations were critical of the fact that because of the weakened powers of local government in Northern Ireland, many of the services (provided by non-departmental public bodies) were excluded from the remit of the Race Relations Order. This deficiency was taken up strongly, notably in an anti-racist seminar at the 1997 West Belfast Festival, by Clark-Glass, who called for stronger monitoring mechanisms and legislation against racially motivated crime. Certainly, the monitoring and investigation powers of the Fair Employment Commission are considerably stronger than those available to the CRENI. Another concern of the Alliance Party – and indeed many other parties in Northern Ireland including, for instance, the Deputy

Lord Mayor of Belfast, Jim Rodgers (UUP) and the ex-Lord Mayor, Sammy Wilson (DUP) – was the (reports of) increased attacks on ethnic minority persons in 1996–97, particularly upon the Chinese community (Hainsworth 1996; CWA 1997b).

Some of these attacks came from loyalist elements in the Donegall Pass area of Belfast. An important role in mediation was provided by the small Progressive Unionist Party (PUP) leadership, in collaboration with CWA. A late starter as a political entity, the PUP, following a sympathetic resolution at the 1996 party conference, emerged as a strong supporter of ethnic minorities, translating party manifestos into ethnic minority languages (again with ethnic minority help) and even appointing an ethnic minority spokesperson (Dawn Purvis). The PUP claimed to be 'in the forefront of enlightened Unionist thinking' and, as evidence, welcomed the race relations legislation, regretted the delay in introducing it and was dismayed that constructive criticisms of the British Race Relations Act had not been taken on board (Progressive Unionist Party 1997). Moreover, Purvis was critical of an intervention by a member of the Conservative Party's Monday Club who, in a letter to the *Belfast Telegraph* (12 September 1996), personally questioned the merits of race relations legislation and urged all unionist MPs to reject it. Of course, it was the Conservative Party which – in one of its swansong acts of office – brought in the Race Relations (Northern Ireland) Order 1997 although, after 18 years in government, this should not be construed as enthusiasm for the legislation. Conservative candidates in Northern Ireland made no apparent references to the legislation in their 1997 Westminster election campaign and literature. In a letter to the author (31 August 1997), one of these candidates (Stuart Sexton) even opposed his party's initiative: 'In my view the race relations legislation which has applied in Great Britain was and is a big mistake, and this makes a further mistake in extending it to N. Ireland.' Perhaps, this was a maverick view and did not reflect party policy. Nevertheless, critics were right to point to the tardiness in bringing in the race relations legislation to Northern Ireland and to Conservative government feet dragging over consent for an EU racism monitoring centre. However, Labour Party criticisms here had a certain hollowness since Labour in office had passed over opportunities to extend protective race relations legislation to Northern Ireland. Small Labour political parties in Northern Ireland, too, had surprisingly little to say about ethnic minority issues and race relations – despite the aforementioned submission to the consultative exercise.

As regards Northern Ireland's other smaller, non-tribal, political parties, there was appreciable support for ethnic minorities. For instance, the Northern Ireland Women's Coalition (NIWC) – again, a recent creation – placed great emphasis (in their 1996 Forum election manifesto (NIWC 1996a) and accompanying policy papers) on the

principle of 'equity for all', including a call to put the PAFT legislation
on a statutory footing (NIWC 1996c). Referring specifically to issues
of inclusion and accommodation, the NIWC stated that it was 'prepared
to help in the negotiation of a political accommodation which takes
account of all sides of the key divisions in Northern Ireland and allows
for cultural and political diversity building a multi-cultural, multi-ethnic
and multi-religious society'(NIWC 1996f). Respect for human rights
– 'regardless of characteristics such as age, sex, race, religious or
political beliefs, sexual orientation or disabilities' – was deemed to be
the cornerstone of any future constitutional settlement or arrangement
for Northern Ireland (NIWC 1996e). Furthermore, equitable access
to health services was seen as a priority: 'This is particularly crucial
for services for travellers and ethnic groups' (NIWC 1996d). Monitoring
of equity and adequate resourcing to recognise various cultural traditions
was equally important: 'These traditions include not only the two main
communities, but a variety of ethnic and minority groups' (NIWC
1996b). The NIWC emerged as a new political entity particularly at
the Forum election, making much less impact at the Westminster
election but, here too, candidates campaigned to 'nudge traditional
politics and established politicians to new ways of thinking'.

The Green Party shared many of these same goals, with party
'leader' Peter Emerson pointing to two ethnic minority individuals on
party local lists in 1996–97. The Greens' manifesto for the 1997
Westminster election proclaimed the party to be based on 'an inclusive
philosophy, restricted neither by class, gender, race, religion, nor
nationality' (Green Party 1997:1). A major target of the Greens was
'majoritarianism and the arrogant insensitivity which it has bred': the
party looked forward to its 'phasing out', so that 'the rights of all
minorities – the travellers, the disabled, the gay community and all
ethnic minorities – may be naturally incorporated into a healthy
pluralist society' (Green Party 1997:8). While not having a great deal
to say about the details of ethnic minority concerns, the Greens nevertheless provided a sympathetic voice, with prohibitive costs ventured
as the only reason for failing to translate election material into ethnic
minority languages.

The Workers Party's main contribution to this debate was a 1996
four-point plan to tackle racism and a call for the Forum and the NIO
to be proactive against racism. The plan supported race relations, backed
by a permanent, anti-racist commission (comprising *inter alia* of non-
governmental organisations, parties, employers, trade unions and
churches) and a body to enforce the legislation. Significantly, too, the
Workers Party linked racism (particularly racist attacks in 1996) to sectarianism in Northern Ireland – both were seen as stemming from the
same politics of 'difference': 'Recent attacks on Chinese, Black and
other ethnic members of our community are equally vicious and

divisive in their commissioning and have their origins in the politics of "difference" – the homeground of mainstream political life in Northern Ireland' (Workers Party 1996). Constructively, the party warned against the practice of racist denialism and demanded a special unit inside the RUC to counter the reportedly growing attacks on ethnic minority persons. With the victory of the British Labour Party in the 1997 election, the Workers Party put forward their proposals to the new Secretary of State for Northern Ireland, Mo Mowlam. The above focus indicated that the Workers Party was clearly interpreting racism as a core issue bound up with the question of what kind of society was wanted in Northern Ireland.

The Democratic Left (DL), a breakaway from the Workers Party, contested the Forum but not the Westminster election and addressed the issue of racism in the context of citizenship, with the party's electoral leaflets declaring: 'Northern Ireland must never treat any of its people as second class citizens' (Democratic Left 1996a). The party's main statement on racism came as part of a 1996 DL document, *Rebuilding Politics: Setting the Agenda for Conciliation*. Essentially, the DL emphasised the diversity of society – seeing Northern Ireland as 'a multi-lingual, cultural, religious and ethnic' entity – and supported protective race relations machinery: 'Discrimination is a real problem to those of ethnic minority origin ... these people are among the most vulnerable in our society.' Thus the party pointed to 'well co-ordinated acts of physical abuse and vandalism aimed at ethnic minority communities'. Among the demands of the DL were more research into the effects of racism on society and the creation of voluntary and statutory organisations to combat racism. Interestingly, the party linked the recent peace process to the cause of ethnic minorities: 'We are of the opinion that the peace process does not belong to white Catholics and Protestants but to all races, creeds and colours, of which there are many on this island' (Democratic Left 1996b:20–1).

The reference here to the peace process is significant because, while the general population in Northern Ireland exhibited an understandably feel good attitude to cease-fire developments in the mid-1990s, there were also some anxieties that the process might have a downside for ethnic minorities. Irwin and Dunn (1997:97–8) researched the experiences of ethnic groups since the paramilitary cease-fire of August 1994. The authors' survey revealed that 12 per cent of Travellers believed that they now attracted more (unwanted) police attention and about 15 per cent of the Chinese community felt that crime had increased. Moreover, over half (57 per cent) of the Chinese respondents interviewed thought that changes brought in with the cease-fire would affect the position of their community. Asked a straight question: 'Do you think these changes will make things better, or will make things worse for your community?', 63 per cent answered 'worse' and 32 per cent said 'better'. Again, according to Irwin and Dunn: 'Of all the reasons for explaining the pessimism of the Chinese community towards the changes, the most important is that half of this community blame recent changes on an increase in racism.' As regards attacks on the Chinese community, NICEM's co-ordinator Patrick Yu assessed the situation: 'In the past, the tension here was between Catholics and Protestants but with the ceasefires attention was drawn for the first time to the ethnic minorities. In particular, the attacks are coming from the strongly loyalist areas' (*Guardian*, 12 November 1996). For the CWA, Race Relations Officer Eleanor McKnight made a similar analysis that, since the cease-fire, 'there appears to be a slight rise in harassment – people may be looking for a vulnerable target, another source of victim' (*Belfast Telegraph*, 28 April 1995), while the Multi-Cultural Resource Centre's co-ordinator, Fee Ching Leong, contended that ethnic minority communities saw 'the potential here for racism to grow and they are afraid' (*Belfast Telegraph*, 4 December 1995). Finally, the *Guardian*'s Northern Ireland correspondent, David Sharrock, interpreted the above situation as a case of 'bigots who thrived on sectarian violence turned their prejudices on minority groups' (*Guardian*, 12 November 1996). This assessment echoed some of the above analyses of the small, left-orientated parties (notably the Workers Party and the Democratic Left), but also it was significant that both Patrick Yu and the RUC pointed to crude economic gain as the prime *raison d'être* for attacks. Whatever the reason – economic, racist or possibly an element of both – attacks on ethnic minority persons or property tended to aggravate feelings of vulnerability and lack of police protection. Attacks on ethnic minority persons, it should be pointed out, have not been confined to loyalist areas and Travellers have been the victims of quite generalised stereotyping, hostility, physical threats and violence. I now turn to an examination of some of the politics of Travellers in Northern Ireland

Travellers, Politics and Racism

According to McVeigh (1992c:373), in a specially commissioned analysis for the Standing Advisory Commission on Human Rights, 'while Travellers are not directly involved in the "troubles", they are not untouched by them'. The same author explains that, in the working-class districts where Travellers have been sited or housed, they have experienced hostile paramilitary activity. Loyalist paramilitaries, for instance, are seen to have intimidated Travellers off some sites in certain areas, and republican paramilitaries have intimidated them in various ways. For example, as regards the latter, Travellers have not always been welcome in fixed abodes on nationalist housing estates –

a theme taken up and illustrated by (Traveller and non-Traveller) participants at a seminar on racism at the 1997 West Belfast Festival (*Irish News*, 7 August 1997). McVeigh also records an instance where a sedentary Traveller was forced to drive a car bomb to a police station and another where a Traveller's van was 'commissioned' for cross-border gun-running. The effect of these events was to intimidate Traveller families off a housing estate. Again, the well-known Dungannon priest, Fr. Denis Faul, criticised the Irish Republican Army (IRA) for shooting two Travellers in South Armagh – accusing it of operating a 'shoot to kill' policy.

Pressures on Travellers were experienced in different ways in loyalist areas. In the 1980s, Gerry O'Hanlon (chair, Northern Ireland Council for Travelling People) pointed to loyalist paramilitary threats against Travellers in Downpatrick, County Down – 'They are victims of racism in their own land' (*Irish News*, 24 June 1987) – while, a few years later, the Ulster Defence Association was reported as threatening to burn down Traveller caravans if a site was located at Brownlow, Craigavon (*Sunday Life*, 6 October 1991). The NICTP's Paul Noonan also underlined the point that Travellers had been attacked by both loyalist and nationalist gangs (*Sunday News*, 27 July 1986).

Whereas physical attacks on Travellers were obviously most immediately dangerous for Travellers, other would-be threats and diatribes from some politicians have been instrumental in nourishing anti-Traveller prejudices. Probably the most notorious comment against Travellers came from the Independent Unionist ex-Deputy Mayor of Belfast, Frank Millar, who contended that Travellers were 'dirt' ('Never mind this dirt who come into Belfast to foul our pavements') who might be expedited to the City incinerator (*Belfast Telegraph*, 2 July 1982). In another instance, the former UUP chairman of Fermanagh District Council (Bert Kerr) said that he would be 'tempted to use his shotgun' if any more Travellers came into the county (*Fermanagh Herald*, 9 July 1997). Although statements such as these rank as some of the more virulent attacks on Travellers, other strident comments have been all too prevalent from political representatives. In fact, an aggressive and reductionist discourse is discernible, focused largely around the issue of Travellers' accommodation. At times, too, this discourse is inclusive of sectarianised overtones and denialism of Travellers' ethnicity and nomadic way of life. Both the main unionist parties in Northern Ireland contest the idea of Travellers as a distinct ethnic group. What is striking here is that politicians who are so conscious of defending their own group and historico-cultural identity are not prepared to accept the same rights for others. An illustration was the aforementioned contribution by Ross in the House of Commons: 'One group that causes immense concern in Northern Ireland is the travelling community ... Are we saying that every group has the right to propagate its culture and way of life, in the way that speakers of Irish have tried over the past 70 years to widen the gap between themselves and the British population of Northern Ireland? Would it not be better to try to make society more homogenous, or are we going to allow groups to become more separate?' (House of Commons 1997:11–13).

As regards the sectarian aspects, McVeigh (1992c:352) refers to 'the commonplace construction of Travelling People as an "invasion" from the south of Ireland'. However, according to an editorial in the *Andersonstown News* (3 August 1985):

> In the history of this country there have always been thousands of travelling people earning their living and plying their wares up and down the country. They are as much a part of our history and heritage as our language, music or song, and they should be encouraged to retain their way of life if they so wish and every modern facility and convenience should be provided.

Yet, unionist politicians have played the 'green' card to protest against Travellers. In 1989, for instance, DUP Derry City councillor William Hay called upon Travellers to 'go back where they came from', rather than trying to secure a serviced site in a unionist-dominated part of the city (*Sunday World*, 2 July 1989). Elsewhere, too, unionist politicians – for example, in Ballymena – have opposed the provision of a serviced site in their area for fear it would provoke a cross-border transit of Travellers, 'milking the Northern Ireland economy' (*Ballymena Guardian*, 6 September 1984). Again, in 1990 in the Craigavon area, local UUP politicians complained about Travellers having 'an Irish brogue' and also urged them to get 'back to where they came from' (*Irish News*, 19 September 1990). An SDLP elected representative, Brid Rodgers, likened this to a 'no room at the inn' approach and urged local councillors to 'take a Christian point of view' on providing sites for Travellers (*Belfast Telegraph*, 4 December 1990). The same theme was reiterated by SDLP local councillor Hugh Casey: 'It's a good thing some of the councillors here didn't have the letting of the stable in Bethelem otherwise Jesus would have been born in a field' (*Lurgan Mail*, 6 December 1990).

Elsewhere, though, SDLP representatives have been accused of blocking site provision for Travellers and going against the party policy of supporting serviced accommodation. For instance, Geoff Sirockin (Belfast Committee for the Rights of Travelling People) criticised the party in West Belfast and Downpatrick for being 'blatantly anti-Traveller' and encouraging racism – charges strongly rejected by the SDLP (*Irish News*, 26 May 1986). In Downpatrick, the NICTP condemned the use of an election flyer by a prominent SDLP elected

representative, Eddie McGrady, to highlight that he, unlike the rival
Sinn Féin candidate, had opposed provision of a local site for Travellers
(*Irish News* 18 June 1986). Certainly, this apparent playing of football
with a genuine problem faced by Travellers contrasted somewhat with
the attitude of yet another SDLP local politician, Len Green, in Derry.
Taunted in 1989 (by the DUP's William Hay) for losing his council
seat because of his support for the Travellers' cause, Green commented:
'If my stand against racism cost me my council seat I'm happy with
it' (*Sunday World*, 2 July 1989).

Without doubt, DUP politicians have been in the forefront of
opposition to Travellers' sites. For example, in the 1980s, DUP elected
politicians took a leading role in opposition to the location of a Traveller
site in Tattykeel, Omagh. The UUP publicly disassociated itself here
from a rally and protest march past Traveller residences: 'marches such
as that organised on Monday evening are only a covert type of intimidation and provide the enemies of our Province with excuses to
misrepresent Ulster Protestants'. However, the UUP's disassociation
should not be taken as a welcome for Travellers since the party
statement continued: 'The Ulster Unionist Party's policy remains, as
in the past, opposed to building accommodation for the itinerants'
(*Strabane Weekly News*, 7 May 1983). Again, in February 1991, the
DUP's Bert Johnston boasted: 'I am the one and only councillor who
is opposed to a gypsy site anywhere in Fermanagh ... anywhere in this
tourist county – the hub of Ulster's tourism.' Johnston called upon
other political parties 'to oppose the provision of a site for these unde-
sirables who are not citizens of Fermanagh and ... can never be
accepted by the settled people anywhere in this County' (*Impartial
Reporter*, 7 March 1991). This draconian view of Travellers was
supported by local UUP politicians, such as Sammy Foster, whose anti-
Traveller language was particularly virulent: 'They are dirty and
unclean. There is an excuse for being poor, but there is no excuse for
being dirty and irresponsible' (*Irish Times*, 13 March 1991).

Responsibility is indeed an important consideration. As Noonan
(Chapter 8) explains, local authorities in Northern Ireland are not
obliged to provide serviced sites for Travellers and the main public sector
housing authority, the Northern Ireland Housing Executive (NIHE),
is not empowered to make such provision. In this catch-22 scenario,
Travellers are placed precariously. However, in addition, Traveller lifestyles and ethnicity are not accepted by some politicians. Three
examples from the same location illustrate this situation. First, in
1990, a former DUP councillor (Bob Dodds) in the Craigavon district,
advocated that Travellers 'should be *directed* [my emphasis] to live as
the ordinary community, in normal housing, and in such circumstances they could make a contribution to society. People should be
prevented by law from living in such fashion. There is no need to in

this day and age' (*Lurgan Mail*, 13 December 1990). Again, in 1992 the Mayor of Craigavon, Joe Trueman (UUP), suggested (following an attack upon a house allocated to a Traveller family): 'It's a difficult problem just to know how to deal with them. How are we going to get them to live respectably and not annoy the rest of the full time residents' (*Irish News*, 3 June 1992). A further comment of this ilk came from another unionist local Craigavon councillor, Yvonne Calvert (DUP), who asked 'why can't they live in houses like other people?' (*Irish News*, 5 December 1990). A more sensitive assessment came from the ex-Commissioner for Complaints in Northern Ireland, Maurice Hayes, when launching a report on 'Accommodation Guidelines in Relation to Travellers': 'people should stop trying to integrate travellers into the community. They should have the right to travel; the system should be built around the travellers' way of life and not the other way around. We all know what happens when we try to eliminate minorities and people who do not have a lot of clout' (*Irish News*, 12 May 1993). Moreover, as regards the above suggestions about housing, it is worth recalling that Travellers are not always welcome when they do live in houses like other people. Also, politicians who have supported the allocation of public sector housing to Travellers – as was the case with, for example, some Sinn Féin elected representatives in Derry in the 1980s – sometimes have had to face condemnations from other residents, including their own electors. Both Sinn Féin and the SDLP support the principle of serviced accommodation sites for Travellers but, equally, the two parties are concerned to speak out for the sedentary population – and obviously votes are a consideration here. Thus, in West Belfast, SDLP councillor Alex Attwood has suggested: 'The conditions in which the travellers live may well be intolerable but so too is it for the residents of the Glen Road' (*News Letter*, 26 July 1985). The Sinn Féin West Belfast councillor Alex Maskey phrased this equation slightly differently: 'I am in sympathy with these residents and their plight. But I also understand the needs of Travelling families' (*Sunday World*, 21 May 1995). Both the SDLP and Sinn Féin maintained that unionist councils were reluctant to facilitate the provision of Traveller sites. Again, Maskey explained the concentration of Travellers in West Belfast: 'Councillors never looked for sites other than in West Belfast because they wouldn't have got it through a Unionist-dominated Council.' In similar vein, nationalists in Newry complained about settlement of Travellers 'on one side of the river only' (*Irish News*, 28 September 1984). An interesting contribution to this debate was made by Fionnuala O'Connor: 'Loyalist and Unionist politicians are uniformly hostile to the Travellers, as a supposed entirely Catholic and Republican group, originating south of the Border ... [Sinn Féin] publicly supports the travellers, but has privately been equally concerned by the prospect of angered local residents in

Catholic West Belfast calling in the RUC to deal with their complaints'
(*Irish Times*, 18 September 1984). To conclude this section, it is
instructive to hear a Traveller's view on the problems faced by this
community in trying to maintain its nomadic identity. As Nan Purcell
explained: 'In 1966–7 you could stay anywhere, even in the Shankill
Road and the Springfield Road, but not now' (*Guardian*, 14 April 1993).

Conclusion

This chapter has concentrated upon some of the political dimensions
of racism and on party political perspectives on ethnic minorities in
Northern Ireland. Political parties, it has been argued, have been slow
to take up ethnic minority concerns. Travellers, in particular, have faced
an uphill struggle in getting political parties to fully support their calls
for satisfactory accommodation provision and recognition of their
chosen lifestyles. Moreover, coming to terms with the diversity of the
population and society in Northern Ireland has been an uneven process
and learning curve for political parties. As has been pointed out,
parties played a secondary role in the important campaign to bring in
race relations legislation – with doubts and opposition also in evidence
here. Suneil Sharma, chairperson of NICEM (interviewed on BBC TV's
Hearts and Minds programme (Sharma 1997)), referred to the political
party input to this campaign as disappointing and tokenistic. The
absence of party submissions to the 1992–93 consultative exercise has
already been noted and again it is noteworthy that only one MP from
Northern Ireland (William Ross) participated in the Commons debate
which brought in the race relations legislation. Also, only one or two
of the parties have thought it worthwhile to appoint a specific ethnic
minority officer whilst there is no ethnic minority voice at the levels
of MP, MEP or district councillor. Furthermore, while virtually all the
parties (albeit with the reservations noted above) have just about
accepted or even welcomed the race relation legislation, denialism (of
racism), stereotyping of Travellers and racist discourse have been in
evidence too. Of particular concern are the suggestions that recent cease-
fire and peace initiatives have left ethnic minority communities even
more vulnerable. Unsurprisingly, ethnic minority spokespersons have
called for an all-inclusive peace process and warned against the danger
of sectarianism feeding into racist aggression.

On the positive side, though, there is in party rank and files a
growing awareness of ethnic minority concerns and this has been
reflected in the manifestos and literature discussed above. The increasing
practice of translating party electoral material is appreciated by ethnic
minorities. Indeed, ethnic minority spokespersons have urged parties
to be more proactive and outreaching rather than resorting simply to

tokenism or assuming that ethnic minorities are not interested in political debate in Northern Ireland. Jonathan Stephenson, chairperson of the SDLP (interviewed on the aforementioned *Hearts and Minds*), suggested that it was difficult for ethnic minorities to participate in local politics in Northern Ireland: 'it takes an extra effort to move out of their own setting into someone else's' (Stephenson 1997). If this is perceived to be the case, then it is incumbent on political parties to make an extra effort to practise a more inclusive politics. For instance, although the race relations legislation is a positive step forward, political parties might lend their support to ethnic minorities in their quest to improve the machinery. Also, at the European level, there are moves – notably by the EU's Consultative Committee on Racism and Xenophobia – to draw up a code of anti-racist good practice for political parties. With ethnic minority organisations and political parties across Europe involved in the discussions, there is scope here for contributions from Northern Ireland. Constructive support for ethnic minority bodies and concerns (see the recommendations by Mann-Kler 1997) in Northern Ireland and a willingness to devote space and culturally sensitive attention to ethnic minorities are the requirements of the day.

Acknowledgements

I am particularly grateful to Paul Noonan for providing access to the archive resources of the Belfast Travellers' Education and Development Group, and to the following individuals for reading and commenting upon the chapter: Brice Dickson, Carolyn Mason, Paul Noonan, Martin O'Brien and Patrick Yu. Many individuals, organisations and political parties also provided literature to assist in the writing of the chapter. They are too many to list here but their contributions (evident from the above) at least merit general acknowledgement.

3 The International Context

Brice Dickson and Mark Bell

In any society ethnic minorities will look first and foremost to that society's own law for protection against discrimination. If that law is inadequate they will turn to international law. By drawing upon the standards set there, local groups will hope to persuade their society to change its law. This, indeed, is the experience of ethnic minority groups in Northern Ireland. They have discovered that a sound appreciation of international legal developments in the area of minority rights protection can assist greatly in the campaign for more effective laws and practices at the local level. The purpose of this chapter, then, is to review the steps that have already been taken to assist ethnic minorities within international law. We will look first at the efforts made under the auspices of the United Nations (UN) and then turn to more specific measures at the European level.

Intergovernmental agreements are now so numerous in this field that many international lawyers assert that racial discrimination and genocide have become unlawful by virtue of 'international custom and practice'. This would mean that even governments which have not yet signed a specific international agreement on the matter could still be considered bound by the general principles underlying it. As yet, however, international custom and practice cannot avail an individual who seeks redress for discrimination before an international court or tribunal: he or she must instead bring a claim under the terms of an international agreement. As we shall see, not many of those agreements allow for such individual rights of action. They tend to operate at the collective level, sometimes even leaving the enforcement of rights to governments. Those which do allow an individual right of action often make it very difficult for such an action to succeed. International law, moreover, does not as yet impose *criminal* sanctions on states that breach its rules; such legal actions that can take place are, in national terms, *civil* in character.

Protection of Ethnic Groups and Races by the United Nations

The need to acknowledge and protect the special claims of ethnic minority groups has been part of international concern on the legal

52

plain since long before the present century (Thornberry 1991b, Chapter 2; MacEwen 1995, Chapter 2). It acquired special prominence at the Congress of Berlin in 1878, and in the Treaties signed after the First World War the concern was concretised for the first time through the setting up of an international court, under the auspices of the League of Nations, to adjudicate upon disputes between minorities and nation states. Strenuous efforts were made to internationalise the problems faced by minorities at this time because, in the words of US President Wilson in a speech given at the Peace Conference on 31 May 1919: 'Nothing, I venture to say, is more likely to disturb the peace of the world than the treatment which might in certain circumstances be meted out to minorities.'

Sophisticated and ambitious though they were, the measures taken in the 1920s and 1930s to operationalise the protection given to minorities by international law (Thornberry 1991b, Chapter 3; Sohn and Buergenthal 1973, Chapters 4 and 5) were of course ultimately unsuccessful for, whilst the Second World War was primarily a struggle by democratic forces against totalitarian regimes seeking to subjugate whole nations, it was minority groups within those nations which bore the brunt of the Axis powers' viciousness. It was to be expected that at the end of that war the victors would want to ensure that no such oppression of minorities could ever occur again. The lesson taken from the previous 30 years, though, was that protection of minorities as such might not be the most effective way of preventing oppression; it was decided that a better way of ensuring this goal was through protecting the human rights of individuals.

The Charter of the United Nations, consequently, makes no mention of minorities and a common view is that, with the exception of the arrangements made in Austria, the post-Second World War treaties were less accommodating of minority rights than those following the Great War (Modeen 1969). Instead, the UN Charter focuses on the principle of non-discrimination between individuals, whether on the basis of race, sex, language or religion (Articles 1, 13, 55 and 76). The Universal Declaration of Human Rights, adopted by the UN's General Assembly in 1948, likewise omits a 'minorities' article, despite the efforts of countries such as Denmark, Yugoslavia and the USSR to have one inserted (Thornberry 1991b, Chapter 13).

Since the 1940s, however, some ground has been made up. Most significantly, a specific provision on minorities was eventually inserted into the International Covenant on Civil and Political Rights (ICCPR), adopted by the UN General Assembly in 1966: 'In those States in which ethnic, religious or linguistic minorities exist, persons belonging to such minorities shall not be denied the right, in community with the other members of the group, to enjoy their own culture, to profess and practise their own religion, or to use their own language' (Article 27).

Even here, though, we should note that the wording relates more to the rights of individuals than to those of the collectivity. And the rights in question, though important, are few in number. In the 1960s, states with large-scale immigration, such as countries in Latin America, did not wish to have a text that could be read as according a special status to particular groups within the population, while on the other hand 'multinational' states, such as the USSR, feared the consequences of secessionist trends (Lerner 1993:89).

The ICCPR created two enforcement mechanisms, one weak and one strong. The weaker mechanism requires all states which have agreed to be bound by the Covenant to submit periodic reports to the UN's Human Rights Committee on how they are complying with their obligations. The Committee publishes 'General Comments' on what it expects to see addressed by member states in relation to each Article of the Covenant and, since 1992, it has issued short reports of its own on what has been submitted to it by each member state (Boerefijn 1995). These country reports draw attention to the principal concerns of the Committee as well as making recommendations for reform.

The stronger enforcement mechanism allows individuals to take their grievances directly to the Human Rights Committee for adjudication, but only if the state in question has submitted to the jurisdiction of that Committee by accepting what is known as the first Optional Protocol to the Covenant. By mid-1998, 92 states had accepted that Protocol; Ireland was one of them, but the UK was not. To date, very few cases relying upon Article 27 of the ICCPR have been brought before the Human Rights Committee (de Zayas 1993:264; Thornberry 1991b, Chapters 14–28), probably because the wording of that Article is so general. It simply requires states not to interfere with the cultural, religious and linguistic preferences of minorities, stopping short of requiring any positive action to promote those preferences. There have been claims, for example, by native Canadian Indians, by Scandinavian Sami and by Breton speakers in France. As yet, no case has turned on the rights of a religious minority and no case has been taken by a minority group in either part of Ireland. Invariably, cases brought to the Committee do not rely solely upon Article 27, but upon other Articles in the Covenant as well, such as Article 25 (the right to take part in the conduct of public affairs). In general it is fair to say that the Committee's jurisprudence on individual rights far outshines that on group rights.

This is also true of the work of another important UN body, the Sub-Commission on the Prevention of Discrimination and the Protection of Minorities. This body does not consider complaints from individuals, but deals with issues either in relation to particular countries or more generally. It comprises 26 independent experts not serving in a representative capacity and it reports to the Commission on Human Rights, an intergovernmental outgrowth of the UN General Assembly's Economic and Social Council. The Sub-Commission has achieved much more on the discrimination front than on the minorities front, possibly because preventing discrimination is a 'negative' activity whereas protecting minorities usually requires more positive action. The differential rate of progress is a pity, not least because, as Thornberry notes, it ignores the basic reason for protecting minorities in the first place: '[I]t is important that international law should recognise the validity of diverse languages, cultures and religions in a positive and direct way rather than to expect this as an implication from an imaginatively interpreted standard or rule of non-discrimination. A direct confrontation of the minorities issue is a more honest and clearer approach than any alternative' (Thornberry 1991b:128). This view, however, has recently been challenged. Rodley (1995:64) argues that 'with the exception of indigenous communities, international law does not and cannot reasonably be expected to recognise minority group rights as such'. He suggests that the notion of minority rights 'should be treated as a conceptual diversion', the issues at stake being 'essentially those of equality under the law, nondiscrimination (direct or indirect) and respect for substantive human rights, read either independently or together' (p.71). There is clearly more than one strategy that could be adopted to protect the rights of ethnic minorities; the choices are not necessarily mutually exclusive.

In the more specific realm of anti-discrimination measures, international law has been more productive in the norm-setting stakes (Lerner 1993:91–100). The furthest any of the instruments goes is in Article 2(2) of the International Convention on the Elimination of All Forms of Racial Discrimination, in force since 1969, which obliges states: 'when the circumstances so warrant, [to] take, in the social, economic, cultural and other fields, special and concrete measures to ensure the adequate development and protection of certain racial groups or individuals belonging to them, for the purposes of guaranteeing them the full and equal enjoyment of human rights and fundamental freedoms'. This Convention also requires states to adopt legislation outlawing racist activities or speech. Again, though, as with all other UN instruments, the defining characteristic of this Convention is that states have considerable freedom of choice as to which form of enforcement machinery to subject themselves to. States *must* submit periodic reports to a Committee of Experts (Committee on the Elimination of Racial Discrimination – CERD), but while this Committee has power to question state representatives, thereby causing political embarrassment if the state has fallen down on its obligations, it cannot issue any binding conclusions based on the reports. Only 21 states have so far agreed to give the Committee power to adjudicate upon individual complaints (Marie 1996:73). Presumably because it does not wish to subject itself to international adjudication of this kind, the UK is not one of those states, nor does it intend to become one in the near future. Moreover, Ireland is the only European Union (EU) state not to have even ratified the Convention.

According to recent commentators, the UK has some way to go before it fully complies with the Convention (Oyediran 1992; Foley 1995). In its most recent comments, CERD itself expressed concern that the UK is not fully complying with its obligation to outlaw organisations which promote and incite racial discrimination, that members of minority groups are disproportionately affected by police brutality and harassment, by unemployment and by deprivation of education, that the Irish Traveller community has suffered with regard to health care, social services and housing, and that asylum seekers are denied full access to employment rights and social services. In relation to Northern Ireland, CERD noted with serious concern the absence of comprehensive race relations legislation and 'the lack of positive efforts to bridge the cultural gaps ... between mainstream society and minority groups, particularly the Chinese and Irish Traveller communities' (CERD 1996:paras. 229–35).

The UN also has a Convention against Discrimination in Education (adopted by the UN's Educational, Scientific and Cultural Organization (UNESCO) in 1960) and a Convention concerning discrimination in employment and occupation (adopted by the International Labour Organization (ILO) in 1958). While these certainly seek to protect people against discrimination based on race, colour, religion, political or other opinion, national or social origin, and so on, they are not widely known or frequently invoked. Each has an enforcement mechanism which can actually achieve concrete results, though not quickly. UNESCO's complaints procedure does not allow for stringent investigations, and details of complaints have to be kept confidential, but the 'success' rate is more than 50 per cent (Marks 1992:97). The ILO complaints procedure is also relatively effective, although it cannot as a rule be invoked by individuals, only by organisations representing individuals. There is power to carry out a survey on discrimination, but none has yet been conducted (Swepston 1992).

In the area of so-called 'soft' (that is, non-binding) law, there is UNESCO's Declaration on Race and Racial Prejudice (1978), which affirms the 'right to be different' and stresses the need for affirmative action as far as disadvantaged groups are concerned. Likewise, Article 4(2) of the UN's Declaration on the Elimination of All Forms of Intolerance and of Discrimination Based on Religion or Belief (1981) requires states to 'make all efforts ... to take all appropriate measures to combat intolerance on the grounds of religion or other beliefs' (Dickson 1995). Most recently, the UN's Declaration on the Rights of Persons Belonging to National or Ethnic, Religious and Linguistic

Minorities (1992) asserts that states should 'encourage knowledge of the history, traditions, language and culture of the minorities existing within their territory' (Article 4(4)) and confers on members of minorities the right 'to participate effectively' in decisions affecting that minority (Article 2(3)). But the Declaration does not require protection of minority practices if they are 'in violation of national law and contrary to international standards' and the right to participate effectively must be exercised 'in a manner not incompatible with national legislation'. In March 1993, the UN appointed a Special Rapporteur on Contemporary Forms of Racism. This official has presented an annual report to the UN's Commission on Human Rights ever since. In December 1993, the General Assembly declared the following ten years to be the Third Decade to Combat Racism and Racial Discrimination; it annexed a programme of action to its resolution and this was supplemented by a further resolution adopted by the Economic and Social Council in July 1995 (see Wallace 1997:173–83) and, in 1997, the Assembly opted to convene a World Conference on racism and intolerance by 2001. Other suggestions for improvement to the UN machinery include more frequent references to, and requests for advisory opinions from, the International Court of Justice at The Hague and increased dialogue between parties to conflicts (Alfredsson and de Zayas 1993:8).

From this brief overview of UN work in the field of racism, it should be apparent that, although that august body is very able and willing to agree the adoption of high-sounding principles, it is not so ready to ensure effective redress for individuals or groups who are the victims of breaches of those principles. At this level, international law operates not to bind states to legal rules but merely to persuade them to change their national laws voluntarily. The UN's efforts, in short, are exhortatory rather than mandatory: they encourage but do not oblige states to take more effective steps to tackle racism.

Protection of Ethnic Groups and Races by the European Union

At the European level the achievements to date in securing legal protection for minority groups are equally non-momentous (see MacEwen 1995, Chapter 3). Recent disturbances in Eastern Europe, particularly in the Balkans, illustrate this all too starkly. The chief guarantors for such protection should be the European Union and the Council of Europe. We will show, however, that the former has been very slow to accept, or assert, competence in the field (Bindman 1996), and that the latter has for the most part rested on its laurels – as represented by the European Convention on Human Rights (1950). Nor, as yet, has the Organization for Security and Co-operation in Europe (OSCE) managed to achieve a great deal. To a large extent,

ethnic minorities in Northern Ireland, like such minorities in other parts
of the United Kingdom, have therefore been unable to benefit from
a European-imposed protection that goes much beyond what the UK
government has itself been prepared to confer. There are signs in the
1990s that European organisations are becoming increasingly active
in this sphere, but much still remains to be done.

The Development of EU Policy on Racial Discrimination

The importance of the European Union to Northern Ireland's law on
racial discrimination lies in the ability of the EU to enact binding
legislation, which may then extend rights to individuals, enforceable
at the European Court of Justice in Luxembourg. This is a familiar
forum for combating sexual discrimination, and a number of individuals
from Northern Ireland have pursued cases of sexual discrimination
through it. Much of the potential importance of the EU thus lies in
the possibility that it could enact an 'Anti-Discrimination Directive',
similar to that applicable *vis-à-vis* sexual discrimination, which would
then provide a means of legal recourse for individual victims of racial
discrimination in Northern Ireland and elsewhere in the EU.

Nevertheless, it is only relatively recently that the European Union
has addressed itself to the problem of racial discrimination. Indeed, it
is unlikely that the drafters of the founding Treaties regarded the
absence of any reference to racial discrimination as particularly
noteworthy. The European Communities (EC) were essentially *economic*
organisations and contained no more than 'the rudimentary features'
of a European social policy (Borchardt 1995:64). More importantly,
the integration of ethnic minority communities was not a pressing
social issue for the six original member states. In 1959, 75 per cent of
all 'immigrants' were European Community nationals living in another
member state. However, by 1973, this figure had changed dramati-
cally; 65 per cent of immigrants were non-Community nationals and
they comprised 5 per cent of the total EC labour force (Shanks
1977:31). This change can be explained by the member states' reliance
on immigrant labour to rectify the problem of labour shortages caused
by the intensity of post-war economic growth. However, the import
of foreign labour was perceived as a purely temporary phenomenon;
the member states anticipated the workers would return to their
countries of origin once the labour shortages had passed (ESC 1984:para.
2). This perspective helps explain why little thought was given, at that
time, to the need for Europe-wide policies to promote the better
integration of immigrants and to combat racial discrimination.

This situation was transformed during the 1970s. As unemployment
rose sharply, member states drastically curtailed the opportunities for

any new immigration and encouraged existing immigrants to return to their country of origin. Yet, by the early 1980s, it was evident that attempts to end, let alone reverse, such immigration had been a failure; some eleven million non-EC migrants were still resident within EC territory (Webber 1991:12). Not only had member states' immigration policies become 'a source of frustration', there were also worrying signs of a growth in racism (Sciortino 1991:89).

It was in this context, bearing in mind also the results of the 1984 elections for the European Parliament (in which several racistly inclined candidates had been successful), that the need for a Community-wide response to racism came to be recognised. In 1985, the European Parliament convened a special 'Committee of Inquiry into the Rise of Fascism and Racism in Europe'. The inquiry found that xenophobic sentiment was rising with 'alarming intensity' and set out a wide-ranging action plan to help combat fascism and racism (EP 1985:67). However, the only recommendation immediately acted upon was the call for a 'Joint Declaration against Racism and Xenophobia', which was signed on 11 June 1986 by the European Parliament, the Commission and the Council of Ministers. The Declaration stressed 'the dangers of racism and xenophobia, and the need to ensure that all acts or forms of discrimination are prevented or curbed' (OJ 1986 C 158/1). The declaration was intended to be a symbol of the commitment of the Community to combating racial discrimination. In fact, it has since come to symbolise all that afflicts the Community's actions in this sphere – an endless stream of solemn declarations and determined resolutions, but a failure to proceed beyond the rhetoric into the realm of substantive policy actions.

Any momentum generated by the Joint Declaration quickly dissipated. Nothing about racial discrimination was inserted into the Single European Act in 1986. It became evident that the Council of Ministers viewed the Joint Declaration as an end in itself, rather than as a precursor to an active policy commitment. This position did not begin to change until 1989 and the signing of the Community Charter of Fundamental Social Rights of Workers (better known as the Social Charter) by eleven of the twelve member states, the UK being the exception. This was another non-binding declaration, designed 'to set out formally the broad principles underlying our model of workers' rights' (Delors 1989). Significantly, the Preamble of the Charter stated that 'in order to ensure equal treatment, it is important to combat every form of discrimination, including discrimination on grounds of sex, colour, race, opinions and belief' (CEC 1990). Whilst the accompanying Social Charter Action Plan left the implementation of this principle to appropriate action by the member states and the two sides of industry (CEC 1989:Part I, para. 5), the inclusion of a reference to racial discrimination provided the Commission with an authoritative basis for future action in this sphere.

Recent Steps Taken by the European Commission

Pragmatically, the Commission concentrated initially on a variety of non-legislative means to combat racial discrimination. For example, it significantly expanded its expenditure commitment. Whereas the Community spent a meagre ECU 50,000 on combating racism in 1990, from 1992 to 1994 the combined budget for measures to combat racism expanded to ECU 1.75 million. This expenditure was directed towards a variety of initiatives, such as the 'Cities' Anti-Racism Project'. Commencing in 1995, and with a budget of ECU 2 million in that year, this project aims 'to promote local partnerships to tackle a few closely defined priority issues' (CEC 1995:para. 2.2). Dublin has benefited from this scheme, but as yet, to our knowledge, Belfast has not.

Further financial support was made available through the designation of 1997 as European Year against Racism. Under this project, the Commission provided ECU 4.7 million to co-fund anti-racism initiatives during the course of 1997 (*European Voice*, 24–30 October 1996). The kinds of activities carried out included a UK campaign for racial equality in the health service and for health workers, and the introduction of teaching modules on racism in schools in Ireland (CEC 1997:7–8). However, the Commission has increasingly acknowledged that a comprehensive and effective policy against racism cannot be sustained merely by Community grants and non-binding recommendations. In 1994, it signalled the need for the Community to move beyond such measures and to adopt binding legislation to prohibit racial discrimination: 'the Commission therefore believes that, at the next opportunity to revise the Treaties, serious consideration must be given to the introduction of a specific reference to combating discrimination on the grounds of race, religion, age and disability' (CEC 1994:Chapter VI, para. 27). Furthermore, in December 1995, the Commission issued a 'Communication on Racism, Xenophobia and Anti-Semitism'. This drew together the Commission's activities in the area and set out plans for the future direction of policy. Crucially, it recognised the importance of European legislation to the further development of EU policy on racism: 'the Commission believes that Community legislation designed to guarantee minimum levels of protection against discrimination throughout the Community would constitute a highly significant step towards full achievement of the Treaty objectives' (CEC 1995:19).

Changing Attitudes Within the Council of Ministers

There has been a steady evolution of support within the Council for an enhanced Community dimension to the fight against racism. This change in attitude followed a significant upsurge in racial violence and a marked augmentation in electoral support for extreme right-wing parties since the mid-1980s (Eatwell 1994). These developments have in turn been linked to the higher rates of unemployment since the late 1980s and the problems member states have had to face in managing immigration. These are truly European phenomena, and many member states have begun to recognise that matters such as immigration, asylum and the integration of ethnic minorities demand a common European policy response.

In June 1994, on a Franco-German initiative, the member states agreed to establish a Consultative Commission on Racism and Xenophobia. This was charged with formulating 'recommendations, geared to national and local circumstances, on co-operation between governments and the various social players to promote tolerance, understanding and harmony in relations with foreigners' (Bulletin of the EU 6-1994, point I.29). Consisting of one representative from each member state, a representative of the European Commission, two Members of the European Parliament and an observer from the Council of Europe, the Consultative Commission delivered its final report to the June 1995 Cannes European Council. This recommended a variety of initiatives which the member states and the EU could adopt to combat racism, in the fields of information, education and justice (Consultative Commission 1995).

Flowing from these recommendations, the Council of Ministers proceeded to adopt three new measures on racism. First, in autumn 1995, the Council agreed two new resolutions on racism, one on the Fight against Racism and Xenophobia in the fields of Employment and Social Affairs (OJ 1995 C 296/13), and the other on the Response of Educational Systems to the Problems of Racism and Xenophobia (OJ 1995 C 312/1). Whilst they are weakened by their non-binding nature, they do state with greater specificity the measures member states are urged to adopt, such as including respect for diversity as an element in the training of public officials, and to this end assist in forging a common policy approach to racism amongst the member states.

The utility of non-binding measures is a contested issue in this field. Many commentators reject such initiatives as simply yet more words, when what is needed is action. At least one MEP has criticised the Council for being 'long on rhetoric and short on action' (Lomas 1989). Nevertheless, as we have seen in relation to the UN, non-binding instruments may prove to be a necessary precursor to the adoption of binding legislation (Sciarra 1995:340). If nothing else, they form an important reference point which could be usefully employed when lobbying governments at the national level.

The two Council resolutions in autumn 1995 were to have been complemented by the concurrent adoption of a resolution in the Justice and Home Affairs Council on racist groups and racist propaganda. However, the fraught nature of policy-making in this sphere was demonstrated when this initiative was blocked by the British government (European Report no. 2087, Section IV, 13). This illustrates the underlying difficulty in making progress where decisions require unanimity. Another example of this problem was given in December 1996 when the British government again employed the requirement of unanimity to block the creation of a European Monitoring Centre on Racism (European Report 11 December 1996, Section IV, 1). The UK objections must be located within the general opposition of the then UK government to further European integration, especially in respect of social policy. The Conservative government maintained that racism was a matter best left to the member states – 'problems of discrimination (particularly on such sensitive questions of race and religion) are best dealt with ... through national legislation' (FCO 1996:para. 57).

Nevertheless, agreement on both of the aforesaid measures was eventually forthcoming. On 15 July 1996, the Justice and Home Affairs Council passed a 'Joint Action Concerning Action to Combat Racism and Xenophobia' (OJ 1996 L 185/5). Whilst legally unenforceable, the Joint Action places member states under a political obligation to ensure 'effective judicial co-operation' on a range of racist offences. The offences covered include public incitement to racial hatred and 'participation in the activities of groups, organisations or associations, which involve discrimination, violence, or racial, ethnic or religious hatred' (Title I(A)). The European Monitoring Centre on Racism was finally agreed in June 1997 (Regulation 1035/97, OJ 1997 L 151). The establishment of the Monitoring Centre should act to institutionalise the commitment of the EU to combating racism. Its aim will be to gather information on racist activity within the member states and to co-ordinate research into the causes and possible policy responses to racial discrimination.

The adoption of the various Council Resolutions, the European Year Against Racism initiative and the Monitoring Centre all demonstrate the existence of a certain dynamic in EU policy on racism. However, the continued evolution of the EU's contribution depends heavily on a move beyond non-binding measures. As stated earlier, this has been recognised by the Commission and endorsed by the Consultative Commission. In particular, the latter lent its support to the idea of a directive against racial discrimination, based on the principle that 'all individuals, regardless of their colour, race, nationality, ethnic or national origins or religion should have the right of equal access to employment, equal pay and fair treatment from an employer' (Consultative Commission 1995:39). Moreover, the Consultative Commission noted that 'effective record keeping and monitoring are central to the effective implementation of equal opportunities policies and action plans' (1995:40). This fits with the experience in Northern Ireland in respect of religious discrimination, and is an important voice in favour of extending existing monitoring to include details concerning the ethnicity of current and potential employees.

Towards Treaty Revision

The recommendation of the Consultative Commission that there should be EU legislation to prohibit racial discrimination in employment dovetails with the 'Starting Line' campaign (Dummett 1994). The 'Starting Line Group' was created in the early 1990s at the initiative of a variety of state agencies and non-governmental organisations, such as Britain's Commission for Racial Equality and the Brussels-based Churches' Commission for Migrants in Europe. These bodies enlisted legal experts from across the EU to prepare a draft directive for the elimination of racial discrimination. This draft directive was submitted in 1993 and received the express endorsement of the European Parliament (OJ 1993 C 342/19, para. 4). However, the adoption of Community legislation demands a specific legal basis within a treaty and, as mentioned above, neither the founding Treaty of Rome nor successor treaties contain any reference to racial discrimination. As a result, the Commission rejected the Starting Line directive on the grounds of an absence of a Treaty legal base. The European Parliament, on the other hand, has argued that the necessary legal powers for European legislation on racial discrimination *do* already exist, if only the Treaty were given an imaginative interpretation.

The response of the Starting Line Group to this initial setback was to submit a further proposal, this time for an amendment of the Treaty which would unequivocally allow for the adoption of EU legislation on racial discrimination. The European Parliament had already raised the issue of possible amendment of the Treaty during the negotiations leading to the Treaty of European Union agreed at Maastricht in 1991 (OJ 1990 C 324/219). However, on that occasion, the Parliament's proposal was not taken up by either the Commission or the member states. The Starting Line's proposal, called the 'Starting Point', would insert two clauses in the Treaty; one to include the elimination of racial discrimination as an objective of the EU, and the other to provide the EU with legal competence to enact legislation on racial discrimination (Spencer 1995:136). This proposal has subsequently been endorsed by almost 300 organisations from across the member states, including several from Northern Ireland, such as the Northern Ireland Council for Ethnic Minorities and the Chinese Welfare Association (Starting Line Group 1996).

The recommendations of the European Commission, the European Parliament, the EC Economic and Social Committee, the Consultative Commission and many NGOs did not go unheeded, and the member states were largely in agreement from the outset of the EU's Intergovernmental Conference (IGC), first convened on 29 March 1996 by the Italian presidency, as to the need for an amendment to the Treaty of Rome. The Treaty of Amsterdam 1997, therefore, provides for a new Article 6a in the Treaty establishing the European Community: 'Without prejudice to the other provisions of this Treaty and within the limits of the powers conferred by it upon the Community, the Council, acting unanimously on a proposal from the Commission and after consulting the European Parliament, may take appropriate action to combat discrimination based on sex, racial or ethnic origin, religion or belief, disability, age or sexual orientation' (EU 1997).

The insertion of Article 6a creates a clear expectation that the EU will move swiftly to adopt binding legislation on racial discrimination. The arguments in favour of such legislation were strengthened by a 1996 report published by the Dublin-based European Foundation for the Improvement of Living and Working Conditions. Entitled *Preventing Racism at the Workplace*, the report was the product of research in each of the member states into legislation on racial discrimination and it reveals a clear need for European-level legislation: 'across EC countries, measures to combat discrimination are variable in their scope and effectiveness, and in some cases hardly exist' (Wrench 1996:147). Member states, the report said, are unlikely to introduce measures which are truly effective unless encouraged to do so by a Directive at the European level. The adoption of such a Directive would be of genuine assistance to victims of racial discrimination throughout the member states and would be a practical demonstration of the EU's commitment to combating racism.

Protection of Ethnic Groups and Races by the Council of Europe and the OSCE

Protection Under the European Convention on Human Rights

The European Convention on Human Rights is, rightly, the proudest achievement of the Council of Europe. But the Convention does not contain a specific clause protecting minority rights. The closest it comes to doing so is in Article 14, which says that the rights conferred by the Convention 'shall be secured without discrimination on any ground such as sex, race, colour, language, religion, political or other opinion, national or social origin, association with a national majority, property, birth or other status'. Despite what the casual observer might think, this is not such a far-reaching provision in view of the fact that there are many rights *not* conferred by the Convention in the first place – social, economic and cultural rights, for example, but also the right to a nationality, the right to personal documents, the right to access to the media or to public services, the right to elections to non-legislative bodies, the right to establish oneself in a profession and the right to non-contributory social security benefits. Attempts to add a Protocol to the Convention to protect these and other rights frequently denied to members of ethnic minorities have so far come to nothing.

What has made the European Convention the world's most successful human rights instrument is its effective enforcement machinery, which allows cases to go before a European Commission of Human Rights and then, if declared admissible by the Commission, to a European Court of Human Rights. Cases which are not referred to the Court after having been declared admissible by the Commission are examined by the Council of Europe's Committee of Ministers, a political body. However, a survey of the 700 or so decisions taken to date by the European Court of Human Rights, and of the thousands of decisions on admissibility of complaints taken by the European Commission of Human Rights, shows that Article 14 has not been applied in a way that significantly improves the lot of ethnic minorities (de Zayas 1993:274–83; Harris *et al.* 1995, Chapter 15; Gomien *et al.* 1996:345–56). To a degree, this again reflects the fact that the rights protected by the Convention are individual, not group, rights, but the enforcement organs themselves, when they have had a discretion in the matter, have sometimes interpreted Article 14 rather narrowly.

The record with regard to the right to free speech, protected by Article 10 of the Convention, is not much better, especially when the question at issue has been 'hate speech', speech which incites hatred of a minority group. The Commission and Court have sometimes relied upon Article 17 of the Convention in order to deny the Article 10 right to someone who wants to stir up hatred on ethnic or national grounds. Article 17 reads: 'Nothing in this Convention may be interpreted as implying for any State, group or person any right to engage in any activity or perform any act aimed at the destruction of any of the rights and freedoms set forth herein or at their limitation to a greater extent than is provided for in the Convention.' But the key decision is that of the Court of Human Rights in *Jersild* v. *Denmark* (A-298, [1995] 19 EHRR1), where a journalist had made a television programme giving publicity to the racist views of a group of youths calling themselves 'The Greenjackets'. Although the Danish courts, including the Supreme

Court, upheld a fine imposed upon the journalist, the European Court (as well as the Commission) took the view that the reasons adduced for the conviction were not sufficient to establish convincingly that the interference with the enjoyment of freedom of expression was, as required by Article 10(2), 'necessary in a democratic society'.

Other Forms of Protection

Recognising the limitations inherent in the European Convention as a means of protecting ethnic minorities, the Council of Europe has diversified its strategy. As with the UN's work, it is necessary to distinguish between steps it has taken to assist minorities in general and specific measures it has taken to combat discrimination. The former have culminated in the adoption by the Committee of Ministers of the Framework Convention for the Protection of National Minorities in 1994. The latter have included measures aimed at the education of young people and at the protection of language and cultural rights.

The Framework Convention had at least three precursors worth mentioning. The first was the proposal for a European Convention for the Protection of Minorities, issued in 1991 by the European Commission for Democracy through Law (the Venice Commission), a body of experts which advises the Council of Europe on matters of constitutional law. As explained by Malinverni (1991), this proposed Convention conferred on minorities, as such, 'the right to the respect, safeguard and development of their ethnical, religious or linguistic identity' (Article 3(2)) and 'the right to freely preserve, express and develop their cultural identity in all its aspects, free of any attempts at assimilation against their will' (Article 6(1)). The control machinery suggested was a European Committee for the Protection of Minorities, which would be able to examine reports regularly submitted by state parties as well as act as an adjudicator should the state party concerned so consent. The second precursor was a draft additional Protocol to the European Convention on Human Rights, presented by the Austrian government to the Committee of Ministers in 1992. Third, the Parliamentary Assembly of the Council of Europe adopted its own draft additional Protocol to the Convention in 1993 (Klebes 1993).

By opting to produce a whole new Convention, rather than a Protocol to the Convention on Human Rights, the Council of Europe has abandoned any prospect of giving the power to enforce the Minorities Convention to the existing Commission and Court of Human Rights. Instead, the Framework Convention, like the Venice Commission's proposed Convention, requires states to transmit regularly, to the Council of Europe's Secretary-General, full information on the legislative and other measures taken to give effect to the principles set out in the Convention. There is no provision for a judicial or quasi-judicial body to adjudicate upon a state's compliance. It is also noteworthy that the Convention eschews any definition of 'national minority' and predominantly deals with issues by addressing the rights of members of minorities rather than the minorities as groups (Klebes 1995).

The Framework Convention will enter into force for those states that have ratified it (although this often requires parliamentary approval in the state in question) once the twelfth ratification has occurred. As two-thirds of the member states of the Council of Europe signed the Convention within a day of its adoption (signing being the first step on the road to ratification), the prospects of its coming into force in the near future are bright. The UK is one of those states which has already signed, but it is still unclear what changes, if any, the government proposes to make to laws in the UK if the Convention is to be fully implemented there.

As regards the measures taken by the Council of Europe to combat discrimination, following the Vienna Summit in 1993 (the first ever for heads of state and government in the Council of Europe), a European Youth Campaign Against Racism, Xenophobia, Anti-Semitism and Intolerance was launched (Council of Europe 1993). This has committees in all member states, working singly and collectively to promote the Campaign under the slogan 'All Different, All Equal'. In Northern Ireland, the local Campaign Steering Group works alongside the Northern Ireland Youth Forum. Here, as throughout Europe, the Campaign has been a fairly low-profile affair, perhaps because of the small budget allocated to it. Whether it will reduce the incidence of racism remains to be seen.

The Council of Europe has also opened for signature a European Charter for Regional or Minority Languages (1992), which will require at least five ratifications to come into force, and the Committee of Ministers is overseeing the preparation of a draft additional protocol 'complementing the European Convention on Human Rights in the cultural field by provisions guaranteeing individual rights, in particular for persons belonging to national minorities'. The Parliamentary Assembly of the Council of Europe has already suggested twelve rights that could be included in any such protocol, such as the right to express, preserve and develop one's cultural identity, the right to use a minority language in dealings with administrative authorities, the right to display local street names in a minority language (important in Northern Ireland) and the right to unimpeded contacts with the citizens of another country.

Protection Under the OSCE

Side by side with these developments within the Council of Europe,
there have been a number of significant steps taken by the OSCE (Brett
1996). Although originating out of the Helsinki Final Act of 1975, this
organisation came of age in 1990 with the adoption of the Charter of
Paris for a New Europe and with the issuing of the Copenhagen
Document. As Brett explains: '[T]he commitments on minorities in
the Copenhagen Document are still considered to be more advanced
than provisions on minorities made by the United Nations and Council
of Europe ... The Copenhagen Document not only includes detailed
standards on use of the mother tongue, educational provision, freedom
of association among themselves and across borders, and so on, but
also on the fundamental right of individuals to choose whether or not
to identify themselves as members of a minority' (Brett 1996:685).
Again, though, the problem lies in enforcement, since there is no
effective way in which the OSCE's standards can be properly policed.
One suggestion is that the enforcement function should be given to
the existing organs implementing the European Convention on Human
Rights (Breitenmoser and Richter 1991), but that looks increasingly
impracticable.

The 1990 Charter of Paris marked the end of the then *Conference*
for Security and Co-operation in Europe as an intergovernmental
talking-shop and the beginning of an institutionalisation process which
has since included the establishment of the Office for Democratic
Institutions and Human Rights in Warsaw and the Centre for Conflict
Prevention in Prague. Most notable of all, for present purposes, is the
appointment of a High Commissioner for National Minorities
subsequent to the Helsinki follow-up meeting in 1992 (Rosas 1993;
Wright 1996:200). The Commissioner (a former Dutch Foreign
Minister, Max van der Stoel) has primarily a conflict-prevention role
although, at the insistence of the UK, Spain and Turkey, he cannot
exercise this in countries where there are organised acts of terrorism.
If there were to be a permanent cease-fire in Northern Ireland it is not
beyond the bounds of possibility that the Commissioner might find a
role there.

Conclusion

It is obvious that there is no shortage of international standard-setting
when it comes to protecting minority rights and outlawing discrimination. The main problem lies in ensuring that those agreed standards
are adhered to. Political considerations can easily get in the way, as
with the Kurds in Turkey or the Chechens in Russia. This highlights

the fact that legal rights alone are not sufficient for minority protection (Gilbert 1996:171). Giving minorities some political control of their own affairs may also be necessary, as may reformed administrative procedures to ensure that the special needs of minority groups are satisfactorily catered for in practice. There is only so much that international law, *per se*, can achieve in this context. It is a necessary but by no means a sufficient guarantee for full minority rights protection. On the other hand, the difference between the effects of hard law and soft law, or between legal and political obligations, can be exaggerated. Arie Bloed has rightly pointed out: 'A commitment does not have to be legally binding in order to have binding force; the distinction between legal and non-legal binding force resides in the legal consequences attached to the binding force, not in the binding force as such. Violation of politically, but not legally binding agreements is as unacceptable as any violation of the norms of international law' (Gilbert 1996:172).

4 Law, Policing and the Criminal Justice System

Ciarán White

This chapter will examine the manner in which the state, through its laws and policies, accommodates persons of minority ethnic origin in Northern Ireland. It therefore discusses the legal and administrative mechanisms of relevance to minority ethnic persons. The focus is, first, on the legal mechanisms for protecting minority ethnic persons from racial discrimination by government, private employers or service providers and for punishing those who engage in racist attacks or behaviour; second, on policing and elements of the criminal justice system; and, third, on significant programmes, policy initiatives and developments pertinent to minority ethnic persons.

Protection from Discrimination and Racist Attack

Race Relations Legislation

The single most significant legal mechanism for protecting minority ethnic persons in Britain, the Race Relations Act 1976, was not extended to Northern Ireland. However, in August 1997, the Race Relations (Northern Ireland) Order 1997 came into force, resulting in the outlawing of racial discrimination in Northern Ireland for the first time (White 1997). This Order is extremely similar to the 1976 Act outlawing racial discrimination in the workplace; in education; in the availability of goods, facilities, services; the disposal and management of premises; providing a mechanism for victims of discrimination to obtain redress; as well as establishing the Commission for Racial Equality for Northern Ireland. There are two main types of discrimination recognised by the legislation – direct and indirect. Direct discrimination involves treating another person less favourably on racial grounds. Indirect discrimination occurs where conditions or requirements are imposed which, while superficially free from racial bias, operate in a disproportionately disadvantageous way upon persons

70

of a particular racial group. The definition of indirect discrimination, in Article 3(b), has four elements: a requirement or condition is applied equally to all; but the proportion of persons from the same racial group as the alleged victim who can comply with it is considerably smaller than the proportion of persons not belonging to that racial group; such a requirement or condition cannot be shown to be justifiable; and the requirement or condition operates to the detriment of the alleged victim because he or she cannot comply with it.

Whether the group to which the victim of discrimination belongs is a 'racial group' for the purposes of anti-racism legislation is governed by the criteria set out by the House of Lords in *Mandla* v. *Dowell Lee* (1983) 2 AC 548. In that case, a young Sikh boy, who wished to attend a private school, was denied admission on the basis that he could not comply with the school policy on uniforms, because he wore a turban over his unshorn hair, in accordance with the tenets of his religion. Religious discrimination legislation does not apply in Britain and his complaint was that he had suffered racial discrimination. The success of his case hinged on whether he was discriminated against because of his ethnic origins. Thus it was vital to establish whether Sikhs were an ethnic group protected by the legislation. Lord Fraser set out what he considered were the criteria to judge whether a group was an ethnic one. There are two essential criteria which a group must possess: a long-shared history of which the group is conscious and distinguishing it from other groups, and the memory of which it keeps alive; and a cultural tradition of its own, including family and social customs and manners, often but not necessarily associated with religious observance. There are also a range of non-essential criteria. Compliance with these is not essential but does serve to reinforce the view that the group is an ethnic one. These are: a common geographical origin or descent from a small number of common ancestors; a common language, not necessarily particular to that group; a common literature particular to that group; a common religion, different from that of neighbouring groups or from the general community surrounding it; being a minority, or being an oppressed, or dominant group, within a larger community.

In the Mandla case, Sikhs were considered as an ethnic group. Jews have also been considered an ethnic group (*Seide* v. *Gillette Industries Ltd.* [1980] IRLR 427), as have English Romanies (*CRE* v. *Dutton* [1989] QB 783). Welsh people (*Griffiths* v. *Reading University Students' Union, EOR Discrimination Case Law Digest*, Spring 1997:3) and Scots (*Northern Joint Police Board* v. *Power* [1997] IRLR 610) are also 'national groups' covered by the legislation. However, judicial interpretation has determined that Rastafarians (*Crown Suppliers (PSA)* v. *Dawkins* [1991] IRLR 327) are not an ethnic group. A significant difference between the English Act and the Northern Ireland Order is that, in Article 5(2)(a) of the 1997 Order, Travellers are specifically included as an ethnic group protected by the legislation. They are defined as 'the community of people commonly so called who are defined (both by themselves and by others) as people with a shared history, culture and traditions including historically, a nomadic way of life on the island of Ireland'.

The Race Relations Order specifically withholds protection from those groups defined by reference to religious belief or political opinion (Article 5(3)(b)). This means that Catholics and Protestants, for example, will not be in a position to use the legislation where they allege discrimination on the basis of their religious identities. Instead, they must bring a complaint under the fair employment legislation, if possible. However, if they can prove that the discrimination was on the basis of their 'Irishness' or 'Britishness' they may be protected by the 1997 Order.

Employment

The prohibition of discrimination in the field of employment is quite wide. Trades unions and employers' organisations, professional regulatory bodies, those involved in vocational training, partnerships, barristers and the police are all prohibited from discriminating against employees or potential employees. In certain circumstances, preferring a person of a particular ethnic group for a job does not amount to unlawful discrimination. If it is a 'genuine occupational qualification' that a person be of a particular ethnic group then an employer will have an effective defence (Article 8) (*Tottenham Green Under Fives Centre* v. *Marshall* (no. 2) [1991] IRLR 162). Where it can be demonstrated that it is a *bona fide* requirement for the post holder to be of a certain ethnic origin, then it is not unlawful discrimination to prefer such a person. This exception only applies in respect of certain prescribed occupations – dramatic performances/entertainment, artistic or photographic modelling, or food and drink outlets – where such a person is required for reasons of authenticity.

This defence also applies to the provision of personal services promoting the welfare of a particular group, where these services can most effectively be provided by a person of that racial group. Employing a Chinese person to act as a health visitor to the Chinese community, therefore, is not a discriminatory action under the legislation, provided that the individual is best placed to deliver those services to the Chinese community. However, employers cannot avail themselves of this defence where they already have employees of the racial group in question, who are capable of carrying out the relevant duties and whom it would be reasonable to employ on those duties and whose numbers are sufficient to meet the employers' likely requirements

(Article 8(4)). Therefore, if an employer has a sufficient number of employees of Chinese origin to carry out health visiting services to Chinese people, it would be unlawful discrimination to appoint more.

Positive discrimination – for example, preferring a black person to a white person for a vacant position because black persons are under-represented in the workforce or because historically they have suffered discrimination – is unlawful. It could only be lawful if it were a 'genuine occupational qualification' (see above) that, say, the person be of Afro-Caribbean origin. Although the legislation does not authorise positive discrimination, it does allow for what are generally termed 'affirmative measures'. These provide exemptions from the Order where access to training facilities is provided for, or encouragement directed at, members of a particular racial group only. These only apply, however, because that racial group has 'special needs' or because there is no representation, or an under-representation, of persons from that racial group in a particular workplace sector of the workforce.

Education

Discrimination by either public or private educational establishments in relation to an application for admission to a school, college or university or in the treatment of existing pupils in those establishments is prohibited by Article 18. This prohibition applies to all levels of education, from primary to tertiary. Education and Library Boards and the Council of Catholic Maintained Schools (CCMS) in Northern Ireland are under a further duty not to discriminate (Article 19), when exercising any of their statutory obligations under the various Education Orders. Aside from these specific measures there is a general duty on public sector educational establishments to 'secure that facilities for education, and any ancillary benefits or services are provided without racial discrimination' (Article 20). This general requirement should, therefore, persuade educational establishments to 'equality-proof' their provision.

Goods, Facilities and Services

Goods, facilities and services made available to the public, or to a section of it, whether for payment or not, cannot be provided or made available in a discriminatory manner. The legislation helpfully provides examples of what amounts to 'facilities' and 'services'. These are: access to public places; availability of accommodation in hotels, boarding houses or similar establishments; facilities by way of banking or insurance for grants, loans, credit or finance; entertainment, recreation or refreshment facilities; education facilities; transport or travel services; and services provided by a profession or trade, or by a local or public authority.

A major limitation on the applicability of the above provision resulted from a House of Lords decision. In *R* v. *Entry Clearance Officer*, Bombay ex p Amin [1983] AC 818, 'goods, facilities and services' was interpreted as applying to acts which were at least similar to acts which could be done by private persons. In that case, the Entry Clearance Officer was not providing a service, but performing the duty of controlling would-be immigrants. This suggested that there was potentially a range of public activities not covered by anti-racism legislation, thereby allowing the state to discriminate with impunity in those areas. The Commission for Racial Equality (CRE) in Britain has argued that an appropriate amendment should be made to the legislation to ensure that it applies to all governmental activities (CRE 1992:30).

Clubs and Premises

'Associations' whose main object is 'to enable the benefits of membership to be enjoyed by persons of a particular racial group, defined otherwise than by reference to colour' are not subject to the legislation, provided they do not discriminate on the basis of colour. Thus the Zimbabwean Students' Association, for example, although restricting membership to one racial group, would not be guilty of discrimination because non-Zimbabweans are not permitted to join. However, such an association would be guilty of discrimination if it refused to admit white Zimbabweans. Landlords, estate agents, rental agencies and anyone selling, letting or in any way disposing of premises in Northern Ireland may not discriminate on racial grounds. This prohibition extends to both the public and private sectors. Refusing to sell property to a minority ethnic person would amount to discrimination, as would charging a higher price or imposing a condition that would not be imposed on a person of a different racial group.

District Councils and the Duty to Eliminate Racial Discrimination

Every district council, too, is under a duty to 'make appropriate arrangements with a view to securing that its various functions are carried out with due regard to the need to eliminate unlawful racial discrimination and promote equality of opportunity, and good relations between persons of different racial groups' (Article 67). This is a directive to be proactive about eliminating racial discrimination and in that sense is similar to, though more extensive than, the general duty on public sector education establishments found in Article 20. It differs from almost all of the provisions examined so far in that they prevent unlawful discrimination, whereas this duty obliges councils to consider how they might go about eliminating it, and how they might promote good relations. Given that district councils in Northern Ireland are responsible for a narrower range of activities than their counterparts in Britain, this duty is not as significant an innovation in Northern Irish law as it might have been. In order to equalise the position between Britain and Northern Ireland, this obligation would have to be extended to the various agencies within the latter which have responsibility for functions, such as housing, and health and social services – which are carried out by local authorities in England and Wales.

The Commission for Racial Equality – Duties and Powers

The Race Relations (NI) Order 1997 created the Commission for Racial Equality for Northern Ireland (CRENI) which has seven commissioners and is the equivalent body to the CRE in Britain. Its functions are to work towards the elimination of discrimination, promote equality of opportunity and good relations between persons of different racial groups generally, keep the legislation under review and submit proposals for amending it – on its own initiative or at the request of the Department of Economic Development.

The Order provides the Commission with a range of powers to fulfil these statutory duties. It may therefore provide financial or other assistance to organisations concerned with 'the promotion of equality of opportunity, and good relations, between the persons of different racial groups' (Article 43) or it may undertake, or commission, research or educational activities (Article 44). The CRENI is also empowered to issue Codes of Practice (that is, non-binding guidance on how to comply with the legislation) about eliminating discrimination and promoting equality of opportunity between different racial groups, in employment and housing. One of the more important powers available to the Commission is the ability to conduct a 'formal investigation' (Article 46). Formal investigations are examinations of particular firms, companies, organisations or industries to ascertain whether equality of opportunity operates in particular workplaces and spheres of life or because it is suspected that unlawful acts of discrimination are being perpetrated. They may be initiated by the Commission or the Department of Economic Development. In addition, as a result of judicial interpretation of its formal investigation powers, the CRE now has the power to conduct two types of investigations: (1) 'named persons investigations' and (2) 'general investigations'. The former arises where the Commission intends investigating a particular person or organisation identified in the proposed terms of reference. General investigations are more exploratory in nature and may relate, for example, to a particular industry in a locality. As regards enforcement of the Order, this is to be carried out chiefly in the industrial tribunal and the county courts. The enforcement provisions are broadly divisible into those that relate to enforcement by individuals and those that relate to enforcement by the CRE. Complaints by individuals about discrimination in employment must be made to the industrial tribunal within three months of the alleged discriminatory incident. Where individuals consider that they have been victims of discrimination in the provision of goods, facilities or services and the disposal or management of premises these allegations must be made, to a county court, within six months of the alleged discriminatory act, except where the complaint is one relating to an educational establishment or the performance of statutory duties by Education and Library Boards, or the CCMS, then the limitation period is extended to eight months to allow the Department of Education to be notified of the complaint.

We have seen that the CRE may enforce the Order through its formal investigation powers. The Commission alone has enforcement powers in relation to a number of specific activities, namely discriminatory advertisements and pressurising or instructing others to discriminate. If it considers that either of these activities has occurred, it may bring forth proceedings (Article 60). If the matter relates to employment, the Commission's application is made to the industrial tribunal; in all other matters, applications are made to a county court. In situations where the Commission fears that similar acts of unlawful discrimination are likely to be performed, then it may apply to a county court for an injunction to restrain such activity (Article 60(4)). Alternatively, the Commission can undertake a 'named person investigation'. Moreover, the Commission is given the power to deal with 'persistent' discriminators, even though they have been censured in the past for unlawful behaviour.

The enactment of anti-racism legislation in Northern Ireland is an important step in the recognition of minorities and their rights and concerns. However, as successive studies in Britain have shown, it will be no panacea (CRE 1992). In particular, such legislation will not invalidate discriminatory legislation already enacted or which may be enacted in the future. Thus the Local Government (Miscellaneous Provisions) (NI) Order 1985 – which provides the legislative basis for the 'designation' policy directed at Travellers (see Chapter 8) – will not be invalidated automatically by the enactment of race relations legislation, nor will the latter require the repeal of the 1985 Order. Neither will the more draconian Proposed Local Government (NI) Order 1997, which may replace the 1985 Order, be directly affected by the new Race Relations Order. Such legislation could only be invalidated if it was considered to contravene an anti-discriminatory provision of a Bill of Rights, something which does not (yet) exist in Northern Ireland or the UK.

Outlawing Racist Speech and Incitement to Hatred

Persons of minority ethnic origin can be subjected to racist speech and legislation in Northern Ireland has outlawed this for a number of years now. Incitement to hatred legislation was first introduced to Northern Ireland in the Prevention of Incitement to Hatred Act (NI) 1970. The present public order offences concerned with combating race hate speech are found in Part III of the Public Order (NI) Order 1987, which broadly mirrors the relevant legislation in England and Wales, the Public Order Act 1986 (Dickson 1997b). Article 9 provides that it is an offence to use – or display – threatening, abusive or insulting words or behaviour with intent to stir up hatred or arouse fear of a section of the Northern Ireland community, whether that group is defined by religious belief, colour, race, nationality or ethnic or national origins. Indeed, an offence is committed if, having regard to all the circumstances, hatred or fear is likely to be stirred up, or aroused, by the use, or display of such material. Thus the intent of the speaker is irrelevant if, to the objective onlooker, there is a likelihood that this will be the outcome. Written material includes signs, symbols or illustrations. Therefore, the offence includes daubing an area with racist graffiti, particularly if the graffiti directs others to attack persons of colour.

Related offences are found in Articles 10, 11 and 13. The first two Articles make it an offence to: publish or distribute written material, and distribute, show or play recorded or taped material which is threatening, abusive or insulting, with the intention of stirring up such fear or hatred or in circumstances where it is likely that such fear or hatred would be aroused. The third of these articles criminalises the possession of such material, where the person in possession intends to publish, display or distribute it. In order for the offence of publishing or distributing racist material to be committed, publications must be made available to the public or a section of the public. Publication or distribution to a single person is unlikely to constitute an offence. Therefore, if an organisation leaflets an area with racist material the offence would be committed, though not if it bombards one individual with this material. This 'loophole' could certainly be exploited by a cunning racist organisation and might be a particularly effective strategy where persons of colour find themselves physically isolated in Northern Ireland.

The police may arrest persons suspected of committing an offence under Article 9, but have no arrest power in respect of the other offences. The punishment for committing these crimes is not more than six months in prison and/or a fine not greater than the statutory maximum – £2,000 – if convicted in the magistrates' court or a term of imprisonment not longer than two years and/or a fine if convicted in the Crown Court. However, a prosecution for any of these offences cannot be instituted except by, or with the consent of, the Attorney-General (Article 25) and, in fact, no prosecutions have been brought for the offences in Part III of the 1987 Order. Indeed, it would appear that since 1970 only two prosecutions for alleged 'hate speech' have ever been taken. The first was under the 1970 Act and it was to prove the only prosecution under that Act. The unsuccessful nature of the prosecution may explain, at least partially, why the legislation was never used again. In 1971, John McKeague, then of the Shankill Defence Association, was prosecuted, along with two others, for his part in publishing a Loyalist Orange Songbook (*Belfast Telegraph*, 14 December 1971). It appears that it was accepted that the words used were threatening and abusive, but defence counsel requested the jury to consider the words in context and to ask whether the song was meant to be taken seriously. The defendants were all acquitted (Hadfield 1984:242). (At that time, under the Prevention of Incitement to Hatred Act it was necessary to prove that the speaker *intended* to stir up hatred or arouse fear.) The other prosecution involved George Seawright, then a Belfast City councillor for the Democratic Unionist Party (DUP). In 1984, he was convicted of using, at a public meeting, threatening, abusive or insulting words which were likely to cause a breach of the peace, in violation of Article 6(1)(a) of the Public Order (NI) Order 1981. During a meeting of the Belfast Education and Library Board, a discussion arose about complaints received from some Catholic parents who were unhappy at the fact that the British national anthem had been played at a joint ceremony between Catholic and Protestant schools. This angered Seawright who commented that all Catholics and their priests ought to be burned. He was fined £100 and given a six-month gaol sentence, suspended for three years (*Belfast Telegraph*, 29 November 1984).

Travellers and their representative organisations called for a prosecution when, in 1982, the then Deputy Lord Mayor of Belfast, Frank Millar, advocated that all Travellers be sent to the council incinerator (*Belfast Telegraph*, 2 July 1984). However, no prosecution was brought. Millar even repeated this comment in 1988 (*Anderstown News*, 5 March 1988) and alleged that Travellers were possibly providing a way for the Provisional IRA to move guns and explosives around Northern Ireland. No prosecution was brought on this second occasion either. There are, therefore, no examples of the legislation being used where the remarks were racist, rather than sectarian in tone. Given that Travellers are to be specifically protected as an ethnic group under the new anti-racism legislation, it would be sensible to amend the 'hate speech' provisions of the Public Order (NI) Order 1987 to ensure that there is no doubt that inciting others to hate Travellers is illegal. This has already been done in the Republic of Ireland.

It is difficult to explain why incitement to hatred laws have not been used more often. However, the low incidence of prosecution is not unique to Northern Ireland. Very few prosecutions have been initiated in England and Wales for the corresponding offences there. Between 1979 and 1994, only 44 prosecutions had been brought for incitement to racial hatred, 15 of which were under the Public Order Act 1986 (Foley 1995). Two general criteria are used by the Office of the Director of Public Prosecutions (DPP) when deciding whether to prosecute or not. The first is whether there is sufficient evidence to give rise to a reasonable chance of prosecution, and the second is whether prosecution is in the public interest. Both of these present their own problems. In order to satisfy the first, it would be preferable if the speech were recorded in some particular way or if , for example, there were witnesses with a very good recollection of the content of the speech. As regards the second criterion, the DPP may need to consider whether prosecution for a 'hate speech' offence might make someone a political martyr. A further explanation for the infrequent use of the legislation may lie in the fact that it specifically requires 'hatred' to be stirred up, which is a very specific emotion. Some commentators have suggested amending the legislation to require the emotions evoked to be 'ridicule and contempt', rather than hatred (Hadfield 1994).

The two latest anti-racism public order offences created by the Criminal Justice and Public Order Act 1994 – section 154 (offence of harassing or distressing somebody using threatening, abusive or insulting words or behaviour) and section 155 (giving the police the power to arrest persons suspected of publishing or distributing material intended, or likely, to stir up racial hatred) – do not apply to Northern Ireland. The main advantage of the first of these offences is that it would fill the 'loophole' identified in Articles 10, 11 and 13, because it would make it a criminal offence to target a particular individual, as opposed to a section of the public. The advantage of section 155 is that it would give the police the power to arrest someone for committing an offence under Article 10.

Policing and the Criminal Justice System

Evidence from Britain suggests that ethnic minorities are disproportionately disadvantaged by the criminal justice system. For example, as Fitzgerald (1993:12) has written: 'As a group they [Afro-Caribbeans] are likely disproportionately to suffer from the system's capacity for inequitable treatment.' It is impossible to draw similar conclusions about the Northern Ireland criminal justice system; not because the system is incapable of inequitable treatment, but because the issue of racial discrimination does not appear to a have been addressed or acknowledged in any systematic way thus far. For example, vital statistical evidence is unavailable. Here, therefore, I am confined to examining elements of the criminal justice system relevant to ethnic minorities by considering the minority ethnic person, in turn, as the victim, the suspect, the accused and the convict.

The minority ethnic communities in Northern Ireland had argued for a number of years that the police should recognise and record racially motivated crime. They claimed that racial abuse and discrimination were taking the form of racially motivated physical attacks on persons and property and that the failure by the police to recognise this hampered appropriate police strategies and responses. As a result of lobbying, the Community Affairs branch of the Royal Ulster Constabulary (RUC) began monitoring racially motivated crime on a force-wide basis in 1995. The scheme operates on the basis of guidelines issued by the Association of Chief Police Officers (ACPO), which define racially motivated crime. In the first full year of the scheme's operation, 66 such crimes were reported. (No figures are given in the Chief Constable's 1996 report.) However, the police believe that, while it is difficult to calculate the real level of unrecorded racially motivated crime (RUC 1996:23), the official statistics seriously understate the actual scale of the problem. The racial monitoring scheme was tested in a pilot scheme run in a number of locations throughout Northern Ireland in 1994. Following this test procedure, force instructions were drafted to implement the scheme. A review of the ACPO guidelines is to take place in the near future to consider how they might need alteration for Northern Ireland.

As a result of serious criminal attacks, the RUC has now become more proactive in investigating offences committed at the homes and businesses premises of the Chinese community, organising a dedicated team under the Serious Crime Squad to investigate these matters. Crime prevention material is now available in several ethnic languages, including Chinese, Hindu, Bengali, Arabic and Urdu. There has also been an increase in interest from the Police Authority for Northern Ireland (PANI) in minority ethnic communities. In April 1996, in response to approaches from the communities, PANI set up a Working Party, chaired by its Vice-Chairman to examine, *inter alia*, the relationship between minority groups and the police (PANI 1997:53). Two sub-groups have been established, one of which will learn more about the problems faced by ethnic minority groups, and a report is due from the Working Group. Another recent innovation has been the extension of the RUC's community awareness training, that all new police recruits undergo, to include inputs from representatives of the minority ethnic communities. It could not be said, nonetheless, that a significant number of RUC officers have undergone anti-racism training, though this may change and become force policy in the future (RUC 1997:44).

Racist behaviour by a police officer would clearly amount to the disciplinary offence of 'discriminatory behaviour' as listed in the RUC's Discipline Code (Schedule 1, RUC (Discipline and Disciplinary Appeals) Regulations 1988). Persons of colour who feel that a police officer has behaved in a racially discriminatory manner towards them can therefore make a complaint. However, one of the major flaws with the police complaints mechanism in Northern Ireland is that the investigation of complaints against the police is carried out by the police themselves. An investigating officer, from Complaints and Discipline Branch, is appointed to examine the complaint, with the function of the Independent Commission for Police Complaints limited to overseeing the investigation and ensuring that it is satisfied with the way in which it is being conducted (Dickson 1997a). Indeed, supervision of the investigation is carried out for some complaints only. Furthermore, many complaints are settled by informal resolution and persons of minority ethnic origin may not feel confident in pursuing a complaint, feeling that it is better to agree to an informal resolution. Significantly, the English Court of Appeal, in *Farah* v. *Commissioner for the Metropolis* [1997] 1 All ER 289, held that when assisting or protecting members of the public, a police officer was providing a service to the public. Therefore, if he or she racially discriminates against members of the public in those situations, they are personally liable. The police officer's employer, in this case the Commissioner of Police for the Metropolitan Area, is not vicariously liable, however.

As is the case in England and Wales, the Codes of Practice under the Police and Criminal Evidence legislation provide safeguards that may be of use to minority ethnic persons where they are suspected of committing crimes. The Police and Criminal Evidence (NI) Order 1989 (hereafter referred to as PACE) is the legislation under which most persons suspected of committing non-paramilitary offences are likely to be arrested. Codes of Practice have been issued, under Articles 60 and 65, setting out guidance for police officers when a suspect is detained for questioning under PACE. These Codes are not part of the law itself and thus police officers are not required to observe them. However, failure to observe the Codes can have very serious consequences and this is usually enough to ensure that they are complied with.

Where a suspect has a genuine difficulty in understanding English and the interviewing officer cannot speak the person's language, then the latter individual must provide an interpreter at the former's request (Code C, 13.2). Any action taken to call an interpreter and any agreement to be interviewed in the absence of an interpreter must be recorded on the custody record (Code C, 13.11). The interpreter cannot be a policeman for the purposes of giving the detainee legal advice, and a police officer can only fill this role if the detainee consents, in writing, to this (Code C, 13.9). The police should make every reasonable effort to make clear to the detainee that an interpreter will be provided at public expense (Code C, 13.8). The suspect may not be interviewed in the absence of an interpreter, except in exceptional cases where delay will involve an immediate risk of harm to persons or serious loss of or damage to property. The task of the interpreter is to translate questions put by the interviewing officers and the suspect's replies, but also to make a note of the interview in the suspect's own language, should he or she be called to give evidence. The interpreter must certify its accuracy and it is the task of the interviewing officer to make sure that such a note is made, except in cases where the interview is taped. The suspect must be given an opportunity to hear the note read and to sign it as being an accurate record or to indicate which parts are considered to be inaccurate. Statements must be taken down in the language in which they are made and again the suspect must be given an opportunity to sign the statement. An official English translation should be made subsequently (Code C, 13.4). Moreover, suspects should be aware that only conversations with lawyers are privileged; those with an interpreter are not. Therefore, an interpreter may be required to testify in court as to the content of any conversation with the suspect, except for a conversation between the lawyer, client and interpreter (Cape 1995).

If the Codes of Practice are not observed and, in particular, if an interview is not conducted in the presence of an interpreter, then it is possible that any resultant confession will not be admitted at a court hearing, thus rendering it more difficult for the police to secure a conviction. This is not always the case. Whether or not the confession is admitted is a matter for the trial judge, exercising discretion under Articles 74 and 76 of PACE. Article 74 states that where it is alleged, or where the court has a suspicion, that a confession was obtained by oppressing the suspect or by means which are likely to render the confession unreliable, then, unless the prosecution can convince the court beyond a reasonable doubt that this allegation is not true, the court must exclude it. Article 76 allows a court to exclude evidence if, having regard to all circumstances, it would be unfair to admit it. But, as stated earlier, the fact that a judge has this discretion can often be enough to deter the police from acting in breach of the Codes and from interviewing without an interpreter being present.

The ethnic status of prisoners in Northern Ireland gaols is not recorded, and whilst provision is made for recording the nationality of prisoners the system is not a useful one. The nationality of non-Irish or of non-British prisoners is not always recorded and, when it is, it is only as a broad category of 'Others'. The Northern Ireland Prison Service does not have a race relations policy as such, though its equal opportunities statement does prohibit staff from discriminating unfairly, *inter alia*, on the grounds of race. It is unclear, however, how this aspect of the statement is implemented and what is its effect. The Prison and Young Offenders' Centre Rules (NI) 1995 also contain some provisions which may be of relevance to minority ethnic persons. Thus every prisoner 'shall be provided with sufficient food ... which takes into account ... as far as practicable, religious or cultural requirements' (Rule 82). Foreign nationals, refugees or stateless persons must be given facilities to communicate with appropriate diplomatic representatives, or relevant national or international interests (Rule 24). Special arrangements are to be made to accommodate foreign nationals with linguistic difficulties (Rule 24(3)). No equivalent provision is stipulated for UK citizens with linguistic difficulties, but Rule 23, which requires all new prisoners to be provided with information sufficient to understand the disciplinary and other requirements of the prison, states that 'in the case of a prisoner who cannot read or *who for any reason has difficulty in understanding* the governor shall ensure that the necessary information has been properly explained to him [sic]' (my italics). Ethnic minority prisoners, like all prisoners, have a right to practice their religions (Rule 56). To this end, prisoners are allowed access to appropriate religious books or materials (Rule 64) and, where they belong to denominations for which no chaplains have been appointed, the governor shall do what is reasonable, if so requested by the prisoner, to arrange for regular visits by a minister of the prisoner's denomination.

Relevant Programmes and Policy Initiatives

Law is not the sole mechanism for tackling racism or racial disadvantage. Government programmes and policies also play a key role, thus making the resourcing of projects and organisations equally important. The funding of minority ethnic groups in Northern Ireland is not underpinned by statute, unlike the situation in Britain. Money is channelled instead on a non-statutory basis through administrative units like, for example, the Central Community Relations Unit (CCRU), an agency of the Central Secretariat of the Northern Ireland Civil Service. Thus, Making Belfast Work (MBW) and the Londonderry Regeneration Initiative have funded projects affecting minority ethnic persons. In 1994, MBW made £63,000 available to the Chinese Welfare Association (CWA) and Travellers' projects, and £60,000 in 1995, while the Londonderry Regeneration Initiative was supportive of the Derry Travellers' Group in 1994. The Department of the Environment

(DOE), the Training and Employment Agency and CCRU have all provided grant assistance to a range of organisations with ethnic minority concerns. In particular, since April 1995, CCRU has provided CWA with a 90 per cent grant towards the cost of a community interpreter and bilingual advocate. To complete this picture of governmental assistance, two other developments are worth noting. First, Health and Social Services Boards have jointly provided for a part-time interpreter to work with the Chinese community and, second, the Belfast Education and Library Board has provided two peripatetic primary teachers in English as a foreign language to assist with the education of minority ethnic children. These projects and initiatives are included here as examples of funding. In the future, the CRE(NI) should also play a significant role in funding communities and organisations using its powers under Article 43 (see above).

The Policy Appraisal and Fair Treatment (PAFT) guidelines and Targeting Social Need (TSN) are two other policy developments – perhaps the most important -which are intended to improve the position of minority ethnic persons (as well as many others) in Northern Ireland. The aim of the PAFT guidelines is 'to ensure that, in practice, issues of equality and equity condition policy-making and action in all spheres and at all levels of government activity, whether in a regulatory or administrative function or the delivery of services to the public' (CCRU 1996). Thus civil servants must consider the likely effect of policies and policy changes on a whole range of groups including, for example, people of different gender, sexual orientation, and age, as well as minority ethnic origin. PAFT guidelines have been in effect since 1 January 1994 and apply to all government departments and Next Step Agencies (for example, the Child Support Agency, and organisations with responsibility for activities formerly carried out by and which remain responsible to government departments). Because the relationship between Departments and Non-Departmental Public Bodies (NDPBs) is not uniform across the administration, the applicability of the guidelines is unclear. Departments have been instructed to 'use all appropriate means' to ensure that quangos comply with PAFT and, in particular, parent departments expect PAFT to be dealt with in the annual reports of such bodies. Departments are required to ensure that, as far as possible, private bodies to whom services are contracted out also comply with the guidelines. Consideration would need to be given to PAFT if, for example, it was intended to cut the level of peripatetic education provision, because this might impact adversely on Chinese people, for some of whom English as a second language education is very important.

Introduced in 1991, TSN predates PAFT and is an initiative with a narrower focus. The government has not published a report or policy paper on TSN but references to it by ministers and government departments show that its main effect should be 'to reduce unfair social and economic differentials by targeting resources more effectively on people and areas in greatest need' (CCRU 1995:10). It thus complements PAFT, though CCRU asserts that there is a distinct difference between the two in that 'TSN is primarily concerned with socio-economic differentials based on religious background. PAFT, however, is not confined to socio-economic issues and concerns a much broader range of social groups' (CCRU 1995:10). TSN, therefore, has not been of much benefit to minority ethnic persons because it has been orientated towards the majority ethnic population. There is no reason why the government should have limited the initiative to the two main sections of the community in the past and certainly no justification for this restrictive interpretation of TSN in the future. Therefore, if statistics reveal a significant disparity between annual per capita income levels of minority ethnic persons and those of the general population then consideration should be given to taking remedial action under TSN.

The PAFT initiative is monitored by CCRU, which has produced annual reports detailing the response to it of various government departments and agencies. However, neither PAFT not TSN appears to have made much practical impact and, as a result, there is some suspicion that the government is engaged here in 'window dressing'. For example, although the government cited both PAFT and TSN in its most recent submission to the United Nations' Committee for the Elimination of Racial Discrimination (CERD), it failed to provide any detail about improvements made due to policy implementation. Whether the developments that are said to result from the application of PAFT and TSN are those that would have taken place anyway and have simply been repackaged to suggest that the two policies were the catalysts for them is impossible to say. For instance, the 1995 PAFT annual report (CCRU 1996:13) lists three major items relating to persons of minority ethnic origin: the commitment to introduce anti-racism legislation; a research study into the demographic, social and employment profiles of ethnic minority communities; and the DOE's interdepartmental review of policies affecting Travellers. However, the introduction of anti-racism legislation owes as much, if not more, to the pressure exerted by CERD, local civil liberties organisations like the Committee on the Administration of Justice (CAJ), and the minority ethnic communities themselves, than to the impact of PAFT. Additionally, the research study in fact pre-dates the introduction of PAFT and was, it seems, a recognition that little 'hard' factual or statistical evidence existed, thereby hindering those charged with the delivery of services to those communities. The Department of the Environment's review of policies relating to Travellers did examine policies in the light of PAFT, but such a policy review would likely (*or should*) have taken place anyway.

Nevertheless, there is some evidence that PAFT is having an effect. For example, via the 1995 report, the DHSS announced that, following the application of PAFT to the special signing-on arrangements for Travellers at social security offices, changes were planned to have these brought into line with those for other customers. In addition, CCRU reported that it had contributed to the cost of producing the Multi-Cultural Resource Centre (MCRC)'s *Childcare reference book on ethnic minorities*, which provides information about religious traditions, customs, diets and lifestyles of various ethnic minority communities. It is intended primarily as a reference source for professionals in Northern Ireland coming into contact with children from these communities. In 1995, CCRU also sponsored research into the history of settlement of the Indian community in the region and contributed to an anti-racism package produced by the MCRC in 1996. Furthermore, other helpful practical measures are being taken by government departments and agencies, such as the publication of more information leaflets in the main minority ethnic languages. For instance, the Social Security Agency is producing posters and leaflets on benefit schemes for ethnic minority groups and the Child Support Agency has a Chinese version of the main client leaflet.

One significant development with regard to PAFT resulted from a judicial review action brought by the trade union UNISON, regarding Compulsory Competitive Tendering (CCT) in respect of the North Down and Ards Community Health and Social Services Trust. The trade union argued that the PAFT guidelines had not been considered by the Trust before embarking on CCT, notwithstanding the fact that there was evidence from the Equal Opportunities Commission (EOC) in Britain that CCT has a discriminatory impact, adversely affecting more women than men. Because the Trust had not been furnished with a copy of the guidelines, Mr Justice Kerr (in the High Court) could not conclude that the Trust's decision had been unlawful for failing to consider the guidelines. However, he held that if the Trust had known of these, he would have expected it to have considered them as part of its market testing operation. The Management Executive of the Health Service subsequently distributed the guidelines to health boards, trusts and agencies, while all government departments issued them to relevant quangos. Therefore, government entities that have been made aware of the PAFT guidelines should now consider them before embarking on, or implementing, a new policy; otherwise, they are likely to be acting unlawfully. Unfortunately, for the reasons discussed above, they are not required to enforce PAFT, merely to consider the guidelines. Hence the argument has developed that PAFT should be enacted in legislative form (Hutson 1996; McCrudden 1996). This is likely to be a lively topic of discussion in the next few years. Further consideration was given to the effect of the guidelines in *Casey* v. *Department of Education for Northern Ireland* (High Court of Northern Ireland (Queen's Bench) 16 October 1996, transcript available on Lexis). This was a judicial review of a ministerial decision to abolish student grants for students attending private higher education institutions in the Republic of Ireland. The applicant contended that this development had a greater impact on Catholics, than on Protestants. Girvan J. stated, in dismissing the application, 'the approach to interpreting governmental policy must be somewhat different from the approach adopted in relation to the construction of a statutory or contractual provision and if the policy is so formulated as to leave a degree of flexibility to the relevant government department in the application of the policy, the court could not conclude that the policy had been breached if the relevant department has acted within the degree of flexibility conferred by the policy'. He went on, 'the Department must have a margin of appreciation both in respect of the interpretation and the application of the policy'. The net effect has been to render the PAFT guidelines less of an effective tool for the groups mentioned in the guidelines when challenging governmental action, though future judicial interpretation may alter this.

PAFT is, therefore, limited in its effect because legislation takes precedence over non-statutory guidance. Indeed other, competing claims may also supersede it. In explaining 'the potential for tensions between the philosophy of PAFT and aspects of other government policies', the 1995 annual report makes the point that 'this may sometimes involve assessing the competing claim of different policies and this may ultimately be a matter for ministerial judgement as to public interest. The ominous conclusion is that 'it cannot be assumed that PAFT considerations will always predominate' (CCRU 1996:12). In their evaluation of PAFT, Osborne, Cormack and Gallagher (Osborne *et al.* 1996) identified a range of matters that need to be addressed to ensure the full and vigorous implementation of the guidelines. These matters included the status of the guidelines; how CCRU is to fulfil its monitoring functions; and how the departments will implement PAFT; in particular, whether they should take a mechanistic or a 'broad-brush' approach to implementation. The Committee on the Administration of Justice (CAJ), in its submission to the Employment Equality Review, a review supervised by the Standing Advisory Commission on Human Rights, also highlighted the 'patchy', uncoordinated implementation of PAFT and TSN. It commented that although every department and quango is responsible for implementing both these policies, there is a 'real risk being run that nobody is responsible' (CAJ 1996a:45).

Conclusion

It is clear that however invisible minority ethnic persons were in the
past, they are increasingly being considered as a distinct section of the
public in Northern Ireland, with particular needs and problems.
However, whilst progress has been made, we are still some distance
from the reality of a multicultural society where difference is respected
and equality expected. Considerable development of the initiatives
mentioned here, along with the creation of new programmes backed
up with the force of effective laws, is needed before we can say that
we have achieved the goal of an anti-racist society.

5 Health Issues and Ethnic Minorities in Northern Ireland

Carolyn Mason

This chapter aims to provide an overview of health issues affecting ethnic minority groups in Northern Ireland, within the wider policy context of the United Kingdom. In so doing, it is hoped that the gap between the rhetoric of health policy and the health experiences of people from ethnic minority groups will become apparent. The chapter begins by outlining the framework for health care delivery in Northern Ireland. The estimated makeup of the ethnic minority population is provided, along with a brief exploration of the problematic nature of the terms 'race', racism and ethnicity. There follows a summary of health policy relevant to black and minority ethnic groups, and a contrast is drawn between formal recommendations and the reality of fragmented and often irresolute action by health service management. The main focus of the chapter is on the health experiences of people from ethnic minorities, including difficulties with access, communication, and obtaining culturally appropriate services. It is argued that the inter-connection between these experiences, racism and social exclusion creates a reality of disadvantage and marginalisation for many members of the ethnic minority communities in Northern Ireland. The chapter concludes with suggestions for the future, including a recommendation that minority ethnic health care should be incorporated into mainstream service provision, which should, as a core function, be flexible in responding to the needs of people from a range of backgrounds.

Health Provision in Northern Ireland

Northern Ireland's health service is part of the UK-based National Health Service (NHS), which consists of an internal market with purchasers and providers of health care. The Labour government has announced its intention to abolish the internal market but to retain the separation between purchasers and providers of health care.

Currently, health purchasers in Northern Ireland are four geographically based health and social services boards and fundholding general
practices, while providers of health care include hospital and community
trusts, along with general practitioners (GPs) and an increasingly
diverse range of private and voluntary sector organisations. Although
this system was designed to promote efficiency and quality, it has
fragmented the health service into a wide array of discrete and competing
units, each with different objectives and agendas. Superimposed on
these divisions are distinct professional, managerial and other staff
groupings, with separate interests and varied lines of accountability.
In this situation, there is potential for central health policy to become
diffused and weakened and this, arguably, has been the case with
respect to government initiatives to promote racial equality in the
health service. There is strong evidence to suggest that the central policy
thrust towards ethnically sensitive healthcare has not been translated
into action (Doolin 1994; CWA 1996) and this will be explored further
in the later section on health policy.

Strategic direction for the health and personal social services in
Northern Ireland is set by the Department of Health and Social
Services (DHSS) in the *Regional Strategy for Health and Social Wellbeing
1997–2002* (DHSS 1996a). The four health and social services boards
are charged with assessing the health needs of their populations, setting
the strategic direction for health and social care in their areas and
ensuring equitable service delivery. In this respect, the boards have an
important responsibility towards ethnic minorities and, in keeping
with the Regional Strategy emphasis on community participation,
should be working with the minority ethnic communities to develop
an ethnically sensitive and non-discriminatory service. Until recently,
there has been little evidence of concerted effort in this respect. In
contrast, a major consideration for resource allocation has been the
well documented link between lower social class and poorer health
chances (Marmot and McDowell 1986; Townsend *et al.* 1992). It could
be argued that the focus on social class has diverted attention from
potentially important health factors associated with 'race' and culture
in the context of Northern Irish society.

In addition, Northern Ireland has special circumstances which
compound the general factors that militate against the development
of ethnically sensitive health and social care. The Catholic/ Protestant
sectarian division has been paramount in Northern Ireland politics,
and one crucial consequence has been the tardy introduction, in
August 1997, of the Race Relations (Northern Ireland) Order and establishment of a Northern Ireland Commission for Racial Equality (see
Chapter 4). A second consequence of the 'invisibility' of black and
minority ethnic groups is that central funding has been provided for
health research using Catholic/Protestant religious affiliation as a

variable (Stringer 1992; Campbell and Stevenson 1993; Moore *et al.* 1996), while similar funding for a major investigation of racial and ethnic factors relevant to health has not happened. A third, more subtle dimension of health and social care provision in Northern Ireland is the concern amongst health workers to be apolitical and provide a universalist service to clients irrespective of their background. Mason (1991) described how community nurses working in North and West Belfast recognised cultural and religious differences amongst clients, but avoided exploring or discussing these. Cameron (1996) argues that the standard response of social services departments, when challenged for not providing day care facilities for ethnic minority elders, is 'we treat everybody alike'. The notion of 'one standard of service to all' has tended to dominate as a philosophy for avoiding sectarianism and this, coincidentally, may have created an unwillingness to consider pluralism, including racial and cultural pluralism, as a social dynamic relevant to health care.

Estimates of the size of the ethnic minority population in Northern Ireland vary. McVeigh (Chapter 1) estimates this population to be in the range of 20,000 – about 1.5 per cent of the population. The Belfast based Multi-Cultural Resource Centre (MCRC 1994) provides a total figure of 12,000, comprising of at least 60 different ethnic communities (Cameron 1995). The largest is the Chinese community, with an estimated population of 7,000. According to MCRC estimates, there are approximately 1,200 Travellers, 1,000 Indians, 500 Pakistanis and 500 Jewish people. More recently, Irwin's (1996) enumeration produced figures, for the four largest minority ethnic communities, of 3,125–5,125 Chinese (but these figures are contested by the Chinese Welfare Association (Northern Ireland) as an underestimate), 1,050 Indians, 641 Pakistanis and 1,366 Travellers. Their age profile was found to be much younger than that of the general population, although the Indian community tended to have an older age profile compared to the other three ethnic groups. Over half of those enumerated were born outside Northern Ireland, and it is suggested that there is likely to be a sustained population growth in the ethnic minority population in Northern Ireland for the foreseeable future.

'Race', Racism and Ethnicity

The terms 'race' and 'ethnicity' are problematic and full analyses of the related issues, applied to health, are provided by Sheldon and Parker (1992) and Ahmad (1993). 'Race' is a biological concept which categorises humanity by means of sets of phenotypical features that appear to distinguish between varieties of people (Sheldon and Parker 1992:58). One problem with the biological concept of 'race' is that consistent categorisation by means of a set of characteristics, such as hair or skin colour, is impossible. Populations merge, differences intermingle and the term becomes meaningless. More often, the term 'race' is used *socially* as a means of differentiating between human populations, and this is where the process of racialisation occurs. Arbitrary criteria (that is, skin colour but not height or eye colour) are used to denote 'race', which can become an instrument of oppression when it is used as the basis for denial of rights. Used in this way, 'race' is a human construct – an ideology with regulatory power within society (Miles 1986). Racism occurs when 'race' is assumed to be the primary and 'natural' means of categorising people (Ahmad 1993:18), and when one ethnic group is considered to be 'naturally' superior (Benedict 1943).

In recent years, there has been a resurgence of interest in the implications for health care of ethnicity and cultural variation. Ethnicity refers 'to shared national identity and language, cultural characteristics or common history' (Sheldon and Parker 1992:60). The term 'ethnic group' might appear uncontroversial, but there is a risk that ethnicity can become the explanation for health behaviour and illness patterns, while important social and economic determinants are ignored. For example, the prevalence of rickets amongst British working-class communities before the Second World War was largely attributed to poverty. In contrast, early explanations for rickets in Asian patients in Britain concentrated on 'the Asian lifestyle'. Thus, the illness was blamed on cultural prohibitions on skin exposure to sunlight, alleged inadequacy of 'the Asian diet' and reported failure of Asian women to take antenatal advice (see Donovan 1986:47–52).

Ultimately, the characteristics used to separate people into different 'races' and ethnic groups are socially determined (Rathwell and Phillips 1986). In this chapter, it is accepted that 'race' is a socio-political construct. In recognition of this fact, and following a recommendation by Sheldon and Parker (1992), the convention 'race' is used throughout. Finally, it is worth mentioning that the phrase 'black and minority ethnic groups' is popular in the official government literature as an inclusive term to incorporate white minority ethnic groups, for example the Polish or Romanian communities in Britain.

Health Policy

There is 'a growing and impressive' (OPM 1996:13) range of policy initiatives designed to combat racism and promote equality in employment and service delivery in the NHS (Smaje 1995). In particular, within the past four years:

[T]here have been at least four major Departmental initiatives on minority ethnic people as service users and NHS employees. Add to that the numerous programmes and projects, of varying scale, taking place in health authorities, social services and NHS Trusts, and one could not be faulted for thinking that, by the end of the decade, minority ethnic peoples in the UK will be enjoying unprecedented improvements in service provisions and delivery. (Wedderburn Tate 1996:7)

One such policy initiative was the Patient's Charter (DOH 1992a) which stipulates that patients have a right to 'detailed information on local health services and access to a health service that has respect for privacy, dignity and religious and cultural beliefs'. Guidance for managers (Balarajan and Soni Raleigh 1993) and 'ethnic checklists' (Gunaratnam 1993) have been issued, as well as directives on equality in employment (NHSME 1993) and collection of ethnic group data (NHSME 1994a). The NHS Ethnic Health Unit was established in March 1994, in Leeds, with a three-year remit to ensure that black and minority ethnic people, Travellers and refugees in England benefit fully from the implementation of NHS policies and, for the first time in 1994, the NHS Priorities and Planning Guidance for 1994/95 (NHSME 1994b) included advice to health authorities to address issues of access to health care for ethnic minorities. Coinciding with this raft of government measures, some professional organisations set up sub-groups specifically to examine racism, employment practice and service provision within their professional arenas. Examples include the Royal College of Nursing Race and Ethnicity Committee and the British Medical Association Racial Equality Working Party. Additionally, the National Institute of Social Work has an associated registered charity, the Race Equality Unit.

Health services in Northern Ireland are subject to the above guidance and policy initiatives, within the overall context of the Race Relations (NI) Order (see Chapter 4). However, the framework for fair treatment in the public services in Northern Ireland differs from that in the rest of the UK. Primarily, the Policy Appraisal and Fair Treatment (PAFT) guidelines and DHSS driven Targeting Health and Social Need (THSN) programme form the equality agenda for health service provision in Northern Ireland. The PAFT guidelines, introduced in 1994, are designed to eliminate discrimination on grounds of race, religion, political belief, sexual orientation, gender, marital status, disability or number of dependants. The guidelines, which have been described as confusing and haphazard (Baldwin 1995), are of 'tertiary' legislative status (Osborne 1996),that is, it is legitimate for a government department to proceed with an initiative, on the basis of a full assessment, in spite of PAFT factors that might indicate discrimination (McGill

1996). The THSN programme seeks to direct public resources to areas of greatest need and, as with PAFT, ministers are not bound by its principles (McGill 1996:7). The main form of targeting in Belfast is represented by the *Making Belfast Work* initiative, which funds community-based projects for health and social gain at local level. Until now, projects on ethnic minority issues have not featured highly. However, there has been funding for a Travellers' Youth Project and an English as a Second Language Development Plan based at the Chinese Welfare Association (CWA).

The *Health of the Nation* White Paper (DOH 1992b) requires health authorities in England to review the way they are meeting the needs of black and minority ethnic groups. Strangely, there is no such call in the *Northern Ireland Regional Strategy 1997–2002*. The latter document briefly refers to the cultural origins of ill health as an area for 'longer term investigations' and its sole reference to any specific minority ethnic group is to Travellers, in the context of reducing perinatal mortality rates (DHSS 1996a:42). Some awareness of multicultural-ism is evidenced in the Northern Ireland *Charter Standards for Community Services* (HPSSME 1995:6) and the *Strategy for Community Nursing* (DHSS 1996b). However, the racial dimension is most explicitly confronted in the Children (NI) Order (DHSS 1996c). For the first time in law, this legislation requires that child care agencies must give 'due consideration' to religious persuasion, racial origin and cultural and linguistic background. Child health services are mandated to be flexible and sensitive to individual racial and cultural needs. This raises issues around child health assessments, staff training, interpre-tation services, protection from stereotyping and consultation with community groups. It presents the greatest challenge so far to childcare agencies with respect to 'race' and ethnicity and, along with the Race Relations (NI) Order, should operate as a lever for ethnic minority groups to challenge and change existing systems.

Having looked at the way health policy is supposed to create an equitable and ethnically sensitive health care system, I now move on to assess the extent to which the rhetoric of government policy has translated into action.

Black and Minority Ethnic Health Experiences

Action on Ethnic Minority Health

Despite growing awareness by government and critical commentators of discriminatory practice in health care in the UK, there is little evidence of widespread, co-ordinated action at senior management level (Smaje 1995), while racism appears to remain endemic (Esmail and Everington 1993; Gillespie 1993; McAlpine *et al.* 1994). The evidence suggests that official policy on 'race' and ethnicity has not been translated into action (Beishon *et al.* 1995; Carr-Hill and Rudat 1995; Jamdagni 1996). For example, one study of purchasing authorities in England found that 'minority ethnic health did not feature in purchasers' mission statements nor in their stated priorities and health gain targets in this area had not yet been developed' (OPM 1996:9). This study showed that there was 'no felt pressure' among commissioners to drive forward an agenda on minority ethnic health, which was perceived as 'not a mainstream issue' (OPM 1996:17). Purchasers work in an environment of severe financial constraints, with a 'huge turnover of middle and senior managers' (Wedderburn Tate 1996:7) and intense demand to fulfil an annual contracting cycle. In this context, health and 'race' issues, which should be integral to the work, unfortunately are often marginalised or ignored.

Commissioning authorities in Northern Ireland face similar pressures to those in other parts of the UK. Some health needs assessments of ethnic minorities have been carried out by the boards (Ginnety 1993; ChildCare NI 1994; NHSSB 1995). However, ongoing assessment of the health needs of people from ethnic minorities is hindered by the absence of census data on ethnicity and lack of ethnic monitoring by DHSS, the boards and almost all the trusts. On a more positive note, the Eastern Health and Social Services Board (EHSSB) recently formed a creative link with representatives of its Chinese population. One outcome of this partnership has been the development of a set of quality standards for health service providers relating to accessing interpreter services, the provision of culturally sensitive care, and compliance with the Race Relations (NI) Order. Board representatives and a member of the Chinese Welfare Association visit each health and social services trust, together, to monitor the extent to which hospital and community health service providers are complying with the required standards. This is proving to be an effective method of changing practice at ground level. A second outcome of the partnership has been the establishment of a Chinese Interpreting Service. This is a one-year, EHSSB-funded pilot project to supplement the existing service which proved inadequate to meet demand. According to Mr Shek Yung Lee, Chairman of the Chinese Welfare Association (Lee 1997), 'the Eastern Board is the leading health authority to make an impact in the shaping of culturally sensitive services for its Chinese population and should be held up as a model of good practice for others to replicate'.

Racism in the Health Services

Racism in the NHS as a whole is reflected in patterns of employment of minority ethnic staff. In 1990, black nurses were concentrated in the lower grades, did not have equal access to training and career development opportunities, and left the profession in disproportionate numbers. Fewer black candidates were applying for nursing, and their applications were disproportionately unsuccessful (King's Fund 1990). By 1995, the situation had not improved (Beishon *et al.* 1995). Within medicine, discriminatory employment practice was demonstrated by Esmail and Everington (1993), who found that job applicants with a 'white'-sounding name were twice as likely to be shortlisted as those with 'ethnic' sounding names. The situation on representation of ethnic minority groups on the boards of health authorities is equivocal, with 'encouraging progress' (Aanchawan 1996:27) between 1993 and 1995 in some areas, associated with support from the Ethnic Health Unit. However, up to 30 June 1995, there was still no black or ethnic minority chair of a regional health authority. In Northern Ireland, employment practices are closely monitored with respect to religion, but not 'race'. It is therefore impossible to assess the extent of job discrimination, on racial grounds, within the Province.

Racial harassment of ethnic minority nursing staff by patients and colleagues is widespread (George 1994a). A Policy Studies Institute survey of over 14,000 nurses in England, along with more than 150 interviews of nurses and managers, found that 'racially abusive behaviour had come to be the norm in the nursing workplace' (Beishon *et al.* 1995:229). The professional health journals contain a wealth of examples of racial abuse: one midwife was called 'a black bitch' by patients (Payne 1995); a black nurse's manager told him that a toy monkey looked like his baby (*Nursing Standard* 1996); and the manager of a nursing agency telephoned a patient to ask if she minded being seen by a black nurse. This latter example of discrimination was found not to be unlawful because the 1976 Race Relations Act exempts employment in a private household (Healey 1996).

In Northern Ireland, many ethnic minority NHS staff are doctors. Porter (1993:600–2) has documented racist comments by nurses in the intensive care unit of a large metropolitan hospital in Northern Ireland:

A staff nurse opens the door to enter a clinical room where she discovers a Palestinian doctor at prayer. After mumbling polite apologies, she retreats from the room. However, almost immediately the following interaction occurs.
Staff nurse: That bloody Arab is praying again in the treatment room. How am I supposed to get my work done?
Domestic Assistant: Huh, if he wants to go down on his hands and knees every ten minutes, you'd think he'd go to his own country and do it.
Staff nurse: Arabs.
She moves off shaking her head.

The Health Status of Black and Minority Ethnic Groups

The health status of black and minority ethnic groups in Britain has been widely investigated and found, in some respects, to be poorer than that of the majority (Balajaran and Soni Raleigh 1993; Chan 1994). Perinatal deaths in Pakistani babies are twice that of the national rate (Chan 1994; Smaje 1995). Mortality from coronary heart disease is higher in people from the Indian subcontinent and African Commonwealth than in the majority population, and mortality from stroke and hypertension is higher in Caribbeans, Asians and Africans (Marmot *et al.* 1984; Donaldson and Taylor 1993). Psychiatric hospital admissions are high amongst Afro-Caribbeans, who are three to six times more likely to be diagnosed schizophrenic than are white people (Dean *et al.* 1981; London 1986; McGovern and Cope 1987; Littlewood and Lipsedge 1988; Cochrane and Bal 1989). High rates of suicide and attempted suicide have been reported amongst young Asian women (Burke 1976; Merrill and Owens 1986), while genetic conditions such as sickle cell disease and thalassaemia affect specific populations.

A major difficulty with these epidemiological studies is the risk, already mentioned, of equating ethnicity with ill health. Ethnicity can be mis-interpreted as the *cause* of ill health. Aspects of biology, behaviour or culture may be blamed for disease in a process of racialisation, while the complexity and interaction of aetiological factors is ignored. Authors sensitive to these issues tend to provide balanced overviews of the positive, as well as negative aspects of minority ethnic health status (Leong 1995). Smaje (1995), for example, emphasises that, despite widespread socio-economic disadvantage amongst most ethnic minority populations, many studies report smaller differences than may have been expected. Respiratory disease and most cancers tend to be lower in the majority of ethnic minority populations (Marmot *et al.* 1984). The main causes of hospital admission – accidents, respiratory disease, circulatory disease and problems of the digestive system – are identical to that of the majority population (Bhopal and Donaldson 1988). The overall picture is complex, with significant variations among ethnic minority populations. Moreover, health status is not static, as illustrated by rapidly falling Bangladeshi infant mortality rates (Andrews and Jewson 1993). Statistics are sometimes quoted selectively to support particular standpoints, while the health effects of the experience of racism have rarely been examined.

One outstanding example of poor health status in a minority ethnic population is that of Travellers (Ginnety 1993; Irwin 1996; Noonan, Chapter 8). Women Travellers have a Standardised Mortality Ratio of 307, compared to a ratio of 140 for women from social class V of the settled population. The figure for men Travellers is 222, compared with 150 for social class V males in the general population (Barry *et al.* 1989). Life expectancy for adult Travellers is 11–15 years below that of the settled community, while Traveller children have very high rates of hospital admission for preventable illnesses and a death rate ten times that of the settled community (EHSSB 1989). The World Health Organization prerequisites for health are 'adequate food, safe water and sanitation, decent housing, basic education and employment' (WHO 1985). Hardly any of these prerequisites were reported by Ginnety (1993:6) to have been met for many of the 400 Travellers living within the Eastern Health and Social Services Board area, where 'approximately half of the Traveller population continues to live without any running water, electricity, postal services or sanitation'. Recent research by Mann-Kler (1997) tends to confirm this picture of serious environmental and socio-economic disadvantage amongst Travellers in Northern Ireland.

Ethnic Minority Experiences of the Health Services

The NHS was created in 1948 to cater for the needs of people from a fairly homogeneous British background. Research evidence and articles in the professional journals suggest that, while there is a growing awareness of racial and cultural diversity, health workers are inadequately equipped to deal with it. With respect to caregiving and ethnic minority patients, nurses have reported frustration and feelings of inadequacy relating to communication, psychological care and knowledge of cultural issues; they have problems building adequate nurse–client relationships and feel they are giving a sub-standard service (Murphy 1990; Rawlings-Anderson 1992; Murphy and Macleod Clark 1993). According to Sally Gooch, Clinical Leader of the Stepney Nursing Development Unit (quoted by George 1994b:23): '[H]ow many of us were taught the signs and symptoms of cyanosis, jaundice, cardiac arrest, and pressure sores in people with hyper-pigmented skin? How many of us know how to care for the skin or hair of an African or West Indian person? How many of us have thought, when struggling to remove sutures from a black person the sutures are usually dark because of an implicit assumption that a patient's skin is white?'

It is unsurprising, therefore, that black and minority ethnic experiences of health service delivery are often negative. For example, a pilot study of 100 ethnic minority patients in Greater London found that 64 per cent were unhappy with the service they received in hospitals, attributing this to 'insensitivity, including lack of comprehension, racist attitudes, rudeness and inattentiveness' (McAlpine *et al.* 1994:15). Problems often centre around difficulties of access, communication and dietary needs, as illustrated by the experiences of the Chinese community in Britain.

In the 1980s, there was an apparent reluctance amongst the Chinese to make requests for social and other forms of assistance. However, this did not indicate an absence of need, as demand was found to increase as soon as intermediaries became available (HAC 1985). Watt (1991) demonstrated that 70 per cent of a sample of 80 Chinese catering workers in Hull had difficulty understanding or being understood by their family doctor (GP). Amongst this sample, in the absence of interpreters, misunderstandings arose; for example, one mother thought that bottle-feeding of babies was compulsory in hospital. As part of the study, Watt interviewed ten families: of these, only two found contact with their health visitor useful. In another study, Tan (1983) took a sample of 50 Chinese families in London and showed how the dietary needs and cultural practices of women were compromised at the time of childbirth, with little cognisance of their requirements for 'hot' and 'cold' food, boiled water for bathing and need for rest indoors following delivery of the baby. In summary, there is evidence that the Chinese and other minority ethnic communities in Britain 'generally have poorer-quality contact with health services' (Smaje 1995:28).

This would also appear to be the case in Northern Ireland. Problems of access to health services can be severe for Travellers who – for instance, when they resided in the Markets area of Belfast – had difficulty obtaining GP registration (Ginnety 1993). This is a crucial barrier since, within the NHS, the GP is the gateway to specialist and allied health services. As a result, one woman suffering from diabetes was unable to get ongoing care, while other Travellers had to make use of Accident and Emergency Departments for primary care. The multidisciplinary Travellers' team in North and West Belfast Community Trust currently believes that Travellers in this area have access to only three GPs. Traveller families, therefore, often have to travel some distance for GP services.

Irwin's (1996) research found that access was problematic for the Chinese community in Northern Ireland, largely due to language difficulties. Of the total Chinese population surveyed, 83 per cent cited language and communication as a difficulty in health care. This finding is supported by Watson (1993) who indicated that, among a small sample of Chinese families in East Belfast, 40 per cent were registered with GPs, one-third had no idea how to contact a doctor during weekends or late at night, and 48 per cent did not know where to obtain information about family planning or child care. Most Chinese people in Northern Ireland come from Hong Kong, where GPs do not act as a gateway to other health services and there is more open access to medical specialists, along with a greater facility for changing doctors. In the Northern Ireland setting, translated information leaflets are not widely available and, without these, many Chinese people are unaware of services or how to obtain them, while the feeling of being 'second class citizens living in other's society' (Yu 1994b: 9) militates against organised activism to demand improvements.

Problems of access and language/communication are also linked for the Asian community in Craigavon, where information is needed in Urdu and Punjabi to raise awareness of available services and to enable Asian people to participate in decisions about treatment and care. Where translated leaflets have become available, these are greatly appreciated (Ali 1996). Lay health worker schemes with the Asian community in Craigavon and the Chinese community in Belfast have been highly successful in communicating information about services, developing health materials and workshops, and building support groups in partnership with local Asian and Chinese women, mothers and elderly people (Barnardos 1995; Ali 1996; CWA 1996). The need for this kind of service is such that the demands of the work can become 'unbearable' (Ali 1996), an experience that appears to be shared by minority ethnic health workers employed in the statutory sector (Ginnety and Ali 1994).

Where interpreters are unavailable, misunderstandings frequently arise. For example, in Northern Ireland recently, four Chinese women did not attend for cervical smear screening because they did not realise they could request a female health professional. Also, there has been a general lack of awareness and understanding of the measles, mumps and rubella (MMR) immunisation amongst the Chinese community (Watson 1996). For Vietnamese people, the term 'weak and dizzy' means 'stressed out' – just one example of how words can have different meanings and create confusion (Chan 1996). Until July 1997, there was only one formally employed interpreter for the Chinese population in Northern Ireland, primarily funded by the Central Community Relations Unit. As a consequence, children have commonly been used as interpreters in often highly inappropriate circumstances and in the absence of any alternative. Misinterpretation, misdiagnosis and negative effects on health may result, and there is potential for acute embarrassment on both sides if intimate information has to be revealed. The misplaced responsibility on the child may now be unlawful under the 1996 Children Order; a test case has yet to be undertaken.

The ethnocentricism of the NHS in general is reflected in Northern Ireland, where there appears to be poor understanding of the cultural needs of the various ethnic minority groups. For example, there is little or no special dietary provision for Muslims who may not eat pork and require specially prepared meat, or for Chinese people who may want a balance of 'hot' and 'cold' foods served in a bowl, with the provision of chopsticks. Furthermore, drug regimes take no account of the fasting needs of Muslims during Ramadan. Weaning practices may differ between various ethnic groups and this is not accounted for during standardised child health assessments. Cultural misunderstandings have arisen between Travellers and health workers who may have little knowledge of living conditions on-site in trailers (caravans), with the result that some Traveller children perceived as acutely ill have been discharged home to very cold and damp conditions (Ginnety 1993). There is little specific provision for the childcare needs of the Chinese community where both parents may work long hours at night in restaurants.

There is a common experience of separation and social alienation by minority ethnic peoples in Northern Ireland (Ginnety 1993; Yu 1994b; Lee 1996b). Pang (1991) portrays a vivid picture of Chinese women who are unfamiliar with the host language, culture and geography. Social interaction outside the home tends to be work based so that, as one woman put it, 'even though I work hard, I feel like I am living in a prison. I can't go anywhere alone because I am afraid, and my husband works all the time.' The problem of social isolation is especially acute for those living in provincial towns and cities, particularly black and minority elders who may have little access to friends and relations, suitable shops and places of worship (Leong 1996). Interacting with the experience of isolation is the experience of racism in the form of verbal and physical abuse (Ginnety 1993; Leeson 1993; Walmsley 1994; Irwin 1996). Together, and superimposed on the specific difficulties of access, communication and cultural difference, this creates a situation of multilayered disadvantage that has, so far, received relatively little attention, action or funding from the statutory bodies.

Suggestions for the Future

In November 1996, the Northern Ireland Council for Ethnic Minorities (NICEM), along with a working group of representatives from the Chinese Welfare Association, the Craigavon Asian community, the Travellers' community, Barnardos and the health and social services boards and trusts, organised a major conference on 'Identifying and addressing the health and social needs of ethnic minorities in Northern Ireland'. The audience consisted mainly of people from the minority communities. The following statements elicited much applause: 'we are citizens of Northern Ireland' and 'we are members of Northern Irish society and wish to be treated as equal in every field here' (NICEM 1996b).

The ethnic minority communities have for long been ignored in Northern Ireland. Emergent awareness within the field of health care, however, has brought its own problems. There is an immature understanding of the politics of 'race' and health. Lip-service has been paid to the notion of 'cultural differences', with the result that 'other' cultures are sometimes perceived by professionals as having unusual, extra and perhaps expensive needs. The process of racialisation inherent in this process appears not to have been recognised. The problem is perhaps exacerbated by the fact that much of the literature to which health professionals have access is disease focused or culture focused, with insufficient consideration of the socio-political, racial context for health care and the risk of labelling minority groups as deviant and blameworthy. There has been underemphasis on the vital need to mainstream minority ethnic health care by creating a service that has, as a *core* function, flexibility in responding to the needs of people from a range of backgrounds. Until very recently, there has been little celebration of the positive contribution of cultural and ethnic diversity to Northern Irish society, and the political will to build a health service with equality of access, communication and cultural sensitivity appears to be weak.

Progress on improving the quality of care for ethnic minorities in Northern Ireland has been impeded by lack of information on ethnic minority health, in the absence of ethnic monitoring. While there has been no large scale, core funded research specifically on the health of ethnic minority communities, it is ironic that the Chinese community is rapidly becoming over-researched for small-scale student projects that are unlikely to lead to change. This demonstrates a requirement for ethnic monitoring in the health services, along with substantive research, designed in collaboration with representatives of the minority ethnic communities, and undertaken with full understanding of the political-racial context for health and social care. Short-term, inadequate and fragmented funding for community projects, lay worker projects and interpreting services has even diverted energy in the voluntary sector away from delivering services to writing proposals. A real commitment to equality by government would mean secure, long term funding for these initiatives as part of mainstream health and social services provision.

The information and communication needs of the minority ethnic communities have been expressed repeatedly. A requirement for better representation of ethnic minorities in the health services and on the boards of health authorities has been made by the Department of Health. The elimination of racism in the NHS is a stated goal of government and of the executive bodies in the health service. Yet, little progress seems to have been made. The challenge for everyone involved in the delivery of health care is to translate the rhetoric into action. Specifically, there must be a commitment by the NHS in Northern Ireland to implement the Patient's Charter standards as they affect ethnic minority users. The challenge for the minority ethnic communities is to provide grassroots pressure and leadership so that the changes are led by the communities themselves. A key feature of change must be talking and listening between health managers and the minority ethnic communities.

It would be incorrect to present an entirely bleak picture of multiracial health care in Northern Ireland. Awareness of the multi-ethnic nature of Northern Irish society is growing and there is 'an escalating demand for anti-racist training and for advice in managing cultural diversity in service delivery' (Cameron 1995:6). Multidisciplinary teams have been formed in several trusts specifically to evaluate and meet the health needs of Travellers and the introduction, in 1991, of client-held child health records provided a degree of continuity of care for Traveller children that had not been possible formerly. Some health visitors and social workers have been welcomed by the Traveller community and valued as advocates. Health professionals, especially social workers and nurses, are examining their practice critically in a genuine attempt to provide racially and culturally sensitive care, while articles on 'race' and health are now routine in the professional journals. Health information leaflets in Chinese and Urdu are available in some areas in Northern Ireland and tools such as the Red Cross (Chinese) language card are in use in the maternity departments of some major hospitals. The EHSSB Chinese Liaison Group, described earlier, represents a promising new partnership-based approach to changing practice consistently across all trusts within one board area. The Race Relations (NI) Order and the PAFT guidelines may have a significant impact in improving cultural sensitivity in service delivery, although this remains to be seen.

The list of improvements is small and the actions are fragmented. A general acceptance of diversity is needed so that the minority communities can articulate their right, as citizens of Northern Ireland, 'to be assertively different' (Cameron 1995:6), and this can be accommodated by the health services. There are also major educational implications attached to the mainstreaming of ethnic minority health care. If equality is to be achieved, an active philosophy of anti-racism and multiculturalism must drive the purchaser and provider agendas. If health care is to be truly multiracial and multicultural, racism awareness and anti-racism training should be integral to courses taken by the health professionals, administrators, planners, managers and finance personnel within the NHS. It is to be hoped that the race relations legislation will provide a statutory imperative to translate this philosophy into action, challenging all those concerned with service provision to think and act in terms of racial and cultural pluralism, within a society that has long been characterised as internally divided by religious difference alone.

6 Fitting In: Ethnic Minorities[1] and the News Media

Liz Fawcett

In 1996, the *Sunday Life* (5 May 1996) carried the first of two articles which linked Chinese triads with a series of violent attacks on members of the Chinese community. Shortly afterwards, the Co-ordinator of the Northern Ireland Council for Ethnic Minorities (NICEM), Patrick Yu, addressed a group of Royal Ulster Constabulary (RUC) recruits. According to Mr Yu, the recruits had read the *Sunday Life* article and wanted to know if it was true that all Chinese people were involved with triads. The article did not make this claim. However, by highlighting the alleged involvement of triads, the newspaper was reinforcing a popular stereotype already promulgated in sections of the British media.

The way in which ethnic minorities are portrayed in the news media has enormous implications for the society we live in. While the precise effect of the media on its audience is a subject of great debate, there can be little doubt that its impact is of particular significance in terms of the way it represents marginalised cultures. In fact, there is a reasonably large body of literature which examines the news media's portrayal of ethnic minorities, drawing on evidence from various Western countries. However, this work has not extended to Northern Ireland. Although much has been written about the portrayal of the conflict involving what are perceived as the 'two communities' in Northern Ireland, the news media's treatment of other groupings has been virtually ignored. This chapter, therefore, examines the way in which Northern Ireland's local news media has dealt with ethnic minorities and with issues of concern to them. As noted below, one can see the same processes at work as in other countries where research has been carried out on this issue. However, the precise way in which those processes are manifested differs in some respects from elsewhere.

This chapter focuses specifically on the local media in Northern Ireland, because the British and Irish national media rarely cover stories pertaining exclusively to Northern Ireland's ethnic minorities. Furthermore, as will become apparent below, media coverage is closely linked in with political discourse and power structures. There is clearly a relationship between the local media and other local elites in this regard in Northern Ireland. However, it must be borne in mind that many people in Northern Ireland receive newspapers and news broadcasts produced in Britain or Ireland. So, before examining the local news media, I shall briefly review existing research on the British news media and other Western media.

The Effect of the News Media

While there is some debate about the extent to which the media influences white[2] attitudes towards ethnic minorities, there is no doubt that the media is a vital source of information for whites on this subject. One of the most comprehensive investigations into this topic was carried out by Teun A. van Dijk (1987). His researchers conducted a series of interviews with 180 white people in Amsterdam and California between 1980 and 1985. He found that the mass media and everyday conversations with other people accounted for more than 90 per cent of the sources of information mentioned by interviewees. As van Dijk pointed out, much of the 'everyday talk' of his interviewees would itself draw on the media as a source of information. Thus his work suggested that the media is *the* prime source of information for whites. His findings also indicated that the media was particularly important in this regard in places where whites had little contact with ethnic minorities – which is the case in Northern Ireland.

Van Dijk's findings supported earlier work carried out by Troyna (1981) and Hartmann et al. (1974), although Hartmann et al. differentiated between the news media and other forms of media. They found that the former, rather than the latter, was an important information source for white people on ethnic minorities and issues connected with race relations. Thus, the way the news media represents ethnic minorities is crucial in providing the facts around which whites in Northern Ireland build their attitudes towards ethnic groups. The work of Hartmann et al. (1974) and Troyna (1981) suggested that the media may reinforce existing negative attitudes among whites about ethnic minorities. However, Hartmann et al. stressed the fact that whites normally attributed such attitudes to their own experience. The authors concluded that there was little evidence to suggest that the media had any direct effect on white attitudes towards black and ethnic groups.

At the same time, Hartmann et al. do consider the possibility that there is a looser connection between news media content and attitudes. In an earlier work, Hartmann and Husband (1972) suggest that the media influences public opinion on race issues by helping to shape the interpretative frameworks that white people use to think and talk about race. This process is much more subtle than any direct, measurable impact on attitudes. The influence of interpretative frameworks on our thinking can be likened to the effect of dropping a vertical, invisible net with large holes into a river. Fish would be forced to swim through one of the holes but the reason why would not be obvious to the naked eye. Likewise, argue Hartmann and Husband, our thinking is shaped by categories which exist as social phenomena but are not as easy to measure as 'attitudes'. The news media plays an important role in shaping these 'frameworks'.

Van Dijk (1987; 1993a) has developed a more sophisticated version of this basic model in which many different kinds of shared thought, talk and symbolic representation are interlinked. Each of these is woven in with our own personal attitudes which consist of a selective expression of these social phenomena. Van Dijk argues that part of this process can be 'captured' through the analysis of news media texts. These contain certain patterns of thought and talk which are present throughout society. Van Dijk refers to these patterns as discourses. However, some discourses are more influential than others. Like Hartmann and Husband, van Dijk attributes an important role in this process to the news media, particularly with regard to ethnic affairs. The news media provides an authoritative platform for those discourses which it reproduces. These discourses are much more likely to be those used by elite groups which hold a disproportionate amount of power in society.

The Ideological Nature of News

The view that powerful groups in society have privileged access to the news media is supported by a great deal of work on this subject, in particular that of Hall *et al.* (1978) who saw elite institutions and groups as the 'primary definers' of news. In their influential work *Policing the Crisis*, Hall *et al.* charted the way in which the British press, together with 'primary definers' like the police and politicians, created a moral panic about mugging which reinforced the stereotype of black youths as criminals. This account asserted that the police, politicians and the judiciary had primacy in the ideological process of media reporting; media organisations were merely 'secondary definers', responding to the ideological cues of the powerful. However, van Dijk (1988) sees the news media as among the primary definers; in other words, as an integral and *active* part of this process. The media actively selects and defines 'news'. It gives greater prominence to some views than to others. This is all ideological work.

Journalists do not, in general, view their job in this way. They see themselves as simply applying a professional judgement about the worth of different stories and aspects of those stories. However, those journalistic principles are an expression, and an integral part, of the reproduction of a culture and ideology which suits those who hold economic and political power. Indeed, elitism is one of the prime news values which governs the selection of stories (Galtung and Ruge 1965; Fowler 1991). Stories about the politically powerful, the wealthy and the famous are perceived as more interesting than stories about ordinary people. Furthermore, the more powerful you are, the more credibility you have both as an interviewee and as a source of information. This has an impact on the use of members of ethnic minorities as both sources of news and as interviewees. In stories concerning issues relating to ethnic minorities, the voices of white 'experts' and authorities are much more likely to be heard than those of ethnic minority groups. Even where the latter's views are represented, the views of white spokespeople are likely to be accorded more prominence (Critcher *et al.* 1977; van Dijk 1993a). Moreover, the views of ethnic minorities tend to be represented only if they fall within the range of opinions considered acceptable within the dominant consensus (van Dijk 1987).

The values which govern the selection of news stories stress the importance of ingredients like negativity, conflict, drama and perceived relevance to the audience (see Galtung and Ruge 1965; Fowler 1991 and Boyd 1994). These are heavily influenced both by the values of the dominant culture, and by the interests of those who hold economic and political power (van Dijk 1993a). Hartmann *et al.* (1974) found that overseas material in British newspapers was far more conflict-oriented and violent than domestic news, a factor which seems likely to influence white attitudes about ethnic minorities at home, given that many whites regard members of ethnic minorities as 'foreigners'.

The application of these news values means that ethnic minorities are marginalised or even excluded altogether from what newsmakers perceive to be 'news' (Wilson II and Gutiérrez 1995). The stories concerning ethnic minorities which do make it tend to concern negative topics, such as immigration problems, crime and violence. More positive or mundane topics, such as the everyday problems faced by ethnic minorities, the cultures of such groups, and their contribution to the economy, tend to be covered less frequently (van Dijk 1991; 1993b). This is partly because journalists see *events*, rather than *issues*, as 'the stuff and substance of hard news' (Tuchman 1978:139). Furthermore, news stories are characterised by a series of negative and often pejorative stereotypes of ethnic minorities. Ethnic minorities are presented as a problematic category, rather than as ordinary citizens (Hartmann *et al.* 1974; van Dijk 1988). While they were once viewed as the 'external threat', they are now portrayed in the British media as the 'outsider within' (Troyna 1981).

This has been particularly evident in Britain in the media's coverage of riots, like those in Brixton and Handsworth in the early 1980s, which criminalised ethnic minorities by suggesting, explicitly or implicitly, that they were responsible for the disturbances (Gilroy and Lawrence 1988; Solomos 1993). Where coverage is more 'favourable', it often reinforces stereotypes of ethnic minorities as 'colourful' and 'exotic', or as being successful because they have conformed to the values and aspirations of the dominant community (Wilson II and Gutiérrez 1995). This latter type of coverage fits into a liberal 'multiculturalist' framework which, in theory, is supposed to bring everyone under the inclusive umbrella of 'us'. However, in practice, it often perpetuates notions of 'us' and 'them', and maintains the subordination of ethnic minorities, via a process of stressing cultural difference rather than economic inequality (Goldberg 1993; Betz 1996; McAllister 1996; Vertovec 1996).

Indeed, McAllister (1996) warns that the active involvement of ethnic groups in implementing multiculturalist policies within parameters set by the dominant community merely means ethnic groups are contributing to their own domination. This analysis could be applied to the dealings of ethnic groups with the media. If ethnic minorities wish to get across their viewpoint in the media, they have to conform to existing news values and, therefore, to the 'core values of the dominant culture' (Ericson et al. 1989:14). Yet, in so doing, one could argue ethnic groups are merely 'fitting in' with the very power structures which marginalise and oppress them.

The pervasive power of the dominant culture can also be seen in the portrayal of racist attacks and right-wing, extremist racist groups in the media. Coverage of these subjects tends to stress the deviant nature of overt racists, particularly in the more 'liberal' media. Yet this portrayal simply takes away the spotlight from the institutional racism which is endemic in Western societies and from the racist nature of public discourse (van Dijk 1991). While the liberal media does cover problems experienced by ethnic minorities, such as poor housing and unemployment, it generally highlights what the dominant white group is doing to help. Therefore, whites and white authorities are represented in a positive light (van Dijk 1993a).

Thus, the available research suggests that the way in which ethnic minorities are portrayed in the Western media mirrors and reproduces their marginalised position in Western society. It also contributes to that position of structural inequality through the media's construction and reconstruction of racist, elite discourse and its impact on the attitudes of whites who are not members of an elite grouping. In order to participate in this elite discourse, ethnic minorities appear to have little choice but to conform to elite values, thereby perpetuating inequality, and adhering to cultural and political values which are not of their own making.

To investigate the extent to which this pattern is repeated in Northern Ireland, I carried out a comprehensive analysis of five key regional newspapers during the months of March, April and May 1996.[3] The newspapers chosen were the *Belfast Telegraph*, the *Irish News*, the *News Letter*, the *Sunday Life* and the Northern Ireland edition of the Dublin-based *Sunday World*. The first is an evening newspaper which is aimed at a broad readership, but tends to be more unionist than nationalist in tone (see Rolston 1991) and has more Protestant than Catholic readers.[4] The *Irish News* and the *News Letter* are both morning dailies, the former appealing to a predominantly nationalist readership, while the latter targets a unionist readership. The *Sunday Life* and *Sunday World* take a cynical stance towards politicians and concentrate on scandal, human interest stories, and 'exclusives' which conform to the news values discussed above.[5] In addition, I examined a selection of articles which featured Travellers taken from the regional and local press over the past ten years.[6] I also carried out a series of interviews with journalists, editors, members and staff of organisations which represent the interests of ethnic minorities, and other relevant individuals.[7]

What was evident from my research was that the same processes described above in connection with the news media elsewhere were also at work in Northern Ireland. However, as already intimated, they have manifested themselves in different ways, to some extent. One of the main differences is the fact that elite discourse in Northern Ireland never constructed immigration to the region as a 'problem'. Instead, the news media spent many years largely ignoring all ethnic minorities with the exception of Travellers who were perceived to be a problem and an 'external threat' to local communities.

Second, I would suggest that the conflictual nature of Northern Ireland politics has had an impact on the way in which local elite discourse deals with ethnic minorities. I would argue that ethnic minorities in Northern Ireland are marginalised almost to the point of invisibility in both political and media discourse. This is undoubtedly due partly to the fact that the priorities for the main parties in Northern Ireland relate to constitutional issues and concerns about civil rights. The latter are constructed within both nationalist and unionist discourse in a way which pays scant regard to the rights of ethnic minorities. However, the conflictual paradigm of politics is probably only one aspect. Another factor which is surely also important is the lack of fully accountable, democratic political structures in Northern Ireland. Moreover, the fact that ethnic minorities are peripheral to political discourse undoubtedly has a direct impact on media coverage, as I hope to demonstrate below.

Elite Discourse and Ethnic Minorities in Northern Ireland

Prior to March 1996, media coverage of ethnic minorities other than Travellers had been extremely infrequent in Northern Ireland. However, in March 1996, the first of a series of violent attacks on Chinese people in Northern Ireland took place. From April, the media began covering the attacks. Furthermore, in the same month, the television channel BBC2 broadcast a documentary on racism in Northern Ireland which attracted some interest in the local media (*The Hidden Troubles*, BBC2, 17 April 1996). During April and May, ethnic minorities suddenly became quite widely debated within both elite discourse and everyday talk.

The way in which the local media handled this series of attacks illustrates the extent to which the media relies on 'primary definers' in the sense that Hall *et al.* (1978) argue. The delay in reporting the attacks can be attributed to the RUC's importance as a source of information on crime. At least 19 attacks had taken place before any of the regional newspapers began to report the fact that there had been a series of assaults on Chinese people. The reason for this appears to have been the fact that the RUC does not normally state the ethnicity or religious affiliation of victims of crime in the reports it gives to the media. Once journalists realised there had been a number of recent attacks on Chinese people, each incident was reported as being the latest in a spate of attacks. From early on in the media's reporting, the Belfast-based Chinese Welfare Association (CWA) was quoted as saying that it did not believe the attacks were racist in nature. The CWA felt that robbery was the motive, a view which accorded with that of the police. Thus the opinion of the CWA was given some prominence but it happened to fit in with the RUC's analysis.

What might have happened if the CWA's view had differed from that of the RUC? There are two incidents which suggest that the media would have favoured the RUC's definition over that of any group representing ethnic minorities, had there been a difference of opinion. First, according to a *Belfast Telegraph* reporter, Elaine Lester, the CWA urged her to 'really go on the racism line' at some point before it publicly stated it did not believe the attacks were racist.[8] It is evident from her account that the *Telegraph* set greater store by what the police were saying at the time than the view of the CWA:

> Now, aside from what I thought personally, my news desk did not, well I think, perhaps was not, utterly convinced of the racial motivation. They were very wary of ... sensationalising something, so we did not go as hard on that [the racist angle] as we could have done ... Speaking to police press officers, often off-the-record [not for attribution], they weren't looking at a racial motivation. I'm not

saying they are the be-all and end-all of defining what is a racial attack, but that was the view that came across from my news desk.

The second instance concerns the two articles referred to at the beginning of this chapter. The first article (*Sunday Life*, 5 May 1996) claimed that the attacks on Chinese people were being carried out by a loyalist paramilitary gang on the orders of Chinese triads. The second article (*Sunday Life*, 12 May 1996) elaborated on this allegation, stating that the RUC's Special Branch believed that a new triad group had arrived in Northern Ireland and that it was commissioning the attacks in order to force the Chinese community to turn to the triad for protection.

The reporter in question, John Cassidy, relied on unofficial RUC sources for his two stories. He said that he only got the first story late on Friday night. He contended that he was unable to contact anyone from the Chinese community who might have been able to comment before his paper went to print on Saturday. However, Patrick Yu, Co-ordinator for the Northern Ireland Council for Ethnic Minorities, rang Mr Cassidy on Tuesday. Mr Cassidy said he included a quote from Mr Yu in his original version of the second, follow-up article. The quote stated, in effect, 'We don't believe we have triads in Northern Ireland.' Mr Yu's comment was subsequently cut out by a sub-editor, apparently because the article was too long. Thus, although Mr Cassidy's articles relied on unofficial rather than official police sources, it is clear that the primary definers in *both* the above examples were the police rather than groups representing ethnic minorities.

The views of politicians, the police and local officials are all given prominence in articles about ethnic minorities. The views of spokes-people for ethnic groups, such as Patrick Yu, are also highlighted. However, in many of the articles examined, their views *accord* with those who generally act as the primary definers of news.[9] As can be seen, where their opinions do not coincide, they can expect their views to be marginalised or ignored. This marginalisation can be seen clearly in relation to local press coverage of Travellers, where the primary definers in this regard tend to be local councillors. This is because proceedings of council meetings form an important source of stories, particularly for local weekly papers. Where the Travellers' viewpoint is given at all, it is generally provided by a spokesperson. As is the case with stories concerning other ethnic minorities, the views of individual Travellers are rarely presented.

One example of this tendency is a collection of three articles on the Education page of the *Belfast Telegraph* (20 May 1996). In this case, the articles portrayed Travellers in a positive light. They focused on some of the problems involved in educating Traveller children in Belfast. The articles were sensitively written and clearly designed to give readers a better understanding of the issues involved and of Travellers' attitudes to education. However, none of the four people quoted in the articles was a Traveller. Two were education officers with the Belfast Education and Library Board, one was a spokesperson for the Catholic Council for Maintained Schools while one was a spokesperson for the Belfast Travellers' Site Project. As with many such articles, the views of an ethnic minority were talked about by the interviewees, but not put over directly by individual members of that group. I would argue that this pattern of coverage helps to render members of ethnic minorities *invisible* to the white community and to give the impression that such individuals are incapable of speaking out for themselves. Where individuals have been given space to speak, they are generally given great prominence and project a powerful image.

While a range of views on issues relating to ethnic minorities is presented in the regional and local press, it tends to fit within a consensus. This consensus is built on a number of assumptions. Some are articulated explicitly but others remain unspoken. I would summarise these assumptions as follows:

- racism is not a big problem in Northern Ireland;
- those who perpetrate racist attacks are deviants;
- white, settled society is doing what it can to help ethnic minorities (it could do more but it is trying its best and its heart is in the right place);
- ethnic minorities, such as the Chinese and Indian communities, are welcome because of their contribution to the *economy*; they are *responsible* citizens;[10]
- Travellers are *irresponsible* – (alternatively, there are good, *responsible* Travellers but there are also bad, *irresponsible* ones);[11]
- ethnic minorities are different, inferior, uncivilised;
- the concerns of ethnic minorities are not the stuff of mainstream politics but something to be added on to the political agenda.

The 'Otherness' of Ethnic Minorities

In Western Europe, ethnic minorities are viewed as 'outsiders'. This perception has powerful historical and cultural roots, being based on a perceived dichotomy between the civilised West and the uncivilised 'other' which stretches back to the Middle Ages (Said 1995; Hall 1992). This historical influence still resonates strongly in the portrayal of both ethnic minorities at home and foreigners abroad in Northern Ireland's press. In the past, ethnic minorities generally only got media coverage when there was a cultural festival, which provided 'colourful' pictures. Such coverage was informative for a white audience who knew little about the food, dress and customs of other cultures. However, it also reinforced a stereotype of members of ethnic minorities as strange and 'exotic'.

This exotic aspect is further reinforced by some of the foreign news stories carried by the regional daily press in Northern Ireland. Foreign news stories tend to be carried only if they contain some element of drama or conflict, or if they are rather lighthearted and quirky. The latter tend to bolster an image of the inhabitants of developing countries as mysterious and uncivilised. For example, the *Irish News* carried an editorial (5 March 1996) headlined 'Tribe loses the head over dam' which explained how the Bukalot tribe in the northern Philippines was threatening to resume headhunting if a dam was built on its ancestral lands. The editorial was very sympathetic towards the tribe. However, this was the only editorial the *Irish News* ran on a foreign story that month. I suspect the subject matter was picked because of the novelty value of the 'headhunting' element rather than any genuine concern for environmental issues in the Philippines. The problem herein is the stereotyped notion of the developing world that is reinforced by this type of news selection.

The tendency to select foreign stories on the basis of the extent to which they contain elements of negativity, drama, conflict and violence also has important implications. Many people in Northern Ireland feel outsiders get a distorted picture of their homeland from the violent scenes shown in the news media. However, the image of the outside world offered in Northern Ireland's press to its readers is also distorted. Furthermore, as noted earlier, these images are likely to have an impact on the picture whites have of members of ethnic minorities at home. Many whites still see members of ethnic groups as essentially 'foreigners'; if they are constantly provided with images in the media which suggest that foreign lands are violent, uncivilised places, they are more likely to categorise members of ethnic minorities in the same way.

Despite the fact that many whites in Northern Ireland would still see members of ethnic minorities as 'foreigners', ethnic minorities are constructed in the local press as 'outsiders within', rather than as an 'external threat'. The exception to this rule, however, is the Travelling community. As elite discourse in Northern Ireland never viewed immigration to the region as a 'problem', ethnic minorities were never seen as an 'external threat'. Historically, however, Travellers were perceived in this way. While they have not achieved the status of 'outsiders within', they are often treated by the media simply as 'outsiders' for whom one must make provision. To some extent, however, they are still portrayed as an external threat to local communities.

One example of this type of coverage occurred in March 1996 when a group of Travellers arrived in Downpatrick shortly before the

St Patrick's Day parade. The Travellers had parked their caravans in a car park traditionally used as the finishing point for the parade. The *Down Recorder* decided to run a story because some businessmen and other individuals had expressed concern about the arrival of the Travellers. The reporter assigned to the story, David Telford, told me that he contacted the council officer who was co-ordinating the parade. The officer told Mr Telford that he was concerned about the matter. The Department of the Environment was also contacted as were the police, who were quoted as saying that the Travellers had told them they would be moving on the day after the parade. However, the Travellers were not asked for their views in either the initial article or a subsequent follow-up piece. Mr Telford said it may have crossed his mind to talk to them but he recalled that he had had a hostile response from Travellers when he had tried to speak to them on a previous occasion.[12] However, he gave no clear reason as to exactly why he had not spoken to them. His editor, Paul Symington, was quite clear, however:

> We didn't view we needed it [a quote from the Travellers]. The story was not about them arriving, it was about them in the car park and the possible disruption that it would have caused to the parade, the fact that they were there. It was a question of talking to the DOE. Why did the DOE allow them in? [The DOE (Department of the Environment) had just dismantled a barrier which had been put up previously to stop Travellers using the car park.]

The *News Letter* (15 March 1996) also carried an article on the same subject entitled '"Visitors" mar festive mood', which again omitted the Travellers' viewpoint. The editors of both newspapers said they generally only carried stories about Travellers when there was controversy concerning them, suggesting that the newspapers were contributing to the perception of Travellers as a 'problem'. Both editors felt that many of their readers would not be kindly disposed towards Travellers. Mr Symington said that if the *Down Recorder* advocated a local permanent site for Travellers, there would be 'a wholesale hue and cry'. He contended that the local council, which had previously decided not to provide a site, was 'very mindful of public opinion'. Yet, where does 'public opinion' come from? It was clear from my interview with Mr Telford that the newspaper set some store by the fact that certain local *businessmen* were concerned about the arrival of the Travellers, even though it did not quote them. Furthermore, the *Down Recorder* played a key role in constructing a 'controversy' by contacting the festival organiser about the Travellers' arrival. One can see elite discourse at work here very much in the manner van Dijk describes. Elite discourse rather than 'everyday talk' appeared to rule that the Travellers were causing a problem. Tom Collins, the editor of the *Irish News*, also told me his newspaper would generally only cover stories about Travellers when there was a conflict between the Travellers and the settled community. He felt that most of his newspaper's readers would be 'relatively antagonistic towards Travellers' but that the newspaper tried 'to rise above people's prejudices'.

However, by virtue of tending to cover stories concerning Travellers only when they are perceived to be causing a problem, all three newspapers are perpetuating a negative stereotype of Travellers. It will be recalled that negativity is one of the ingredients which counts when the process of news selection takes place (Galtung and Ruge 1965) and that stories about ethnic minorities tend to be negative (van Dijk 1991; 1993b). The coverage of stories concerning ethnic minorities in the five regional newspapers examined fits into this pattern. The number of articles concerning issues relating to ethnic minorities and racism in Northern Ireland jumped from 8 in March, 1996, to 16 in April, when the media first began reporting the series of attacks on Chinese people, and increased further to 21 in May. Of the 8 articles carried in March, 5 contained a strong element of negativity or 'bad news'. This applied to 12 of the 16 articles carried in April, and to 14 of the 21 articles carried in May. The attacks were featured in 4 stories published in April and 10 stories carried in May.

This coverage fits in with the pattern identified by van Dijk (1988) and Hartmann *et al.* (1974) whereby ethnic minorities are presented as a problem, or at least as problematic, rather than as ordinary citizens. Furthermore, both the *Sunday Life* and the *Sunday World* displayed a tendency to criminalise ethnic minorities; in other words, to indirectly suggest that all members of an ethnic group are criminals. The *Sunday Life* articles, which linked the attacks on Chinese people to triads, were criminalising Chinese people by perpetuating a stereotyped view of the Chinese as triad members. The journalist responsible for that story, John Cassidy, also wrote an article which effectively branded all Nigerians as criminals. It was headlined 'Nigerians in cash fiddle target Ulster' (*Sunday Life*, 7 April 1996). It began:

Cheeky Nigerians want to visit Ulster to get company bosses to open bank accounts for them.

Local businessmen fear the foreigners want to use the accounts to salt away millions of US dollars left behind in wills.

It is the latest in a long line of attempts by Nigerians to get access to the public's accounts in Ulster and the rest of the UK.

When I suggested to Mr Cassidy that the blanket use of the term 'Nigerians', which continued throughout the article, gave the impression that all Nigerians were criminals, he agreed and said he would bear my point in mind next time he was writing a similar story. However, the possible connotation apparently had not occurred to him at the time.[13]

The *Sunday Life*'s rival, the *Sunday World*, printed an article just two weeks later (21 April 1996), headlined 'Irish cops told to watch for Chinese BSE beef trips'. The article informed readers that:

> Gardai on border duty as a result of the alert over Mad Cow Disease have been told to keep watch for vehicles driven from Northern Ireland by Chinese.

> For there are fears some unscrupulous restaurateurs have bought large quantities of beef from stores in Northern Ireland which sold it off cheap to clear their stocks when the scare started.

Needless to say, nobody had even been arrested. Nevertheless, the article effectively criminalised *all* Chinese restaurant owners north of the border. Travellers believe that the news media in Northern Ireland is also fond of labelling their community as criminals. Michael Mongan, spokesperson for the Monagh Bypass Travellers' site in West Belfast, contends that the news media covers crimes committed by Travelling people which would not have warranted any coverage had they been committed by members of the settled community. If this is the case, it may well be partly because the fact that a Traveller has committed the crime gives the story an element of 'novelty', another quality which journalists look for in their selection of what constitutes 'news'.

The Media's Role in Masking Institutional Racism

While the news values of the media do permit some concerns of ethnic minorities to become 'news', many fall by the wayside. This is partly because of the event-driven nature of news. Elaine Lester said she felt very lucky because she was given two weeks to research an in-depth feature on racism. This is very unusual in daily journalism. Generally, editors require some sort of news 'peg' on which to hang a feature of this sort. Thus, an *Irish News* reporter, Jim Fitzpatrick, who had written a news article on the attacks on Chinese people, told me he was working on a more in-depth feature on the topic but had been waiting for a good news story to 'lead into it, you know, to give people a reason to read it'. However, he had got somewhat sidetracked by 'politics' in the run-up to the election for the Northern Ireland Forum in May 1996.

The complaint that excessive coverage of 'politics' crowded out issues like those concerning ethnic minorities was one I heard a number of times. Tom Collins put it succinctly:

TC: We have ... been very obsessed by the mainstream political agenda and we have completely ignored the whole agenda of community politics which just hasn't figured at all in how the newspapers set their news agenda ... I think it is just because the media has been complacent and lazy in many respects. You just take up the stories which are easiest for you and ignore the stories that you have to do any digging on.

LF: And what sort of stories are easiest to cover, then?

TC: Well, ... the pre-planned events, you know ... party political press conferences, managing the fax machine. You know ... more journalists in Northern Ireland ... spend all their time walking around the fax machine, rather than walking around the towns and cities where they are reporting ...

If there is a big party political statement, or a big press conference, you know, you have got a story the next day ... You have got 500 words and it is going to be perceived as relatively important, because everybody in the media perceives it to be relatively important.

The media consensus as to what makes 'news' is crucial. Clearly, this consensus allows the government and the major political parties to play an important role as primary definers of news. Yet, as already suggested above, both marginalise ethnic minority issues almost to the point of invisibility. The government produces scores of press releases every month[14] yet only two pertained to issues concerning ethnic minorities during the twelve months from June, 1995. None of the five main political parties was able to produce any recent press releases on such matters. However, Ian Paisley Junior of the Democratic Unionist Party wrote to me to point out that, in 1995, the party passed a motion, which the press failed to cover, calling for the extension of race relations legislation to Northern Ireland. It was the last in a list of 43 resolutions tabled for debate, a position which speaks volumes about the significance of ethnic minorities within mainstream Northern Ireland politics, whether unionist or nationalist.

The marginalisation of issues of concern to ethnic minorities on both the political and the news agendas, and the reinforcement of negative and/or alien stereotypes all help to mask the extent to which racism is endemic in Northern Ireland in terms of both its institutions and its public discourse. Every act of discrimination, unintentional or otherwise, is a form of racism. Yet both powerful elites and ordinary white citizens are able to construct a worldview which largely absolves them of responsibility for the current state of play. The media contributes to this cosy perception by concentrating coverage on acts of racism carried out by individuals, such as violent attacks. As Fee Ching Leong, co-ordinator of the Multi-Cultural Resource Centre, observed with regard to *The Hidden Troubles*:

At least it informed the general public that racism goes on and sometimes to a horrific scale as well ... But, at the same time, it enabled a lot of white middle-class people to sit back and think 'But I don't do things like that ... I'm not part of that society that would indulge in racist attacks and neither would I allow my dog to defecate in a Chinese take-away' [one of the incidents shown in the programme].

Both Ms Leong and Patrick Yu criticised the programme for focusing much more on individual and dramatic acts of racism than on examples of institutionalised racism, such as the relative lack of information in languages other than English, the inadequate supply of interpreters, and discrimination in the jobs market. Both said that their own attempts to get across such a message in the news media have met with relatively little success.

Conforming to Elite Values

When the news media does cover issues, it likes to be able to encapsulate those issues in examples of real individuals (Galtung and Ruge 1965; Fowler 1991). This puts ethnic minorities at a big disadvantage because straightforward linguistic problems make it much more difficult for individuals to be interviewed by the media. From the journalist's point of view, this is one factor which makes coverage of issues of concern to ethnic minorities more difficult to report on than issues affecting white people.

The existence of this language barrier also helps to explain why, as noted earlier, the newspapers which were examined often quoted spokespeople for ethnic groups rather than individuals when they did cover stories concerning ethnic minorities. Linguistic difficulties are a major problem among Northern Ireland's largest ethnic group, the Chinese community. According to the Chinese Welfare Association, most older Chinese people speak little or no English. There is also a communication barrier between Travellers and journalists. Travellers I spoke to said that they did not like speaking to journalists because they use a different and more 'educated' vocabulary. Bridget McDonagh, a Traveller at the Monagh Bypass site, said that news coverage should adopt a simpler vocabulary: 'If it is for Travellers to read, why don't they put it out in small words, instead of big words like "controversy" ... If a Traveller is going to read it, put it in small words ... Big words, we don't understand.' Moreover, members of ethnic minorities sometimes fail to comprehend the significance of any quotes they do give journalists. Michael Mongan told me that Travellers will sometimes make flippant or inaccurate comments because they do not realise the potential impact of their words in the media. Elaine Lester said that some of her interviewees from other ethnic groups were shocked when they saw their comments in print: 'It was rather terrifying. It was like "We know it [racism] exists and we have finally come out and said it. Are we going to get attacked more?"'

This relates to another point which became an issue of debate within the Chinese community after *The Hidden Troubles* was shown. There was clearly a division of opinion between those who felt that white people should know about what was really happening and those who felt that it was better not to rock the boat. The Chairman of both the CWA and the Northern Ireland Chinese Chamber of Commerce, Shek Yung Lee, was of the latter view. He felt *The Hidden Troubles* had exaggerated the scale of racist attacks in Northern Ireland and was concerned it might affect relations between the Chinese community and white people:

SYL: We want to ... get on well with the local people, you know. We have been living here for so many years, we have never really had ... compared with the recent scale of attacks, we have had no problem, whatsoever. Of course, the majority of our customers are local people and, if we don't get on with them, it will affect our business.

LF: So that matters.

SYL: Yes, that's right ... For example, local people call us names. I don't treat it, you know, seriously. Like, for example, they call us Chinkie. In the older generation, they [whites] maybe have an idea of it being racist, but I think the younger generation, they call us Chinkie, maybe like calling us Chinese people, you know. We don't take it seriously at all.

LF: Well, I mean, it's talking down. You don't find it patronising?

SYL: Well, in my opinion, you know, when they first call us names, you know, we feel a little bit uneasy and unhappy about it. But now, you know, it seems to be getting used to [sic] ... we don't take it seriously, you know ...

I put this point to one of the interviewees featured in *The Hidden Troubles*, Paul Mo. He is a waiter and chef in Belfast and has experienced a great deal of racist abuse. He was scathing in his response:

PM: It's not serious! ... Well, let me tell you something. You, you let me call you names. You even let me call you a *bastard*, you wouldn't even like that, it's not something that *you* would live with, no way! ... I mean, no one would put up with it ...

LF: But have you come across people in your community telling you that you shouldn't ... ?

PM: Yeah, I mean. They said 'You shouldn't went on TV because, you know, I mean, they can't do anything, the Westerners can't do

anything. It's not going to stop them, you know. I mean, living in
here, you're trying to make a living. You shouldn't went on TV.'
That's what they say.
LF: But, how do *you* feel about it?
PM: I just don't care, you know ... I mean, I'm only saying what
I've been through ... Whether the public wants to listen or not, it's
up to them. But, I mean, I'm a very strong person and it doesn't
worry me at all, one bit, what the Chinese people say ...

The willingness of at least some in the Chinese community to fit in
with the patronising and discriminatory attitudes of the dominant
group in society underlines the structural inequality which is masked
by a veneer of cultural difference. Rather than that dominant group
changing to accommodate ethnic minorities, ethnic minorities
compromise to fit in with existing power structures. However, while
some organisations representing ethnic minorities feel that they have
not had a great deal of success in getting across their message, one
spokesperson for Travellers is pleased enough with his record in this
regard. Paul Noonan was Co-ordinator for the Northern Ireland
Council for Travelling People (NICTP) for several years from 1985.
He had a clear understanding of news values and made sure the media
got what it was looking for: '[You have] to kind of pitch it in ... stark
terms, you know, some would say sensationalist ... but to pitch the
story in clear-cut terms, you know – goodies and baddies type thing,
you know.'

This strategy proved fairly successful. Mr Noonan says that, not only
did it earn a fair amount of news coverage for Travellers' campaigns,
but that coverage led to the setting up of a number of research studies
on Travellers. These studies have had an impact on elite discourse about
Travellers. One could argue that the parameters of public debate on
Travellers have shifted to accommodate their needs and concerns. The
downside of such coverage may have been that, in conforming to
news values which stress negativity and controversy (many of the
stories did feature conflict between the Traveller and settled
communities), these stories were also reinforcing a stereotype of
Travellers as trouble-makers. A protest against the *status quo* is likely
to attract media coverage because of the element of controversy.
However, the experience of the NICTP suggests that it may be the
most effective way of moving the parameters of elite discourse, at least
in the short term.

Conclusion

The relationship between the printed news media and ethnic minorities
in Northern Ireland illustrates the process by which ethnic minorities

are forced to fit in with the values and power structures of the dominant group. There is an elite discourse, promulgated by the media and most politicians, which marginalises the concerns of ethnic minorities and fails to recognise the racist nature of society in Northern Ireland. The news values of the press mean that its coverage reinforces the notion of ethnic minorities as being problematic, alien and/or exotic and, in the case of the *Sunday Life* and the *Sunday World*, inclined to indulge in criminal activities. Ethnic minorities are given a voice in the media. However, the evidence above suggests that they tend to be given as much credibility as members of elite groups only where their views fit in with the world-view of those elites. Ethnic minorities suffer, too, from the problem of lack of awareness of the news values of the media, and from linguistic difficulties. However, the experience of the NICTP suggests that, when their publicity efforts conform to news values, the media may give space for their views, even if they challenge the dominant consensus. This is particularly true where there are elements of controversy and drama. Such coverage may also reinforce the notion of ethnic minorities as trouble-makers. Nevertheless, if this type of publicity can help change the parameters of elite discourse, then it may be a strategy other organisations representing ethnic minorities should consider.

In a society where all members have equal rights, however, the onus should not be on those who are marginalised to initiate change. Patrick Yu talked about the 'passivity' of the media in this regard and this reflects the 'passivity' of politicians and other groups who wield power in Northern Ireland. 'Politics' is defined in a very narrow way in Northern Ireland, partly because of the conflictual paradigm within which it is constructed, and partly because of the lack of a meaningful and accountable political system. I would argue that this means issues of concern to ethnic minorities are even further down the political and news agendas in Northern Ireland than in Britain and many other Western countries. Editors and politicians do have the power to challenge and to attempt to change the *status quo*. By failing to do so, they are contributing to maintaining a society which, through its neglect of the rights and needs of ethnic minorities, is quite simply racist.

Acknowledgements

My thanks and acknowledgements go to all the interviewees, and to Eva Logan of the CWA, who acted as interpreter for the interview with Shek Yung Lee and who provided some additional information, and to Sally Quinn who transcribed most of the interviews. I owe thanks also to the Northern Ireland Office (NIO) and to all other organisations which sent me press releases in connection with this research.

Finally, I would like to thank Paul Hainsworth, John Hill and Greg McLaughlin for valuable comments which they made on an earlier draft of this chapter.

Notes

1   I use the term 'ethnic minorities' with some reluctance as I see it as merely reinforcing the marginalised position of such communities. However, I cannot think of a more suitable term. I also use the term 'ethnic group'. In the context of this chapter, these labels refer to those groups marginalised on the basis of their ethnicity. This does not include members of the white, settled (as opposed to non-white and Travelling) Protestant and Catholic communities who form the dominant group within this analysis.

2   'White' is used here to include all members of the white, settled communities.

3   It should be noted that, strictly speaking, the northern edition of the *Sunday World* is a regional edition of an Irish newspaper. Constraints of time and resources meant this study had to be restricted to newspapers, rather than the broadcast media. However, in a survey of white people in Leicester and Manchester, Troyna (1981) found that the press, both local and national, was a more important source of information on 'race relations' than local radio stations for his interviewees. Thus, the content of newspapers is clearly of significance.

4   According to the Northern Ireland Readership Survey, 1996, 60 per cent of *Belfast Telegraph* readers are Protestant while 28 per cent are Catholic and 12 per cent are 'other' (figures cited in *Belfast Telegraph*, 11 February 1997).

5   According to the Northern Ireland Readership Survey 1996, 50 per cent of *Sunday Life* readers are Protestant, while 39 per cent are Catholic and 10 per cent are recorded as 'other' (figures supplied by the *Sunday Life*). According to figures produced by Ulster Marketing Surveys for 1996, 65 per cent of *Sunday World* readers in Northern Ireland are Catholic, while 30 per cent are Protestant and 5 per cent are recorded as 'other' (figures supplied by the *Sunday World*).
    The Audit Bureau of Circulations records the following average sales per issue for the first six months of 1996:

Belfast Telegraph	136,756
Irish News	45,906
News Letter (Ulster edition)	33,260
News Letter (Belfast edition)	66,209[*]

| Sunday Life | 101,118 |
| Sunday World (NI edition) | 68,520 |

Note:* Distributed free of charge. Circulation figures supplied by Verified Free Distribution.

6. I would like to thank Paul Noonan of the Belfast Travellers' Education and Development Group who provided access to his files of cuttings.

7. The following individuals were interviewed during June and July 1996 (the job titles and positions attributed to them are those which they held when they were interviewed):

John Cassidy, reporter, *Sunday Life*
Tom Collins, Editor, *Irish News*
Jim Fitzpatrick, reporter, *Irish News*
Dave Hanna, Chief Information Officer, RUC
Shek Yung Lee, Chairman, Chinese Welfare Association (NI) and Chairman, Chinese Chamber of Commerce (NI)
Fee Ching Leong, Co-ordinator, Multi-Cultural Resource Centre and Honorary Secretary, Northern Ireland Council for Ethnic Equality
Elaine Lester, reporter, *Belfast Telegraph*
Geoff Martin, Editor, *News Letter*
Bridget McDonagh, Traveller, Monagh Bypass Travellers' site, West Belfast
Helen McGurk, reporter, *News Letter*
Paul Mo, chef and waiter
Mary Ellen Mongan, Traveller, Monagh Bypass site
Michael Mongan, Travellers' spokesperson, Monagh Bypass site
Paul Noonan, Director, Belfast Travellers' Education and Development Group
Martin O'Brien, Director, Committee on the Administration of Justice
Raj Puri, President, Indian Community Centre
'Susan', Traveller, Monagh Bypass site
Paul Symington, Editor, *Down Recorder*
David Telford, reporter, *Down Recorder*
Ramesh Vinayak, reporter on secondment, *News Letter*
Patrick Yu, Co-ordinator, Northern Ireland Council for Ethnic Minorities

8. A spokeswoman for the CWA told me that Elaine Lester's contact must have been speaking in an unofficial capacity, as the Association never believed the attacks were racist.

9. This was partly due to the prominence given to the spate of attacks on Chinese people. Other comments from ethnic minority organisations which criticised government policy or highlighted the problem of racism generally got less prominent coverage than the articles on the attacks.

10. An example of this type of coverage is to be found in an *Irish News* editorial (*Irish News*, 29 May 1996) which suggested that, at some future point, Belfast's Lord Mayor should be selected from one of the ethnic minorities. It displays the theme alluded to, along with an example of the priorities of nationalist political discourse:

> It is essential that a nationalist should be given the job [of Lord Mayor] in the immediate future, but it is also important that people from a wide range of backgrounds should play a full role at the city hall.
>
> Members of the Chinese and Indian community have made a significant contribution to commercial life in Belfast. They fully deserve to have the opportunity to provide the city's first citizen.

11. This latter view was voiced by some members of the Travelling community, as well as the editor of the *Down Recorder*. However, the Travellers I spoke to felt that the media brands all Travellers 'irresponsible' by covering the actions of 'bad' rather than 'good' Travellers.

12. A number of journalists and editors said they had received, or knew colleagues who had received, what they felt was a hostile response from Travellers. Both Michael Mongan, from the Monagh Bypass site in West Belfast, and Paul Noonan, of the Belfast Travellers' Education and Development Group, said this was due, at least in part, to anger on the part of some Travellers about the negative portrayal that they feel they get from the media.

13. Mr Cassidy did not accept my argument that his 'triads' stories criminalised the Chinese community. He had written a number of articles on racial discrimination and said it was an issue that interested him.

14. This includes press releases from all government departments and agencies. The figure obviously varies from month to month. The Northern Ireland Press Office gave me the following monthly totals for 1996: April, 110; May, 120; June, 113; July, 65.

PART II

CASE STUDIES

7 Race and Ethnicity in Northern Ireland: The Chinese Community

Anna Manwah Watson and Eleanor McKnight

This chapter aims to give an overview of the Chinese community in Northern Ireland, their origins and ensuing emigration, something of their cultural traditions and beliefs as well as aspects of life in Northern Ireland including their support networks and organisations. It then moves on to specific areas which directly impact on the community: health and social care, housing, education, immigration and racial harassment in order to identify specific needs as well as the problems and discriminatory practice faced by Chinese people there. The community is now the largest minority ethnic group in Northern Ireland but has a relatively short history and to some extent has remained largely invisible. It is hoped that this chapter will remove some of this 'invisibility' and so help establish the community more firmly within Northern Irish society, allowing members to play *their* part in its future.

Origins

The majority of the Chinese residents in Northern Ireland come from the rural area of Hong Kong, the New Territories, where people speak Hakka and Cantonese, dialects of Southern China, and regard themselves as the indigenous Chinese residents, *Yuen Gui Men*, in Hong Kong. In the New Territories, family clans form close-knit communities living in near proximity of each other in villages that have been built for hundreds of years, well before the influx of Chinese refugees into Hong Kong, which occurred when the Communist Party took over China in 1949. Family life in the New Territories has followed the traditional rural pattern of China for centuries with farms and trades being passed down from one generation to the next and children seen as assets and the hope for the future. Family members share a strong sense of identity and they expect loyalty and support from each other.

Unlike the affluent island of Hong Kong and the peninsular of Kowloon, the New Territories have remained under-developed economically, socially and educationally. Subjected to little Western influence and industrialisation, the people of the New Territories still hold very strong traditional Chinese attitudes and generally they have not acquired a command of English as a second language before emigration (Watson 1989).

In the 1950s, with the explosion of the refugee population from China, which brought expertise and capital into Hong Kong, livelihood in the already poor farming villages of the New Territories was threatened by the massive import of agricultural products into Hong Kong. Young people in the New Territories, who had much less educational opportunities than their counterparts in the city, were unable to compete successfully for other jobs when farming was no longer a viable option. Coincidental with the period of decline in the New Territories, Britain was thriving economically in the post-war years. The concomitant increased demand for labour was met by immigrants coming from Commonwealth countries. Both the British and the Hong Kong governments encouraged large-scale emigration until 1962, when the Commonwealth Immigrants Act curbed the flow of immigrants. The implementation of the employment voucher system in 1962 which only issued work permits to certain professionals and workers with jobs already lined up in the UK, effectively limited immigration from Hong Kong to those villages whose members had already established themselves in Britain. Most began in the catering trade. As a result of this legislation, subsequent emigration patterns to the UK took the form of 'chain migration' whereby a restaurant owner secures the employment of a clan member, following the traditional Chinese preference for employing relatives. Work experience in the UK is thus restricted to the Chinese catering trade, and when the employee has saved enough money to fulfil the goal of owning a business, this usually consists of opening a restaurant or a food 'take-away' and reproducing the 'chain' to enable migration of the relatives. During the 1950s and the 1960s, thousands of unskilled young Chinese males uprooted themselves from the New Territories to settle in British towns and cities where the urban environment, the climate and the culture were alien to them. The majority have remained in catering businesses which, although they provide a reasonable profit, demand long and unsociable working hours – a lifestyle that prevents many from establishing a meaningful relationship with their children, engaging in healthy leisure pursuits or educational opportunities and, ultimately, integrating into the wider community (Watson 1993).

In addition to immigrants from the New Territories, some 20,000 ethnic Chinese from Vietnam, known as 'boat people', settled into the UK during the late 1970s and early 1980s. Several thousand Chinese students from Mainland China also were granted residence status in the UK in this period (Yau 1996). After 1991, the British government granted 50,000 Hong Kong families the right of abode in the United Kingdom prior to the change of sovereignty in July 1997. However, only just over half of the 50,000 who were given the right to hold full British passports decided to obtain them. A proportion of these families has now moved to the UK but a significant number has remained in Hong Kong. The 1991 Census found some 159,600 Chinese residents in the UK, with big populations in London, Liverpool and Manchester, although the total number of Chinese people is smaller than that of the equivalent populations in the Chinatowns of New York or San Francisco (Yau 1996).

The Chinese Community in Northern Ireland

Similar to the pattern of immigration into other parts of Britain, Chinese people began to arrive in Northern Ireland in the early 1960s. The first recorded Chinese restaurant, 'The Peacock', was opened in Belfast in 1962, but it closed in 1973 due to loss of trade following the erection of a security barrier, a product of 'the troubles' (Lee 1996a). With the rapid growth in the number of Chinese restaurants and take-away shops in Britain during the early 1960s, Chinese catering businesses began to get competitive. Inevitably, new locations were sought and Northern Ireland was attractive due to its wide geographical spread of towns and villages and relatively cheap property. The civil unrest in the Province since 1969 had, no doubt, dampened the enthusiasm of some Chinese people to invest therein. Subsequently, while the Chinese catering trade reached nearly saturated levels in mainland Britain during the 1970s, Northern Ireland still had few Chinese restaurants. A survey in 1977, for example, listed only 35 Chinese restaurants and estimated a local population of 1,000 Chinese residents (Creaney 1977). The improved political situation and less adverse publicity about 'the troubles' in the 1980s saw the revival of some confidence in Chinese investment into the catering trade. An added attraction was the perceived lesser racial tension in Northern Ireland, in contrast to the situation in some inner cities in Britain. Therefore, it was estimated in 1989 that 'the Chinese community in Northern Ireland has grown considerably in the last ten years, to become its biggest ethnic minority with approximately 4,500 people' (Watson 1989).

Today, the Chinese Community is still the largest ethnic minority in Northern Ireland, whereas in the UK it is only the seventh biggest ethnic group (1991 Census). As already explained, the majority comes from the New Territories, with approximately 150 from Vietnam and a similar number from Mainland China (the latter predominantly connected with the universities). There is also a small number of ethnic Chinese from Malaysia, Singapore and Taiwan. A recent major study of ethnic communities in Northern Ireland (Irwin 1996) estimated the local Chinese population to be between 3,000 and 5,000, a number disputed by the Chinese Welfare Association (see below) to be an under-estimation. The CWA believes that the figure could be as high as 8,000. Irwin's survey showed that 41 per cent of the Chinese population live in Belfast with significant numbers living in Craigavon, Lisburn, Newtownabbey, North Down and Ballymena. The findings indicated a young and growing population with some 53 per cent between the working age of 16 and 44 years and a large proportion of school-age children. Nearly all the Chinese residents are engaged in the catering trade locally with over 500 catering outlets (Lee 1993) all over the Province. In addition, three Chinese supermarkets and two bakeries supply the local Chinese community with food provisions, newspapers and videos.

Cultural Traditions

Chinese religions, festivals and traditions are observed in the Chinese community in Northern Ireland to an extent practicable in overseas Chinese societies. Confucianism (a Chinese philosophy), Buddhism and Taoism are the most popular religions practised by Chinese people. Religion is not institutionalised into the system; in other words there is no special day or place for worship and praying is very much a personal matter which takes place in one's home. It is therefore not the Chinese community's priority to build a Buddhist temple in Northern Ireland – unlike several other ethnic groups which have their own specific places of worship in the Province. Local Chinese restaurants often have their own 'god shelf' on which stands images of the popular deities, such as the three gods of happiness – representing long life, happiness and prosperity. Apart from Chinese religions, there is a Belfast Chinese Christian Fellowship Church, which was initiated by Chinese overseas students and a local minister in 1985. The congregation numbers between 60 and 100 members, some of whom are from the catering trade.

Many Chinese festivals were religious in origin and held to celebrate the birth of, or some deeds of, either a god or a legendary hero. Festival dates continue to be calculated on the lunar calendar. The most important festival for the Chinese is the Lunar New Year, which falls between mid-January and mid-February in the Western calendar, with celebrations hitherto lasting fifteen days, but now mostly reduced to about three days or even less. Each Chinese year is named in sequence after twelve animals; ancient legend telling the story that the years got their names when the Buddha asked all living creatures to come to him but only twelve turned up. To mark their faithfulness, the Buddha named a year after each of them.

New Year is a time to start things afresh and settle old debts or feuds. Special foods are prepared, and houses are decorated with 'lucky' messages and tangerine trees. On New Year's Day, children pay their respects to parents and in return are given red packets known as *lai see* containing money. Most local restaurants close on Chinese New Year and families and friends have their New Year's dinner together. During the Chinese New Year, the Chinese Chamber of Commerce (Northern Ireland) organises a dinner with accompanying cultural performances at a Belfast hotel. The event is well supported and generally 500–600 adults and children turn up to enjoy the gathering. With the demand for more social events, the recently established Oi-Kwan Chinese Women's Group in Belfast has celebrated other festivals such as the Dragon Boat Festival and the Moon Festival with special food prepared and further cultural activities. In addition, a Chinese children's dance group has been established which performs at the above festivals and also participates in cross-community events.

'Respect for Ancestors' is a strong Chinese tradition. When young, children are taught to respect not only adult relatives but also their deceased ancestors, *Jo Sinn*. This form of respect includes a set of rituals to revere the good deeds and achievements of a family's forebearers. In many Chinese homes, a wooden plaque bearing the family name and representing *Jo Sinn* is put on the 'god shelf' alongside other deities. Lighted joss sticks are placed in a small urn in front of the plaque and at festivals flowers, fresh fruit and wine are additional items put before *Jo Sinn* when parents and children take turns to pray and bow in front of the plaque, to pay respect to their ancestors.

Representation: the Chinese Welfare Association, NI

In 1983, in response to difficulties being faced by the Chinese community, a group of Chinese people set up the Chinese Chamber of Commerce (Northern Ireland) (CCC (NI)) and also, in order to maintain language and culture within the younger generation, the Chinese Language School. The latter is part funded by the Belfast Education and Library Board (BELB) and its 200 students attend classes held in a local school each weekend. The CCC (NI) is funded through membership fees, and currently has about 150 members. In 1985, this body bought premises in Belfast in order to serve the Chinese community more effectively and to act as a focal point. In June 1986, the CCC (NI) set up the Chinese Welfare Association (CWA) to provide direct services and to try to bridge the gap between the needs of the Chinese community living in Northern Ireland and the available health, social, educational, legal and welfare services. The CWA has developed from the Training and Employment Agency's Action for Community Enterprise scheme (ACE), originally designed to help the long-term unemployed. The CWA has now progressed to become one of the most effective Chinese support organisations in the UK, providing much-needed information and advice, English-language classes, youth activities, interpreting and translating facilities to the local Chinese community (CWA 1996). In the context of the work of this organisation, it is appropriate to consider first what has been widely perceived as a major area of need, health and social care.

Health and Social Care Needs

Research carried out by Barnardos (1995) and also by the Northern Health and Social Services Board (NHSSB) (1995) revealed that the majority, 54 per cent and 60 per cent respectively, of Chinese residents have lived in the Province for ten years or fewer. As recent immigrants, many of the Chinese people face problems associated with first-generation immigration. For example, Barnardos' survey of 50 families found that 90 per cent of interviewees identified the 'language barrier' as their biggest obstacle to integration with the wider community. As many Chinese people put it, without the language ability, they become 'deaf and dumb' to the outside world. Language difficulties result in inadequate and uneven access to health and social provisions.

As Hong Kong is not a welfare state and has no National Health Service, many of the immigrants from there to Northern Ireland are unaware of the medical and health services available to them as well as their welfare entitlements. Barnardos' survey showed that only 8 per cent of interviewees have ever used dental services despite the fact that the sample included many children. In the NHSSB's sample, 42 per cent said they did not know how to contact a general practitioner (GP) after office hours. Often children are brought to hospital casualty departments at night because parents either do not know how to locate a GP on duty or feel they cannot explain symptoms over the telephone.

The language difficulty has prevented many Chinese citizens from seeking information about existing services and the local health boards or trusts have not made much effort in the past to enable their thousands of Chinese residents to access information and services. Moreover, in the absence of a Race Relations Act until 1997 and related codes of practice, it appears that none of the health boards felt obliged to have any policy on translation and specific service provision to meet the language needs of their black and ethnic minority residents. There are few translated materials to inform the Chinese users about services, health care issues or their rights and entitlements. Over the last two years, some improvement was evident in translating essential information for the Chinese community relating to statutory services. The Craigavon and Banbridge Trust, the Health and Social Services Councils, the Northern Ireland Housing Executive and the Department of Health and Social Services (DHSS) have all produced some translated materials in Chinese and Urdu. A small working group of health workers and minority support groups have been considering translation of leaflets on a regional basis. Although these were very welcome initiatives, they were largely piecemeal attempts made possible by the efforts of some concerned individuals. While translation into ethnic languages has been common practice by many health authorities in the rest of the UK, communication with ethnic minority groups seems to be a low priority for statutory bodies in Northern Ireland.

There is still only one full-time interpreter for the total Chinese population, funded by the Northern Ireland Office's Central Community Relations Unit with contributions towards the interpreter's expenses from two health boards. A one-year pilot scheme funded by the Eastern Health and Social Services Board (EHSSB) established a part-time inter-preting service in the CWA for residents in the Eastern Board area in July 1997. Without adequate interpreting facilities, families use children and relatives to interpret medical consultation with general practitioners (GPs) and in hospitals or at home with health visitors or social workers. For example, a woman with abdominal pain asked her 16-year-old nephew, who was the only English-speaking relative, to accompany her to see her GP. She was extremely embarrassed when the GP asked her about her menstrual cycle and contraceptive methods. Another woman diagnosed as being a carrier of Hepatitis B at a routine antenatal test found out about her condition three years *later* through a Chinese health worker. During those three years the primary care staff of GPs, health visitors and district nurses had all been aware of it and had been given health board guidelines to protect themselves from infection from her. These examples were obviously at variance with the much-vaunted Patient's Charter which stipulates that patients have a right to 'access to a health service that has respect for privacy, dignity and religious and cultural beliefs' (DOH 1992a).

In November 1996, ethnic community support organisations and statutory health workers organised a conference to identify the health and social needs of the ethnic minority communities in Northern Ireland. The event was well supported by ethnic groups but the attendance by statutory agencies was disappointing, which was a con-firmation for many ethnic minority residents that their needs are a low priority for statutory agencies. At the conference, the Chairman of the Chinese Welfare Association, pointed to the primary issues and needs which concern the Chinese community:

- Social isolation and exclusion.
- The language barrier, which leads to difficulties in obtaining equitable access to health and social services, welfare, housing provision, education and training opportunities in areas of economic activity.
- Racist and discriminatory attitudes manifested in the behaviour of local people. These attitudes affect the lives of members of the Chinese community on a daily basis. In addition, there is a lack of coherent policies towards this community on the part of statutory providers, and an unwillingness to understand, assess and address the particular needs of the community and resource support organisations within the community (Lee 1996a).

The Chinese delegates at the conference highlighted problems with the language barrier which have caused people 'misunderstanding, frustration and dissatisfaction of services' (CWA/Ethnic Minorities Working Party on Health 1997). Delegates cited examples of misdiagnosis due to poor communication and to the subsequent loss of confidence in their GPs. Urgent considerations by health agencies to fund more interpreters and liaison health workers were called for. People wanted two-way communication with service providers and information in their own language and consultations in needs assessment and appropriate services. The needs of Chinese youth and elderly people were also highlighted with the call for mainstream funding in these services.

The language barrier has also compounded the problems of isolation experienced by many, especially Chinese women in Northern Ireland. Owing to the strict immigration laws, many Chinese couples have no extended family around them. If they live in a rural area, they may be the only Chinese family residing there, without the support of relatives or friends and unable to establish any social networks through the connections of family, churches, schools or employment – networks that are readily available to their neighbours. The lack of extended family also poses serious difficulties in childcare for many young families. As catering businesses are generally small family concerns, the wife is normally required to work in the kitchen or at the counter of the take-away shop. For parents who need childminding facilities, it is difficult to employ a registered childminder to cover the customary working hours between 5 p.m. and midnight. Some parents are forced, through lack of choice, to send their young children to Hong Kong to be reared by relatives (this at least allows the children to learn something of their language and culture in their early years). Others arrange with local Irish families to have their children fostered privately. Children may only see their parents when the latter go home to Hong Kong for visits, perhaps once a year or less often. Children who reside with foster parents have more regular parental contact, often on a daily basis or at least once a week. Generally, these children reunite with their parents when they reach school age, at a time when they are more able to look after themselves. Such practices obviously can create problems stemming from lack of bonding, at times made worse by cultural and linguistic differences between parents and children who might have been brought up by English-speaking foster parents in a Western culture. In addition, while many local Irish families undoubtedly looked after these Chinese children well, the potential for abuse is evident for any child where private foster parents are neither formally approved nor monitored by Social Services. Over the years, a small number of anecdotal and confirmed incidents of child abuse in local private foster placements and in family homes in Hong Kong as well as at home with their parents have been reported to the CWA. Social workers have also been dealing with several cases of Chinese teenagers rebelling against parents, either as a direct result of the long separation from their parents when they were younger or because of different expectations between children and their parents. The lives of first-generation Chinese revolve almost totally around their business, demanding hard work and long hours if it is to succeed. This can be difficult to reconcile with the needs of their children (Watson 1993).

Without any means of alternative employment outside catering, parents struggle on with running a business and looking after their family. In this context, some children are seen to be neglected or bearing excessive caring responsibilities for their younger siblings, although this is not unique to the Chinese community. Contacts between families and health/social workers have often been frustrating and, at times, ineffectual. Some staff admitted to Chinese workers feelings of inadequacy in providing their social services to Chinese clients, compounded by a general lack of race awareness training and resources for ethnic minority residents, and by the language barrier. One study (Baiden 1994) found that none of the 20 midwifery students interviewed 'knew anything about the Race Relations Act and its relevance to Northern Ireland'. A Chinese woman said of her health visitor in Baiden's research: 'She comes in and looks at the baby and goes away very quickly. We cannot communicate. I cannot tell her if I am worried about the baby or ask her about anything.'

In another revealing case study (known to the CWA) in 1995, a Chinese couple had their parental rights removed when their 14-year-old son was made a 'ward of court', simply to facilitate a police interview with the youth following the parents' refusal to have him questioned by the police. The parents believed that they had told Social Services and the police everything in connection with an incident of 'physical punishment' for their child's misdemeanour. The necessity for the police involvement was not fully understood by the parents and the social workers were not aware of some immigrants' fears of authority and law-enforcing officers. Misunderstandings are not limited to health and social care issues; with increasing numbers of UK-born children of Chinese ethnic origin and an increasing elderly population, another phase in the settlement of the Chinese in Northern Ireland has occurred and this manifests itself in the housing needs of the community.

Housing Needs

Housing concerns identified by the House of Commons' Home Affairs Committee (HAC) *Report on the Chinese Community in Britain* (HAC 1985) were considered in a survey conducted by the Northern Ireland Housing Executive (NIHE) which published its findings in October 1995 (NIHE 1995). The research revealed that over 50 per cent of the 40 households interviewed are owner-occupiers – a similar percentage to that indicated by Barnardos research (Barnardos 1995). Irwin's survey (1996) on a much larger scale, pointed to some 65 per cent of the Chinese community owning their own homes in comparison to 62 per cent of the general population (NI 1991 Census). Irwin's findings showed that only one in ten Chinese households live in public housing, some 20 per cent reside in privately rented housing and a small percentage reside in tied accommodation (see below). Private sector rented housing is often in a state of disrepair and it is usually difficult for Chinese tenants who do not speak much English to ask for repairs or upgrading of their living conditions. As the main purpose of immigration for many Chinese people in Northern Ireland is the search for economic betterment, an ultimate ambition is to own a family business and home. It is common practice for many Chinese restaurant employers to provide 'tied accommodation' (with employment) for new workers arriving in the Province. The worker shares living accommodation with other staff and their families. This is often a terraced house situated near the restaurant they work in. While it is obviously convenient for a newcomer to be given accommodation, such arrangements can increase the vulnerability of the worker and his or her dependence on the employer. Also, families who are unrelated are often put together under the same roof, causing emotional strain on the occupants because of the lack of privacy due to sharing limited space.

The relatively small number of Chinese people renting from local or public authority housing is partly due to the NIHE seven-year residency criterion. This requires applicants to have lived in the Province for at least seven years before they are eligible for public housing (unless they qualify under Special Circumstances Priority Grouping, where emergency housing is provided for homeless people and priority is also given to applicants with special social and health needs, supported by a social worker's or medical report). Immigrants of less than seven years' residency who are in employment and are willing to pay full rent to the NIHE can also obtain public housing. However, unemployed Chinese immigrants are thus prohibited from the benefits of public housing, even though they might have strong housing needs.

Apart from the finding from the NIHE survey that 'overall experience of information or advice services about housing issues provided by the Executive was low' (NIHE 1995) owing to communication problems, the research has uncovered serious concerns regarding racial harassment. The survey revealed that almost a third of the members of the Chinese Community interviewed (thirteen people) had experienced some form of racial harassment, and eight of these were NIHE tenants. Harassment involved physical assaults, attacks on property, verbal racial abuse and racist graffiti. Serious vandalising of homes also occurred in 1995–96, during a series of racial attacks around the Donegall Pass, an inner-city area of Belfast. Some of the Chinese residents were intimidated out of their homes and transferred to other areas. The local police, CWA and the local residents' associations have been meeting in attempts to avoid further incidents.

Caring for and respecting elders has been a Chinese cultural norm and it is often seen as the filial duty of families to live with and care for their elderly parents. With some of the first generation Chinese residents in or reaching old age as well as elderly parents joining settled families in the UK, families face the dilemma of maintaining a cultural norm that is impractical in the West. For three generations to live together in an average family size house or, worse still, in limited space above their take-away food business premises, causes obvious overcrowding problems. Furthermore, many elderly people are often left at home in isolation for much of the day and night when family members are out at work. Few have access to elderly day care centres due to the language barrier. Fewer still are in local authority sheltered housing. In England, it has been shown that even if they were in such housing, their needs are not being met in a culturally appropriate manner (Birmingham City Council Housing Department 1993). There are, however, several Chinese elderly sheltered housing schemes in England and Scotland (Tung Sing Housing Association 1996), with Chinese wardens, enabling independent living and enhancing the dignity of the Chinese elderly.

A recent visit by a CWA Chinese worker was made to one such scheme, in Connaught Gardens, Birmingham (Trident Housing Association 1995) where there is a sizeable Chinese population and where the scheme has a five-year waiting list. On the day of the visit, dozens of elderly Chinese residents were sitting in the common room, chatting or playing Chinese card games. Those approached said they much preferred their self-reliance to sharing accommodation with their children and grandchildren. One woman was very open in telling the worker that she used to quarrel with her daughter-in-law and son frequently, when they lived together, but now enjoys a much better relationship when they come to visit her once a week, bearing gifts of fruit or dim sum.

The Chinese Welfare Association has helped several of its Chinese clients to apply successfully for sheltered housing in Glasgow and Edinburgh. These elderly residents had to leave their families in Northern Ireland to make use of available schemes outside of the Province. In view of this demand, the CWA commissioned a survey to identify the Chinese community's elderly housing needs in August 1997 (CWA 1997a). Belfast Improved Housing Association plans to build a 35-unit sheltered housing property in South Belfast for Chinese elderly in 1998, if the survey indicates sufficient demand for such accommodation. In conjunction with the postal survey, the CWA also held three public meetings in different parts of Northern Ireland, to consult the community regarding the sheltered housing proposal. The response was overwhelmingly positive. It is hoped that such a scheme will also localise the Chinese elderly to enable social services to provide some facilities for this group, at present largely unknown to the local health and social services trusts. In the summer of 1997, an English-language class for Chinese elderly people was set up by the CWA to help this integration process. This is, however, a relatively small area within a wide range of educational and language needs within the Chinese community in Northern Ireland. Meeting these needs is crucial to its development and eventual diversification to other areas of employment.

Education

According to the Runnymede Trust Report, *The Chinese Community in Britain* (1986:6), difficulty with the English language was found to be at the root of many problems experienced by the Chinese in Britain. This applies both to adults (65–75 per cent of first-generation immigrants were estimated to be unable to speak English) and to children, many of whom arrive in the UK in their teens with little English and have difficulty acquiring it. The report goes on to say that examples were found 'of pupils arriving in their teens and receiving only 2 half days of language teaching a week or leaving school after 6 years ... with English not advanced enough to seek employment'. A similar situation exists in Northern Ireland, where many Chinese children continue to under-achieve at school and where this is not always being detected. Inequity of treatment in the school system (for example, racial bullying and withdrawal from chosen subjects) is sometimes exacerbated by parental pressure (or indeed a feeling of moral responsibility on the part of the Chinese youth in line with traditional expectations) to work in the family restaurant. This commitment to the family business can take considerable study-time away from young Chinese people, although many manage to balance their commitments and even fit in time for private home-tuition in English language in the evenings.

Poor English has been identified as one of the major factors for academic low achievement. With increasing numbers of Chinese children registering at schools in Northern Ireland, it is hoped that English as a Second Language (ESL) provision will become increasingly resourced in order to meet the special needs of this community. Indeed, in 1994 the Belfast Education and Library Board revealed that they had 156 Chinese children registered at primary level and 186 at secondary level. For some of the schools in question, these children pose a problem because their teachers may not be equipped with the skills necessary to deal with a child for whom English is a second language. It is difficult even to assess the child appropriately. Many Chinese children, even though born in Northern Ireland, do not hear much English until they start school. The language development of such children from non-English-speaking homes is complex. By the age of three or four, such children will almost certainly have developed an extensive vocabulary in one, if not two, Chinese dialects. Yet these skills cannot be tested, as the child cannot be assessed on a language other than English, and if the latter is poorly developed then placement in an educationally sub-normal or remedial class may be suggested. According to one young secondary-school-age Chinese child: 'Sometimes English people use words and we don't understand what they are saying. I think that's because half the time we have to speak Chinese at home and when we go to school we have to speak English' (quoted in CWA/CCETSW 1987).

Yet language difficulties are not to be confused with 'special' educational needs and 'special educational provision', as stated in the 1981 Education Act (DES 1983a), would not be proposed simply because the present school or individual teachers are not respecting and providing for individual cultural or language needs. DES Circular 1/83 states: 'Under the Act, a child should not be taken to have a learning difficulty because the language or form of language of his home is different from the language of instruction of his school. The problems experienced by such children are essentially linguistic; they should not be equated with learning difficulties in the terms of the Act' (DES 1983b). With the introduction of race relations legislation to Northern Ireland in 1997, current tests will be interpreted as being indirectly discriminatory if they continue to be culturally biased and result in lower assessments being given to a considerably higher proportion of pupils from a particular ethnic group. Of course some advancements do have to be acknowledged. Both the Belfast Education and Library Board and the South Eastern Education and Library Board have been developing their own ESL units and policy guidelines in response to increased demands from schools in their areas. Within the South Eastern Board, the number of pupils of primary-school age requiring English-language support more than doubled between March 1993 and March 1995, from 41 to 97 (Board policy guideline on support for ESL pupils). Future plans, too, include employing a bilingual language assistant to support Chinese pupils and their families in the area.

The introduction of the Race Relations (NI) Order in 1997 should help to eliminate bad practice in relation to children from ethnic minority backgrounds. The Order will also strengthen considerably the new Children (NI) Order 1995 which, for the first time, forces childcare agencies in Northern Ireland to give 'due consideration' to 'religious persuasion, racial origin and cultural and linguistic background'. However, the Order is weaker than its counterpart in Britain, the 1976 Race Relations Act, which also makes it unlawful for a local education authority to discriminate in carrying out functions such as school meals provision, ESL provision, the Youth Service, educational welfare, liaison and psychological services. The Department of Education (Northern Ireland) issued *Policy and Guidelines for the Education of Children from Traveller Families* (DENI 1993) which contained a number of guidelines for ensuring equality of opportunity for Traveller children, but there is no equivalent circular in respect of Northern Ireland's other minority ethnic communities. This should be developed as a matter of urgency.

The needs of Chinese parents should also be addressed alongside the needs of their children. In a small-scale study, Fong (1981) discovered that the parents in 28 out of 31 families in Liverpool claimed to speak Chinese with their adolescent children, and only 3 parents spoke both Cantonese and English, with none speaking English alone (Taylor 1987:143). Further Education colleges run English as a Foreign Language (EFL) classes during 'conventional' school hours and often first thing in the morning. This shows little recognition of the fact that over 90 per cent of the Chinese community are still involved in the restaurant trade and so cannot attend classes at these times. Another important factor why current provision is not taken up is that often those most in need have the least experience of schooling. Many first-generation Chinese were able to gain only a few years of primary education in Hong Kong. It is therefore very difficult in a new country to approach a formal institutional building and even more difficult once there to be presented with traditional, grammar-based English-language teaching.

The CWA (NI) attempts to meet such specific needs in Northern Ireland by running flexible classes in terms of time, numbers and subject material – with English-language classes covering subjects such as

English for driving, dress-making, health and maternity care, as well as catering for students who wish to take EFL examination classes. Increased knowledge of even basic English language builds confidence and self-esteem, lessens feelings of isolation and encourages integration with the wider community. At present, students include a Vietnamese woman who escaped by boat from her home at the age of 13. She landed in Russia and travelled overland to Germany, where she was settled, learning German as a second language, until a family reunification scheme run by a national organisation (Refugee Action) brought her to Northern Ireland where she now hopes to reside. Another woman from Hong Kong came to Northern Ireland in her twenties to join her husband. She now works seven days a week in a Chinese food take-away business but gives up a precious two hours in the afternoon twice a week between lunchtime and evening shifts. A third is an overseas student at Queen's University who wished to make faster progress with her listening and speaking skills in order to sit a Cambridge English-Language Proficiency test. This student was interviewed in English at her assessment and said: 'I think because I'm afraid to talk – I often avoid to speak English. I just try to get along with Chinese people.' Education and library boards in Northern Ireland will hopefully give consideration to improvements in ESL provision and also provide financial assistance to Chinese organisations involved in ESL teaching, as recommended by the 1994 Home Affairs Committee report (1994b) and in line with current resourcing in Britain.

A further recommendation made in the above report, in addition to improved ESL teaching for Chinese adults and children, was that a multicultural curriculum be introduced in every school, so that children can learn from and share each other's culture. In Northern Ireland, this is particularly important in relation to other ethnic minority communities who are also religious minority groups such as the Jewish, Hindu, Baha'i and Muslim communities. In 1985, the Swann Report (House of Commons 1985) unequivocally endorsed a religious education curriculum that followed a pluralist, multi-faith approach. The Committee was concerned that the absence of such a multi-faith perspective would negate any notion of intercultural 'Education for All'. Northern Ireland has its own Education for Mutual Understanding programmes which focus on issues such as 'self and others', 'under-standing conflict', 'interdependence' and 'cultural understanding', but bases these predominantly around the two dominant Catholic and Protestant communities in Northern Ireland.

Additional recommendations made by the Home Affairs Committee include more intensive language facilities for young Chinese entering school; peripatetic language assistants, efficient in both Chinese language and culture, employed to liaise between parents, pupils and the school; more financial resources put into ESL courses; education

and library boards to consult the Chinese community regularly about
its needs; multicultural awareness and anti-racism training as a
compulsory part of all teacher training courses, so that teachers acquire
more confidence and expertise to deal with sensitive issues such as racial
bullying as well as specific language needs; recognition by the boards
and other agencies of the need to finance and maintain mother-tongue
classes for Chinese children. This last point is crucial in the Chinese
community. The local Chinese Language School, run by the Chinese
Chamber of Commerce (NI), has almost 200 students aged between
5 and 16. The school is not only a place to learn to read and write, it
is a place that enables the children to retain their *Chineseness* and to
communicate with their extended family and community network. It
is also worth noting that research has clearly shown that the more firmly
a community language is established, the more successfully other
languages are learnt. Maintaining the Cantonese dialect, for example,
will not act as a barrier to the learning of English as a second language
but rather should be encouraged.

Internal research carried out by the Chinese Welfare Association (NI)
already shows that over half the Chinese population is now British-
born. We are also beginning to see trends which indicate that local
Chinese school leavers are moving to other parts of the UK or even
returning to Hong Kong to look for jobs. Very few teenagers would
wish to follow their parents into the restaurant business, having seen
enough of the hard work and long hours their parents put in. Yet, as
Taylor points out, 'high(er) aspirations may be difficult to realise
because the opportunities for further and higher education and jobs
are very much linked to proficiency in English' (Taylor 1987:278).
Patrick Yu, co-ordinator of the Northern Ireland Council for Ethnic
Minorities, has also pointed out that young Chinese people 'are still
not being accepted by their local peer group because of their colour':

> This is a group which feels even more alienated and confused in this
> society, because they have not only lost most of their original Chinese
> culture, but the Western culture which they have adopted in its place
> is not being easily accepted by their parents. This identity confusion
> can become the core of family disputes if the importance of com-
> munication and understanding is not appreciated. Moreover, with
> regard to education and open employment, our young people are
> also facing a certain degree of discrimination. (Yu 1994)

In a BBC radio interview, which was part of a week against racism in
December 1996, two Chinese teenagers commented: 'Here we stick
out (not like in Hong Kong) and so we are a target all the time'; and
'It's because some people in our class think more of themselves than
we do, and sort of, they're English and we're Chinese'(BBC Radio

1996). The common perception of identifying oneself almost as a 'second-class citizen' is inferred in both these statements.

In 1987, a Chinese Youth Club was launched by the CWA (NI) to begin to meet the needs of young Chinese people in Northern Ireland, as they had remained ignored and uncatered for within Youth Service provision. The Club allows Chinese teenagers to socialise with each other in a group where they can feel 'at home' and enjoy being Chinese. Culturally sensitive and bilingual staff provide a safe environment where the young people can explore their feelings about personal experiences of racism, identity confusion and the generation conflict. Many share an isolated childhood due to lack of knowledge or confidence in English, physical separation from parents, lack of opportunity and time to meet with their Chinese peer group. Most also share the fact that they may be the only Chinese person in their school and so have to work that much harder to be accepted as one of the crowd. Not even Chinese children born and brought up in Northern Ireland escape the labelling so quickly attached to everyone living there. Implicitly racist questions, such as 'Where do you *really* come from?' and 'Are you Catholic Chinese or Protestant Chinese?', are initially treated with good humour but, when repeated with such regular monotony, the same questions become frustrating and hurtful.

Immigration

While second and even third generations of Chinese have been born in Northern Ireland and call it their home, the community still faces major difficulties in relation to immigration and nationality. Northern Ireland had a similar immigration pattern to other parts of the UK, where young Chinese men come to the UK to work temporarily but harbour a dream of one day returning to their home villages in Hong Kong. With the arrival of wives and children, though, the original desire to return has long been lost. In addition, the uncertainty of Hong Kong's future under Chinese sovereignty after July 1997 has also influenced many other Chinese to apply for permanent residence to stay on in the UK and, ultimately, to register as British citizens. However, for Chinese immigrants, lack of knowledge in relation to immigration and nationality matters is still a serious problem. The Home Affairs Committee report (HAC 1994a) contended that the 'Home Office had a duty to publicise the law and regulations much more effectively, particularly among minorities like the Chinese with relatively few English speakers'.

There is considerable misunderstanding about entry clearance (permission for a foreign national to enter the UK), renewing visas and subsequent changes in immigration status. Entering for the purposes of employment is by far the most common reason for Hong Kong Chinese to move to Northern Ireland; followed by requests for study visas (mostly for tertiary education, but Chinese children also board at both primary and secondary school levels) and as spouses of British citizens. Usually when a Chinese person comes over to Northern Ireland to work in a restaurant, a work permit is needed to allow entry and residence. Under the present law, a person has to work for four full years of approved employment before securing exemption from the restrictions on employment and conditions of stay. These restrictions include the need to seek permission from the Training and Employment Agency in Northern Ireland and, also, from the Home Office if the work permit holder wishes or needs to change jobs for any reason. As already suggested, it is not unusual for a Chinese family to work very hard and save up sufficient money to establish their own take-away food business. Moving from employee to self-employment status, however, requires the above permission. The consequences of failing to follow the strict immigration procedures can be devastating for a work permit holder and family. It may mean that at the end of the four year period, instead of being permitted leave to stay on a permanent basis, the visas may not renewed and the whole family may be forced to return to Hong Kong.

Clarification is also sought about the rights of a child born in Northern Ireland to Chinese parents. Before 1983, a child born in the UK was automatically entitled to British citizenship and a full British passport. However, from 1983 onwards, this child only gains automatic right to citizenship if one of the parents is either settled or already has citizenship status – yet many people in the Chinese community still remain unaware of this fact. Further confusion arises out of the relationship between immigration status and welfare benefits. A visa stamp, whether to a student, fiancée or dependants, will most likely include the phrase 'should have no recourse to public funds'. 'Public funds' here should be interpreted as housing (under Part II of the Housing (NI) Order 1988) and income support, family credit, council tax benefit and housing benefit (under Part VII of the Social Security Contributions and Benefits (NI) Act 1992). This quandary about the actual rules and lack of access to information is paralleled by a general fear that accompanies any immigrant community with short-term rights of residence. Families may put themselves under severe financial pressure or live in a situation of continual racial harassment because they are afraid that any application for benefits or housing, or indeed a complaint of any kind (perhaps to their employer in relation to conditions at work), may adversely affect their visa requirements and thus their right to permanent residence. This fear can add considerably to the emotional pressure, vulnerability and insecurity faced by such families.

In addition, much of the information about immigration and nationality tends to get passed around the community by word of mouth. Since each case may vary slightly there is a high risk that information applicable to one person's situation may not be applicable to someone else. This informal information network arises not only out of the above-mentioned fear and the insularity of such a small community, but also because of the lack of professional immigration advice agencies operating in Northern Ireland. Since 1986, the CWA (NI) has worked closely with the Law Centre (NI) to offer a comprehensive package of immigration and nationality advice to Chinese people. Neither the Joint Council for the Welfare of Immigrants (JCWI) nor the Immigration Advisory Service (IAS) have ever been based in Northern Ireland and individual solicitors' knowledge and expertise, through lack of experience, is often limited in this field. An attempt to improve the situation generally and give people the right to accurate information and increased choice led to the setting up of an Immigration Advisers' support group in Belfast which meets monthly to share information and work towards changes in policy throughout the criminal justice system. This group has invited participation from representatives of the Royal Ulster Constabulary (RUC)'s 'Aliens' Registration Office (an archaic and discriminatory name that is constantly challenged but remains unchanged), the department most likely to send officers to accompany immigration staff on raids and follow-up interviews, and also from the Belfast Immigration Office, in order to access information about developments in legislation and current practice.

In the last two years, neither the CWA (NI) nor the Law Centre (NI) have seen a significant increase in the numbers of applications for entry clearance from Hong Kong to Northern Ireland. This leads us to believe that the tight UK immigration controls, alongside people's own preferences (in the years 1990–94 almost three times as many people emigrated from Hong Kong to Canada and New Zealand, and more than ten times as many emigrated to the US and Australia, as chose to make the UK their new home) have effectively prevented any significant increase in numbers coming to this country. Due to some people's fears about the situation in Hong Kong after 1997, however, there has been a slight increase in applications to bring elderly parents to join their Chinese children now resident in Northern Ireland, many of whom have obtained full British citizenship. The immigration rules operate on the principle that entry clearance is refused if the elderly person has other relatives outside the UK, or is not wholly or mainly dependent upon relatives in the UK. This has effectively broken down the extended family network and in turn has serious implications for traditional childcare provision and support for young families. The Runnymede Trust Research Report (1986:12) pointed out that Chinese 'culture and practice is for parents to live with sons rather than daughters and that grandparents traditionally look after the grandchildren and are turned to for advice and instruction'. The report therefore recommended that the rules on the entry of elderly parents are applied flexibly and with due regard for the culture of those affected. This was supported by the Commission for Racial Equality (1986) in its report *Immigration Control Procedures*. Among second generation Chinese, while arranged marriages are not as common in the Chinese community as in some other cultures, such as in the Indian subcontinent, it would still be considered quite acceptable to be introduced to someone during a visit to Hong Kong. If the relationship progressed, there may be a stage when the couple choose to marry. This is where complications set in since, if a British citizen or person settled in the UK marries someone from Hong Kong or other parts of China, then it must be proved that the 'primary purpose' of the marriage was not to enter or stay in the UK. The onus of proof is on the foreign national to prove his or her intentions in entering into the marriage. The harshest decisions are often taken abroad, when the UK-based spouse is living in the UK and the partner is abroad. According to one Northern Irish immigration law practitioner: 'The couple may remain apart during a lengthy appeal process following an adverse decision and the success rate at appeal is frustratingly slow' (Grimes 1996).

The CWA has also seen a recent increase in applications for political asylum from people fleeing from the People's Republic of China (albeit very small; approximately three or four per year). Sometimes, applicants are apprehended and detained pending a decision from the Home Office. At the time of writing, there are currently eight Chinese detainees being held locally in prison. The future is uncertain for anyone found in breach of immigration rules in Northern Ireland. It can mean six to eight months' detention in prison (there are currently no detention centres available for those who have not been charged with any criminal offence), unable to speak to staff or other prisoners, subjected to verbal abuse and harassment and convinced they live in constant fear of being sent back to China, where allegedly they may face torture or even death. Due to the closure of a Belfast prison in 1996, all detainees in breach of immigration rules are now held in Magilligan prison, some 60 miles from Belfast. This has led to the increased isolation of these prisoners and even more infrequent visiting from members of the community, pastoral carers and legal representatives.

The UK Asylum and Immigration Act 1996 includes increased powers and penalties in relation to immigration offences (including the power to search premises) and also creates a new criminal offence, that of knowingly employing someone who is not entitled to work in the UK. It is not difficult to imagine situations where the police and/or immigration officers may be encouraged to 'trawl' areas for likely 'suspects'. Concerns have been raised, therefore, that every Chinese food business will now be treated suspiciously on account of the nature of the workforce rather than for any reasonable doubt. In relation to the issue of checking employment credentials, it is also believed likely by civil liberty and ethnic minority organisations that employers will err on the side of caution if required to make complicated and time-consuming investigations. Such a provision will undoubtedly encourage discriminatory attitudes towards ethnic minorities in the employment market.

Racial Harassment

Throughout this chapter we have identified a number of areas where we are concerned about the racial discrimination faced by Chinese people in Northern Ireland. Some examples are more overt and involve direct harassment of individuals in the community. Ethnic minority support organisations, like the CWA (NI) and the Northern Ireland Council for Ethnic Minorities (NICEM), have spent considerable time in raising awareness about racism and racial harassment, as well as mobilising the community to come forward to record complaints and acting as an advocate on its behalf. A first step has been to ensure that Chinese people know what racial harassment involves in order to identify what is unacceptable behaviour towards them. Racist harassment can take the following forms, but the list is not definitive: attacks on persons, attacks on property, threats and abuse, and racist graffiti. Incidents of racial harassment are a regular occurrence for many Chinese people living in Northern Ireland. These incidents are not a recent development; some of the first families to arrive in the Province have reported early problems and feelings of vulnerability and isolation on account of the small numbers in the Chinese community then. Yet, 30 years on, a culturally racist attitude prevails in Northern Ireland that maintains 'there is no racism here'. There is an acceptance that racism is something which happens in other parts of the United Kingdom but not in Northern Ireland. Moreover, feelings of vulnerability and isolation were accompanied by the knowledge that, there was no grassroots organisation – until the Chinese Chamber of Commerce opened its doors in 1983 – to offer help and support. The wider picture was also depressing. There was a lack of any significant legislative framework to deal with racism and racial harassment, accompanied by political turmoil in the 1970s, and the focus was clearly upon discrimination and harassment of another kind.

Racial discrimination towards Chinese people in the institutions and structures of our society has been discussed in the areas of health and social services, education, housing and immigration. Inequity of treatment through the denial of opportunities and access to services, inadequate resourcing, lack of training, lack of monitoring and lack of accountability have been commonplace for Chinese and other ethnic minority groups in Northern Ireland. The introduction of the Race Relations (NI) Order may help redress such practices from state institutions. Policy and practice will also continue to be challenged by the CWA and other ethnic minority support organisations and, as partnerships develop and consultation increases, the Chinese community is slowly beginning to target the goal of improved equality of opportunity and equity of treatment.

Unfortunately, little change has been recorded in the area of individual racism where incidents of verbal abuse, bullying and vandalism continue to be an everyday experience. During a summer-scheme outing in 1996, a young Chinese toddler who was facing taunts in the playground responded by saying to his mother: 'I don't want to be Chinese any more, I just want to be normal.' In January 1997, an elderly Chinese person living in a local housing estate asked relatives to put bars on the downstairs windows to help counteract fears caused by constant intimidation. These two anecdotal examples illustrate how racial harassment can be experienced at any age. Moreover, when a Chinese person is faced with all the different forms of racism together, the result can be total social exclusion from the wider society in Northern Ireland. A sense of helplessness and insecurity is apparent in responses such as: 'this is someone else's country' or 'we don't want to rock the boat'. But also, there is anger and frustration that such behaviour must be tolerated on a daily basis because, even when a complaint is made, 'nothing ever changes'.

In an attempt to formulate more accurate statistical information on discrimination and harassment (while continuing to record extensive anecdotal evidence), the CWA attempted in 1990 to introduce a recording and monitoring system for Chinese people to register complaints in complete confidence. Initially, figures remained low and the general reluctance to come forward was seen to be due to a number of factors: the language barrier (almost no interpreting facilities), the cultural barrier (not wishing to be seen to challenge authority), fear of reprisals (including stronger immigration checks), no formal legislative protection (the race relations legislation did not apply prior to August 1997) and the absence of prosecutions to date under Public Order or anti-incitement legislation (see Chapter 4) (causing lack of confidence in present mechanisms of protection).

The above barriers also have to be taken into account when looking at figures now produced by the Royal Ulster Constabulary (RUC) at the end of each year. In January 1995, a formal ethnic monitoring scheme was introduced by the RUC into Northern Ireland and was welcomed as a positive step by all of the ethnic minority communities. It will be some time, though, before RUC figures can be accepted as an accurate portrayal of the situation. Fears of and suspicion about the police will often prevent individuals approaching their local police station, choosing in preference to approach their own community association. In addition, the CWA has already put forward a number of suggestions to the RUC to alleviate the language difficulties that will inevitably exacerbate such under-reporting. In the House of Commons' Home Affairs Committee Report (1994a), *Racial Attacks and Harassment*, it was recommended that Chief Constables 'should be encouraged to provide an interpreter service to enable their officers to communicate with victims of racial incidents. [We] therefore recommend that the Home Office should provide ring-fenced resources to these forces to enable them to operate Language Line [a 24-hour telephone interpreting service available to public agencies] or other facilities.' This is of paramount importance if the RUC is to demonstrate a genuine commitment to ethnic monitoring in the future and facilitate access to their services for all members of the public, including those for whom English is a second language.

Apart from the RUC's monitoring scheme, the CWA has received complaints of racial harassment and/or discrimination in the following areas:

- *Business*: small Chinese take-away food shops in the main, but restaurants also, face incidents of verbal racial and sexual abuse, vandalism, customers not paying, bogus delivery orders, demands for protection money (often paid simultaneously to racketeers from both sides of the religious divide), and so on.
- *Homes*: attacks of aggravated burglary with assault on victims; threats of torture and acts of humiliation; daily taunts from local children; and vandalism such as rubbish thrown into gardens, windows smashed and racist graffiti.
- *Education*: racial bullying in the playground and discriminatory treatment by teachers/lecturers (such as ignoring the student, making 'an example' of him or her and unnecessary criticism of students' use of English).
- *Goods/services*: verbal harassment in shops, leisure centres, and so on; and refusal to serve.
- *Health*: lack of equity of treatment from staff; refusal to comply with cultural/religious beliefs and practices, and poor interpreting and translation facilities.
- *Police*: direct harassment of Chinese people by police; slow response to reported burglaries and robberies; failure to record and monitor reports of harassment of Chinese people; inadequate interpreting provision, and treating victims and attackers equally.

- *Immigration*: exploitation by unqualified 'immigration advisers'; random unprovoked house-checks with unreasonable use of force; and lack of access to information, such as basic legal rights.

With regard to the second category listed above, in June 1996, three months after an increase in attacks of aggravated burglary, a young Chinese man was murdered in Carrickfergus, Country Antrim. These attacks lessened over the summer period but by September were continuing at the rate of one or two per week. Victims were sporadically subjected to vicious beatings accompanied by the use of physical threats (in one incident, children were threatened by having a kettle of boiling water held over them). Victim Support (NI) and the CWA (NI) have been working together to offer support to families facing severe emotional trauma after these attacks and some people from the Chinese community have undergone Victim Support training in order to be able to provide support in the victim's own language. During 1996, the RUC reported 43 offences against ethnic minority families, including armed robbery and aggravated burglary, compared to 55–60 the previous year. In June 1997, one suspect was arrested and is currently awaiting trial. Meanwhile, the attacks continue. Both the police and the CWA (NI) have publicly stated that in their view these attacks are primarily financially motivated, but the CWA (NI) and many members of the Chinese community itself are convinced of a racist element also. The perpetrators of these attacks have not only identified the community as a easily targeted group (with workplace and work patterns easily ascertained) but they have also subjected their victims to prolonged and humiliating racial abuse.

Conclusion

The Chinese, the largest ethnic minority group in Northern Ireland, are now in their fourth decade of residence. During the last decade, in particular, there have been many changes as the community has grown and become more established. While many still retain strong family ties in Hong Kong, Northern Ireland has become 'home' for most of these Chinese people. Within the Province, however, the members of this community hold on very strongly to their own unique cultural identity and are concerned about the assimilative pressures facing their children. As already noted, the growth in Chinese-language classes is partly a result of parents trying to maintain cultural values through the subsequent generations. At the same time, young Chinese people are beginning to challenge the traditional, low-profile, 'keep your head down' approach of the older generation. Support organisations like the CWA are now in place to meet changing needs, advocate on the community's behalf and develop closer links with the wider society.

The Chinese community has been largely ignored in Northern Ireland and, when thought of at all, it is only in terms of restaurants and take-aways. Yet, the situation is slowly changing as other aspects of Chinese culture are introduced; for example, Chinese medical centres using holistic approaches to health and Tai Chi Chuan – a slow-motion martial arts health exercise. As the community's confidence grows and more cross-community opportunities develop, it is worth highlighting the comments of Mr Shek Yung Lee, Chairman of the Chinese Chamber of Commerce (NI) and the Chinese Welfare Association (NI), delivered at a past inauguration of the Chamber:

> In the past, owing to the limitations of human and material resources, we only placed emphasis on the provision of services to Chinese people. We did not participate much in local community activities and charitable events. From now on, we shall proceed in this direction, in accordance with the Chinese saying 'What you take from the community, you shall plough back into the community'. (Lee 1993)

The future then will need to be charted along a parallel path – stronger participation by Chinese people in order to break the stereotype of 'the silent minority' and, at the same time, effective race relations legislation in line with an educational process which must ensure equality of opportunity and equity of treatment for ethnic minority communities in Northern Ireland. Another quote from the BBC Northern Ireland Racism Awareness Week radio interviews (1996) provides a suitable concluding comment: 'The Chinese community should be respected as a body, like Protestants and Catholics are, but not to use this to criticise, just to accept it as part of the mixture of Northern Ireland – every part has something to give and to contribute.'

8 Pathologisation and Resistance: Travellers, Nomadism and the State

Paul Noonan

Travelling People represent the second largest ethnic minority in Northern Ireland, yet only 0.07 per cent of the total population (Paris *et al.* 1995a:24). As an indigenous minority ethnic community they are culturally distinguished in a variety of ways from the majority community, but most significantly in relation to their commitment to nomadism, the central element of their cultural identity. This difference has been the focus of a virulent antipathy and rejection (permeating virtually every sector of society). McVeigh (1992a:2) has characterised the key structuring factor of this rejection as sedentarism, a specific form of racism (in its application to ethnic nomads) which can be defined as: 'a system of ideas and practices which serves to normalise and reproduce sedentary modes of existence and pathologises and represses nomadic modes of existence'. The dominance of sedentarism has had negative impact on Travellers and non-Travellers alike. For Travellers, it has meant widespread social, economic, cultural and political exclusion. A growing number of reports from various statutory and voluntary agencies (see below) has exposed the salient features of this exclusion. These include poor health performance, low educational achievement and an unemployment rate of 76 per cent (Advisory Committee on Travellers (ACT) (NI) 1992:7, 8). In addition, reports by human rights agencies have drawn attention to the existence of both individual and institutional racism against Travellers.

That Travellers continue to survive as a distinct community despite rejection and exclusion is testament to the resilience of their culture and their flexibility and ingenuity in adapting to changing circumstances. For members of the non-Traveller community, continued complicity (conscious or otherwise) in the oppression of the Traveller community is a consequence of the continuing hegemony of sedentarism. The continual resistance of Travellers to the various unsuccessful attempts to force them to assimilate has meant, too, a significant waste of resources. McVeigh (1992a:6) has also noted that the historic process of nomadic-sedentary transition was 'associated with a profound sense of loss and unease ... There is a whole historical subtext to the transition which is characterised by a sense of loss and envy amongst the sedentarised.' Moreover, the denial and exclusion of nomadism and Traveller culture, as a significant influence on Irish culture, leads to a distorted view of Ireland itself. In addition, there is an inevitable impediment to communication and social relations caused by the perpetuation of racialised stereotypes of Travellers and by the profound alienation of the Traveller community as a consequence of this negative dialectic.

Traveller Identity and the Origins Issue

The question of the origins of the Traveller community, as Ní Shúinéar (1994:73) and McVeigh (1992c:4, 8) point out, is informed by political perspective. In the absence of verifiable historical lineage, Travellers can be pathologised as a group whose origins lie in their failure to survive in the wider society. The implication of this is that the most appropriate solution for the group is their rehabilitation back into mainstream society. Thus the Itinerant Settlement Movement (ISM) (see below) tended to subscribe to the widely held belief that Travellers were descendants of the peasantry dispossessed during the famines of the nineteenth century and that, therefore, the most appropriate policy to pursue was one of assimilation back into the host society (McDonagh and McVeigh 1996:4). In contrast, others concerned with the situation of Travellers tended to use historical and linguistic evidence suggesting a distinct cultural identity of considerable antiquity, to support the case for recognition of Travellers as a minority ethnic community (with the concomitant rights this should entail). Although some nomadic peoples have maintained both a written and an oral history, this is not the case with the Traveller community whose culture is very much present-time oriented. Such evidence as does exist has been located in the margins of the historical record and derived from the study of the Travellers' secret language, Gammon or Cant (McAlister 1937; McCann et al. 1994). It is clear, though, that Travellers today are a distinct group within Irish society (O'Connell 1994b:110–20). Gmelch and Gmelch (1976:16) concluded that the membership of the group was most likely established over centuries rather than during any specific period and by a diversity of causes which led families to take to the road. Okely (1983:5) defines Travellers, using the terms 'Gypsies' and 'Travellers' interchangeably, as 'a self-reproducing ethnic group with an ideology of travelling ... a preference for self-employment and a wide range of economic activities'. Up until about 40–50 years ago these activities were practised within the context of the rural economy, such as tinsmithing, horse dealing, selling domestic wares, chimney cleaning and seasonal agricultural labour. As Okely (1983:28) noted, the Traveller economy can only survive in the context of the wider economy 'within which they circulate, supplying occasional goods and services and exploiting geographical mobility and a multiplicity of occupations'.

By 1930, the travelling circuit of most families was usually limited to two or three counties or less, camping on the roadside for a period seldom longer than two weeks at a time. Typically, the average group of Travellers on the road comprised two to four families, generally close relatives such as parents, married sons, their wives and children. However, entire extended families would meet on occasions such as funerals, weddings or fairs. Family life still retains its importance as a key element of Traveller culture: 'Ties of kinship are strong and among the factors accounting for this are the traditional pattern of arranged marriages and the Travellers' isolation from the settled community' (McDonagh et al. 1988:24). In the years following the Second World War, wider social and economic forces led to a dramatic change in Travellers' way of life. The mass production of plastics, increasing mechanisation of agriculture, rural depopulation and the increasing mobility of the remaining rural community meant that the demand for the craft skills and services provided by Travellers entered into rapid decline. This was not a peculiarly Irish phenomenon. Throughout most Western European countries, the economic symbiosis between Travellers, Gypsies and rural populations was destroyed between 1945 and 1960, leading to widespread urbanisation of their lifestyles (Liégeois 1987:65–6). In their new urban environment, Travellers attempted to adapt economic practices to avail of other opportunities for income generation such as tarmacing or dealing in scrap, carpets or caravans. Only a minority was able to achieve economic independence, and social security benefits became the main or only source of income for the majority of Travellers. Similarly, in Northern Ireland, the majority of Travellers now live in towns and cities, with 30–40 per cent living in Belfast (Department of the Environment (DOE) (NI) 1993:11).

Travellers and the State in Northern Ireland

Significantly, the first interest shown by the state of Northern Ireland in what was characterised as the 'problem' of Travellers occurred during the post-war period. To those committed to economic modernisation, the presence of a community committed to a nomadic lifestyle (and a lack of attachment to land as property) and to independence from wage labour (one of the central features of industrialised capitalist economies), Travellers (in both rural and urban settings) symbolised anachronistic and deviant values. Mayall (1995:16) argues that the rejection by Travellers of the ways and patterns of the majority population 'means that they have come under regulatory desires of a state keen to suppress a way of life and existence commonly associated with vagrancy, parasitism and criminality'. Much of the early discourse concerning Travellers in Northern Ireland is framed in these terms.

A Stormont Committee on Gypsies and Like Itinerants reported in 1948 on the 'problems' caused by 'persons who have adopted an itinerant mode of life' (Ministry of Home Affairs 1948). The most 'grievous' problem was identified as that of sanitation: 'it requires little thought or imagination to realise the contact danger of these people as a source for the spreading of vermin and disease wherever they go'. In respect of roads and trespass issues, the main problems identified arose from illegal camping and the lack of supervision of horses. The Committee concluded that: 'No very strong evidence of widespread theft or intimidation was produced', although the Ulster Farmers' Union in evidence to the Committee complained of petty pilfering of food and fuel and alleged intimidation of rural families by 'the "evil eye" or some such psychological device'. Under the general category, the Committee made much of the problem of identifying Travellers responsible for misdeeds and bringing them to 'summary justice': 'one gypsy ... is much like another'. There was a recommendation in the report that 'a system of registration and reporting to the Barracks in the various Police Districts should be introduced and that an attempt should be made to check the caravans as they cross and re-cross the Border'.

The Committee also concurred with the opinion of the Royal Ulster Constabulary (RUC) that powers of summary arrest should be conferred on the police 'to enable accused of the gypsy class to be brought before a Magistrate sitting outside Petty Sessions, as in the case of vagrants'. Recommendations were also made that public health legislation should be strengthened notably to empower local authorities to prohibit camping on specific areas of land. Increases in fines for illegal camping were recommended. The 'education of the young of these nomads' was considered to be the problem 'probably the least susceptible to solution. The "running wild" of these children appears to be inherent in the nomadic life and until the people concerned can be compelled, or induced, to adopt a more civilised way of life, their offspring will be without the benefit of modern education.' Interestingly, the report makes reference to a pamphlet circulated at that time which recommends, as a 'practical solution' for the 'tinker classes', the establishment of a concentration camp for the males in which they would have to work to support their families, who would live outside this camp. Although the Committee did not embrace such an extreme proposal with its connotations of a 'Final Solution', the general tone of the report was undeniably pejorative to nomadism.

The Minister, responding to the report in 1949, announced that he was 'considering if it would be possible to frame legislation which would deal effectively with the gypsy [sic] nuisance' (*Belfast Newsletter*, 4 October 1954). In the course of a statement to the Stormont Commons, he claimed 'the most abundant, overwhelming and completely conclusive evidence that in very many instances gypsies [sic] had been far more than a nuisance. They had been a menace in some parts [and he] was fully satisfied that legislation would have to be introduced in order to give the authorities greater power of control over them and their movements.' In 1950, the Gypsies Bill (Northern Ireland) was introduced in the Stormont Senate. It sought to impose stringent fines and imprisonment to prevent camping without the consent of the owner of the land. The Bill effectively sought to criminalise the Travellers' nomadic way of life, while at the same time suggesting that local authorities provide camping sites, without coercing them to do so. The Gypsies Bill (NI) was passed by the Senate but was unexpectedly withdrawn in October 1950 during the second reading in the Commons because of strong opposition by local councils to the inclusion of a slight defence against prosecution for encampment if the local council failed to designate sufficient sites.

In October 1954, the new Minister for Home Affairs, G.B. Hanna, announced the establishment of a committee to investigate and advise on 'the problem of gypsies and other itinerants'. Although described by the Minister as a 'fairly representative body', there appears to have been no attempt to seek Travellers' views. The committee's report commented on 'attempts made in many countries to solve the problem usually by sentencing gypsies to exile under pain of death' and concluded from this that 'the fact that the gypsy and the itinerant have survived clearly indicate that there is not an easy solution to the problem' (Ministry of Home Affairs 1955). Terence O'Neill, who succeeded G.B. Hanna as Minister, commented during the debate on the report that he was 'very pleasantly surprised ... that the number of gypsies and itinerants has fallen by half from 1,012 to 583' (McVeigh 1992c:6). However, the government's response did not please all of its supporters and a resolution was passed at the annual Ulster Unionist Council meeting in 1956, calling on the government to introduce effective legislation immediately to prohibit 'these wandering bands from spoiling our countryside, damaging property and availing themselves of public assistance, free medical and dental services and children's allowances'. Elements of both sectarianism and sedentarism (nomadism is equated with vagrancy) informed the debate at the Council meeting:

Mr David Somerville (Cookstown) ... described gypsies as Eire's chief export and said that if the Government did not do something he feared the people would take the matter into their own hands. [Travellers] come into this heaven-upon-earth state we have here and to qualify for the family allowance take care to have their children born in the six counties. After only five years' residence they could qualify for assistance. After three months' residence they were also entitled to be registered on the British electors' list. (*Belfast News Letter*, 9 March 1956)

However, the government made the period for qualifying seven years, and ruled that they must reside in premises for that period. Thomas Hughes (Pomeroy) claimed at the Council that 'vagabonds' came over the Border to avail themselves of public assistance: 'If they live near the Border they take money back into the Twenty-six Counties and spend it in the shops there. If they live further inland they spend it on riotous living.' The Council unanimously passed a motion expressing: 'Regret that the Ulster Government had as yet failed to pass legislation to control gypsies, tinkers and vagrants at present roaming at large through the Six Counties of Northern Ireland' (*Irish Press*, 9 March 1956).

Both Nan Joyce and Nan Donaghue, describing their travels in Northern Ireland during this time, refer to harassment by the agents of the state:

Some of the police were very hard on us. They would come up at ten o'clock of a winter's night and it didn't matter if it was snowing or freezing, the Travellers would have to pack up ... We'd have to pack up everything in the middle of the night, and at that time we had no motor van or car, it was a horse and wagon. You couldn't say to the police that you weren't shifting because you'd be kicked around the road, the men would be beaten with batons, they'd even be brought into the barracks and locked up. You got no fair play at all if you were a Traveller. (Joyce 1985:39–40)

'Ah now, we're done,' said I. 'Here's the B-Specials, Mick. We're done for. Here's the gammy feens coming. (The "bad men" I called them because if you done anything, they'd kill you. Great big farmers' sons). Oh, the B-Specials would beat you to death.' (Donaghue, quoted in Gmelch 1986:47)

The subsequent harassment of Travellers in the 1950s and 1960s, combined with problems brought on by the destruction of the Travellers' rurally based economy (and emigration to England by many), led to a dramatic reduction in the number of Travellers living in Northern Ireland from 1,012 in 1948 to only 160 in 1965 (Noonan 1994:173).

A report by the Association of Public Health Inspectors in the mid-1960s complained of the inadequacy of existing legislation 'to deal with offending itinerants satisfactorily ... the only method of control generally adopted is to harry them from place to place' (Assisi Fellowship 1966:17).

The situation of Travellers in Northern Ireland in the mid-1960s drew the attention of the Assisi Fellowship, a loosely knit grouping of churches, voluntary organisations and individuals 'concerned with the social welfare of men and women who, for one reason or another have been unable to live a normal life in the community' (Assisi Fellowship 1966:15). The group's analysis, in a 1966 report, was strongly influenced by the undeniably assimilationist *Report of the Commission on Itinerancy in the Irish Republic* (1963) and stated that its fundamental aim was to assist 'the itinerants to become fully integrated – socially, economically and culturally – with the resident community. To achieve such an aim, it will be necessary to settle the itinerant in proper housing accommodation' (1966:15–16). The report suggested that grant-aid be available to subsidise local authority provision of serviced sites as an interim measure towards assimilating the Travelling people into the social and economic life of the settled community. Once these 'authorised and approved' sites were provided, 'the itinerant family should be compelled to use these sites and should not be permitted to camp on unauthorised sites'.

The assimilationist emphasis of the report, its charitable ethos and paternalistic tone proved to be a key influence on the approach of many of those settled people in both statutory and voluntary sectors who were to come into contact with the Traveller community over the next 25 years. Nevertheless, it was the first Northern Ireland report which emphasised the 'social and human' dimensions of the Travellers' situation. In particular, it drew attention to the lack of access for Travellers to education and welfare services. Despite the effective dismissal of their report by the government, the Assisi Fellowship's Working Party on Itinerants continued to lobby at both Stormont and local government level. The following year, a deputation of the Working Party petitioned Belfast City Council to make site provision for Travellers in the Bog Meadows area but met with an equally bleak response. They were informed that 'no Committee of the City Council has any responsibility for the itinerant members of the community' (Assisi Fellowship 1967, 7 September), and that 'there was no likelihood of Belfast Corporation taking any action to provide a proper camp site for itinerants within the Belfast boundary' (1967, 12 October). Further evidence, if it was needed, of the state's studied lack of interest in the representations of the Assisi Fellowship is apparent in the failure to extend the Caravan Sites Act 1968 to Northern Ireland. This 1968 Act was an update of the Caravan Act 1960, and specifically empowered local authorities to provide accommodation for Gypsies 'residing in or resorting to their area'. The Act also enabled the Minister to direct local authorities to provide such sites (Noonan 1994:18).

In 1969, the Belfast Itinerants Settlement Committee evolved from the Assisi Fellowship group and from a Legion of Mary group working with the Belfast Travellers' children (Noonan 1994:18). The Committee's ideology was that of the Itinerant Settlement Committee movement which sprang up in the Republic of Ireland in the wake of the 1963 Commission on Itinerancy Report (Gmelch and Gmelch 1974). The Commission had concluded that there was no alternative 'to a positive drive for housing itinerants, if a permanent solution to the problem of Itinerancy, based on absorption and integration, is to be achieved' (Commission on Itinerancy 1963:62). Comprised entirely of settled people, the Belfast Itinerants Settlement (19 June 1969) Committee aimed to co-operate with statutory and voluntary organisations to 'work in the long term to achieve properly serviced sites'. The logo of the Itinerant Settlement Movement was a winding road leading to a house, in itself a revealing insight into their key objective.

Itinerant Settlement Committees also subsequently developed in Derry, Dungannon, Coalisland, Newry and Omagh during this period. In 1970, the Committees formed a federation known as the Northern Ireland Council for Itinerant Settlement. In November 1970, a member of the Committee, Stormont Northern Ireland Labour Party MP Vivian Simpson, attempted to move two amendments during the introduction of the Housing Executive Bill. The first (based on the Caravan Sites Act 1968 Section 6) sought to make it a duty of the new Northern Ireland Housing Executive (NIHE) to provide accommodation for Travellers 'by means of caravan sites or otherwise'. The second wanted the NIHE empowered to provide adequate sites for Travellers which had working space and facilities for conducting essential activities (Noonan 1994:18). The amendments were voted down by the government at Stormont, a decision which was to have important ramifications for the possibility of site provision for Travellers in Belfast and throughout Northern Ireland. With the reorganisation of local government, the housing and accommodation functions of local authorities were removed to the NIHE, yet district councils still retained the power, but not the duty, to provide serviced sites (under the Caravans Act (NI) 1963). Council officials subsequently responsible for site provision have often stated that this whole area should be within the remit of the NIHE as the public body exclusively concerned with accommodation provision.

In spite of the earlier setbacks faced by the Assisi Fellowship, the Itinerant Settlement Committees continued to lobby for site provision. The first 'breakthrough' came when the Derry Itinerant Settlement

Committee secured the provision of a serviced site, 'Labre Park', next
to the city refuse dump at Ballyarnet; it was officially opened in 1975.
But, within a short period of time, the initiative was considered 'a near
total failure' (Butler 1985:31). Meanwhile, in Belfast, following
continued lobbying by the local Itinerant Settlement Committee, a
proposal to provide a 'serviced' site, was finally carried in March
1974. However, it took six years for the site (located on the Springfield
Road peaceline) to near completion, because of 'local objections and
lack of commitment or incompetence by various officials' (McCart
1985:7). Furthermore, comprehensive vandalism of the site by local
settled residents, just prior to its completion, ensured that it was never
occupied. It was estimated that the site had cost approximately
£100,000 (Northern Ireland Commissioner for Complaints 1984:122).
Travellers were not consulted about the location or design of either
of these sites.

By 1980, the voluntary sector magazine *Scope* was able to comment
that: 'Although travellers only number around a hundred families, not
one permanent facilities site exists for them in any area, and attempts
by voluntary organisations to get District Councils to provide for
those families resident in their area have frequently met with delays
and outright opposition from almost all sources' (*Scope*, September
1980). In a further feature on Travellers in December 1981, the
magazine referred to the Department of the Environment (DOE)'s
'genial wall of silence' and stated that 'it is obvious that provision of
facilities for Travellers is not perceived as a priority'.

The first official report since the 1954 Home Affairs Committee
Report appeared in 1981. The report of the Co-Ordinating Committee
on Social Problems (Northern Ireland Co-Ordinating Committee on
Social Problems 1981) addressed the issues of accommodation,
education, employment and training, health and social work support
as well as the role and potential of voluntary activity. The report's
emphasis was less assimilationist than the Assisi Fellowship report: 'The
underlying principle has been that the travelling people have a right
to a nomadic existence for so long as they wish and to retain their own
identity, without being subjected to pressure to settle' (para. 2).
Stressing that a range of accommodation, from transit halts through
to housing, should be made available to cater for the differing aspirations
within the Traveller community, the report maintained that 'the
provision of serviced sites is the key strategic initiative in the development
of services for Travelling People' (paras. 4 and 22). The report
emphasised interagency co-operation with the lead co-ordinating role
being given to the DOE; whilst the role of the Northern Ireland
Council for Travelling People (NICTP),[1] as the Northern Ireland
Council for Itinerant Settlement was now known, was described as
'crucial'. The DOE Minister, David Mitchell, responded by establishing

a Working Party in April 1983, 'to examine policy options to improve provision of settled sites for the travelling people of Northern Ireland' (Noonan 1994:21). The Working Party, chaired by the DOE, comprised representatives of local authorities and the NICTP and produced its report in July 1984 (DOE (NI) 1984). The report had no legal standing as such, but it recommended the introduction of legislation to cover 100 per cent DOE grant-aid to district councils for provision of serviced sites. Recognising that 'the majority of Travellers desire accommodation on serviced sites', the Working Party also made a number of other significant recommendations including: provision of a Northern Ireland wide network of legal, serviced sites, to be completed by 31 March 1987, in order to eliminate 'wasted effort on evictions, cleansing and provision of welfare and education services'; the setting up of an Advisory Committee on Travellers (ACT) to advise the Minister; the provision of minimum facility transit sites for 'the fifty families who are involved in long-distance trading' – but they were to take second priority to funding of permanent sites for 'static' families; and the collection/collation on a regular basis of population, of health and other statistics relevant to Northern Ireland Travellers (DOE (NI) 1984:20–1). The Working Party report glossed over the short-comings of social, health, educational and training/employment services in a mere 21 sentences, giving the impression that the delivery of these services to Travellers was on a par with those to the settled community.

The legislative consequences of the 1984 Working Party report in respect of grant-aid and additional powers of eviction to 'designated' local authorities were contained in the Local Government (Miscellaneous Provisions) (NI) Order 1985. This legislation empowers but crucially does not oblige local authorities to provide serviced sites (in contrast to the aforementioned Caravans Act 1968 applying to England and Wales). This fundamental shortcoming and the subsequent legislation were referred to by the Standing Advisory Commission on Human Rights (SACHR) – a government-appointed public body – in its reports for 1983–84 (SACHR 1984) and 1985–86 (SACHR 1987). Moreover, while the Working Party report was important as a summary of current government policy, the implementation of its more progressive recommendations was much slower than envisaged. Even by December 1989, only 53 of Northern Ireland's 203 Traveller families were living on serviced sites. The Advisory Committee did not come into being until 1986. By the mid-1980s, the morale of the Itinerant Settlement Groups was at a low ebb. Despite the publication of the DOE Working Party report, there was little confidence in the ability of the relevant statutory authorities to implement its recommendations.

Meanwhile, in the Republic of Ireland, the values espoused by the Itinerant Settlement movement had been challenged by a number of groups adopting a more radical approach, such as the Committees for the Rights of Travellers and the all-Traveller *Minceir Misli* (Travellers' Movement). These groups questioned the domination of the Itinerant Settlement Committees (ISCs) by non-Travellers, stressed the importance of Travellers' distinct cultural identity and criticised the failure of the ISCs to provide any amelioration of Travellers' circumstances and living conditions. Further, they rejected assimilationist ideology, categorised the ISCs' emphasis on philanthropy as a form of social control and placed a firm emphasis on the active struggle for rights (DTEDG 1992:62). In contrast to the low key and behind the scenes lobbying of the ISCs, the rights-oriented groups adopted a high-profile campaign involving marches, media publicity and resistance to evictions whilst attempting to make contact with European Gypsy groupings. Although the Committees for Rights of Travellers and Minceir Misli had relatively short life-spans, they influenced the ideology and practice of groups like the Dublin Travellers' Education and Development Group (now Pavee Point), whose community work activities continue into the 1990s. These new groups sought to resource and motivate the Traveller community to build a national movement for self-determination, which located the recognition of Travellers' distinct ethnic identity as central to their campaign. The combined effect of these developments was also felt north of the Border. A number of the newer members of the Northern Ireland Council for Travelling People felt uncomfortable with the paternalistic and assimilationist ethos inherited from the Itinerant Settlement movement and were attracted to the rights-based approach pioneered in the Irish Republic. At the same time, the resolve of the pro-settlement NICTP members had lessened in the face of continuing setbacks and many had lost interest in the pursuance of their project. During 1985 and 1986, the committees affiliated to the NICTP were in effect disbanded and replaced by a number of Committees for the Rights of Travellers, most of whose members did not have previous involvement in the Itinerant Settlement Movement.

The new Committees developed a more sophisticated and confrontational strategy. This involved encouraging and supporting Travellers themselves to speak out regarding their circumstances and aspirations. Anti-Traveller prejudice and discrimination were characterised as racism, which required the introduction of anti-discrimination legislation. Instances of racism were highlighted in the media and evidence forwarded to SACHR and the ACT. Attempts were made to resist evictions through the courts. On 30 March 1993, for instance, in a judgment in the case of *Belfast City Council* v. *Donaghue and others*, Justice Nicholson awarded adverse possession to 14 Traveller families who had been living on an illegal site at Glen Road for over 20 years (Belfast Law Centre 1993:5). Occasionally, direct action (including pickets and an impromptu road block) was used to focus attention on particular situations. The aim of the new Committees' strategy was to visibly redefine the situation of Travellers in Northern Ireland as one concerning the denial of human rights and to move the focus from Travellers as a 'problem' to those policies and practices of the state which obstructed the full expression of Traveller ethnicity.

The campaign almost immediately drew a strong reaction. In June 1986, the occupation by Travellers of a car park outside the Council Chambers of Down District Council (following a series of evictions from roadside camps around Downpatrick) gave rise to unprecedented vilification and harassment. Three caravans (in another camp) were burnt during an attack by a mob from the nationalist St Dympna's estate during which stones were thrown and a member of the Down Committee for Travellers' Rights assaulted. An editorial in the *Down Recorder* (25 June 1986) called for a public boycott of Travellers – all council facilities to be closed to them; all shops, petrol stations, bars, and so on, to refuse to serve them. The newspaper described Travellers as 'social misfits who suck the blood dry before moving on to another easy prey', 'a cancer', 'a plague of parasites' and as people who 'cock a snoop at all standards of human decency' and concluded by sending out 'the clear message to gypsies – get out now'. The Chamber of Trade issued a public statement that 'no more should these misfits be allowed to rape our environment and disrupt our community. We don't want Itinerants camping legally or illegally on our highways and byways.' Moreover, the political parties represented on the district councils, with the exception of the Workers' Party and Sinn Féin, also added their voices to the chorus of condemnation. Threats of violence were made by loyalist paramilitaries in the area, while the RUC also engaged in petty harassment of the Travellers (*Scope*, July 1986:6).

The Travellers were eventually forced to leave Downpatrick as this pressure continued, but the incident drew considerable media coverage and helped focus interest on other instances of harassment, discrimination and resistance to these which took place elsewhere. Political parties, churches and trade unions were lobbied by the NICTP and its member groups. Alliances were developed during the late 1980s and early 1990s with some of the key voluntary sector agencies, the Committee on the Administration of Justice (CAJ) human rights group and trade unions, based on the premise that the Traveller community and those involved in direct work with them were numerically too small and marginalised to bring influence to bear on the policy community solely by their own efforts. Links were made with other minority ethnic communities, initially with the Chinese community and later with the umbrella group, the Northern Ireland Council for Ethnic Minorities, in the context of the common struggle against racism. The links with the CAJ were particularly valuable in that they enabled access to the international arena. Submissions including reference to Travellers were made to the United Nations (UN) Committees on the Elimination of Racial Discrimination (August 1993, March 1996 (CAJ/NICEM 1996) and March 1997 (CAJ 1997) and the Rights of the Child (August 1994 (CAJ 1994)), generating calls from these bodies for the government to honour its international treaty obligations (see Chapter 3). In May 1997, a submission was made by Belfast Travellers' Education and Development Group (BTEDG) to the UN Committee on Economic, Social and Cultural Rights (BTEDG 1997).

At local level, the campaign drew a number of editorials in the main newspapers. Following a visit by the German-based human rights organisation, *Gesellschaft für Bedrohte Volker*, focusing on the situation of Travellers, the *Irish News* (30 May 1986) asked:

What are we doing to solve the problem besides moving it on to someone else? Councils have already been given the go-ahead by government to provide sites and Stormont Ministers have indicated that the necessary finance – and not much is required – will be available. Yet action is long in coming. The same is true of government plans for a semi-independent body to examine the issue: it has taken so long to materialise, some believe the will to act is not there.

In August 1986, the DOE finally announced that this body – the Advisory Committee on Travelling People (ACT) – had been set up to advise the DOE on ways of improving the living conditions of Travellers in Northern Ireland: 'In particular, members will promote provision of accessible serviced sites, advise on the exercise of eviction powers, and on ways of improving relations between travellers and the settled community where necessary' (ACT 1986, 25 September). The ACT (reviewed below) was initially composed of representatives from district councils, the Eastern Health and Social Services Board, the Catholic Diocese of Down and Connor and the NICTP, with an influential secretariat provided by the DOE.

The overall campaign developed from its initial targeting of accommodation needs, to address the issue of parity of access to the full range of services such as education and training, health and social services and youth provision. Whilst the locally based Committees for the Rights of Travellers, affiliated to the NICTP, continued to place an emphasis on rights issues, they also began to attempt to provide various services to Travellers, including pre-school and youth provision (with a view to demonstrating the need for statutory intervention). It became apparent that, without prior education and training, neither individual Travellers who had spoken out nor the Traveller community as a whole were equipped to sustain a lengthy campaign or to take the lead in developing an effective strategy which would generate an appropriate response from the state. The Committees tended to evolve into Travellers Support Groups from around 1990 onwards. Several of these groups began to examine strategies for empowering and enabling Travellers to take a more active role in determining the future for their community. These included provision such as culturally specific training programmes and arrangement for 'shadowing' various jobs in the service provision sector, such as play worker posts. However, insecurity of funding has resulted in 'breaks' in provision and Travellers Support Groups have encountered considerable difficulties attempting to resurrect projects, including meeting the expectations of Travellers, attracting experienced staff and enduring high staff turnover. Projects of one, two or three years' duration are not sufficient to redress the effects of the longstanding multiple exclusion experienced by Travellers. The impetus of the campaign for Travellers' rights has, however, generated a continuing series of reports from both statutory and voluntary agencies (some of these are Traveller specific, whilst others make reference to Travellers amongst other issues) including the Eastern Health and Social Services Board, Save the Children Fund, the SACHR, the CAJ, the University of Ulster, the ACT, various Travellers Support Groups and Barnardos. The net effect of all this was to stimulate at last some consideration from the statutory and wider voluntary sector for the situation of the Traveller community. To what extent the resultant activity has benefited the lives and circumstances of Travellers is, however, open to question.

In November 1996, the government undertook an interdepartmental review of all its policies relating to Travellers. The review was based on a report commissioned by the ACT (from the University of Ulster) and the responses to this solicited from interested parties during a consultation period. The Paris Report examined developments in the provision of a range of services to Travellers, including accommodation, health, education and training, and made a number of recommendations for policy change. Drawing attention to the lack of baseline data, it concluded that 'it is too early to say definitely whether the increased level of awareness of Travellers' needs is resulting in better service delivery, although there are some promising signs of significant improvement' (Paris et al. 1995a:8). The DOE's response (DOE 1996) emphasised its intention to adhere to the existing policy approach. Virtually none of the key recommendations made by Paris et al. were taken up, except those referring to collection of necessary data and the inclusion of Travellers' needs in the preparation of development plans by the Planning Agency.

A recent report which examined Travellers' access to service provision was commissioned by the government's Central Community Relations Unit to study the situation of the four main ethnic minorities in Northern Ireland and it concluded that serious problems remained:

'Travellers experience high levels of overcrowding in homes, low levels of employment, a low level of attainment in education, and the disturbing statistic concerning low proportions of this community aged over 45 ... These factors taken together point to a community whose existence is unduly affected by disadvantage' (Irwin 1996:83). A review of the current state of service provision, highlighting recent initiatives whilst also drawing attention to their limitations, is outlined below within the context of the comments by Paris *et al.* (1995a) and Irwin's study (1996), as well as the proposals by the NICTP and other Travellers Support Groups for further initiatives and reform of existing arrangements.

Accommodation

Paris *et al.*'s optimistic conclusions are not congruent with the reality of accommodation provision for Travellers. Provision of accommodation for homeless people from the majority sedentary community is mandatory under the Housing (Northern Ireland) Order 1981. The provision of accommodation for people who wish to pursue a nomadic way of life, but do not have access to the most basic facilities (water, sanitation, electricity, refuse collection), is discretionary. As already pointed out, under the Local Government (Miscellaneous Provisions) (Northern Ireland) Order 1985, local councils are empowered but not obliged to provide such sites. The responsibility for providing for the small population of Travellers is diffused to a number of councils. These provisions mitigate against centralised implementation of any long-term strategy for accommodation for Travellers.

The DOE's *Regional Development Strategy for the Provision of Sites for Travellers over the period 1994–2000* (1994) must be seen merely as a limited statement of need. It cannot be considered as a statement of intent, because the DOE does not currently have the powers to compel councils which prevaricate or simply refuse to make provision. Furthermore, given that the budget for capital construction of sites for 1997–2000 is a little short of £400,000, it is unlikely that more that one of the additional ten sites forecast by the DOE as needed during this period will be built. The *Report of the Northern Ireland Working Party on Site Provision for Travelling People* (DOE 1984:20) similarly forecast the provision of a Northern Ireland-wide network of sites to be completed by 31 March 1987. However, by 1997, only 65 per cent of the Traveller population of 1,115 were accommodated on serviced sites, most of which are of sub-standard quality (see below).

The effects of the shortcomings of the 1985 legislation have been a slow rate of progress (despite the availability of 100 per cent grant-aid from the DOE for the construction of sites) and widely varying standards of provision. There are serviced sites (halting sites) in Belfast (2), Derry (2), Omagh, Coalisland, Strabane and Newry. Temporary, 'tolerated', unofficial sites with minimal facilities have been provided at Toomebridge (Magherafelt District Council) and the Monagh Bypass (Belfast). Only the group housing scheme developed in Omagh, the only one of its kind in Northern Ireland, has the unqualified approval of the Travellers resident there. The government has pre-varicated over making funding available for further group housing by arguing that only the NIHE is allowed by law to provide accommo-dation with bedrooms, but that it is not allowed to provide housing to any specific ethnic group. Furthermore, the site provision programme in Belfast has been behind schedule since it started over 20 years ago. District councils elsewhere, such as those in Armagh and Craigavon, have seemingly engaged with the process of investigating such provision merely to deflect criticism on the grounds of anti-Traveller prejudice. In reality, these councils have continued to delay taking a decision to proceed with the development of sites in their areas. Essentially, many councils have been engaged in a game of pretence in which other key agencies, such as the DOE and the ACT appear to have colluded with. Other councils are more open in their opposition to provision for Travellers. For instance, Fermanagh District Council has stated that there are no Travellers living in Fermanagh (a fiction with which the DOE appears to concur) and, therefore, that there is no need to make provision. Again, Newry and Mourne District Council have refused to provide further accommodation to alleviate overcrowding on the deplorable official site at Middlebank, claiming that this is the respon-sibility of some other agency and that the council has 'done its share'.

The legislation on site provision in Northern Ireland also allows for the controversial measure of designation. Articles 9 and 10 of the Local Government (Miscellaneous Provisions) (Northern Ireland) Order 1985 effectively allows for the imposition of a quota of Travellers allowed to live in a particular local authority area, if the local authority can satisfy the Department of the Environment that 'adequate' provision has been made for Travellers who 'normally reside in or resort to' the district. Once an area is designated, Travellers not camped on serviced sites will be evicted at short notice, under criminal law. In effect, whole areas can be declared off-limits to Travellers. At present, designated council areas include Derry, Dungannon, Strabane and Newry. Paris et al. (1995a:7) concluded that 'most councils are only prepared to provide serviced sites for their identified indigenous Traveller population with the objective of obtaining designation'. Evictions of Travellers from illegal sites have continued virtually unabated throughout recent years. Legal instruments which were used to facilitate this process included the Public Health (Ireland) Act 1878, the Housing Act 1963, the Pollution and Central and Local

Government (Northern Ireland) Order 1978 and the Roads (Northern Ireland) Order 1980. Illegal means have included threats from police, paramilitary organisations and residents groups. It has been estimated that the cost of eviction for district councils is £50,000 per family per year. Post-eviction clean-ups have been estimated at a cost of between £3,000 and £8,000 per incident.

There has thus been little tangible progress towards developing the provision of transit sites which could facilitate nomadism, although the need for such sites was identified clearly in the DOE's report on site provision for Travellers in Northern Ireland (DOE 1984:21) as well as by the ACT (ACT 1996). A revealing comment contained in the interim findings of an ACT survey (ACT 1988), which was not made public, confirms a hidden policy agenda focused on containment as a stage towards assimilation:

A common theme running through the responses is that travellers [sic] are committed to their lifestyle and, with only very few exceptions, intend to continue as travellers. The hope has been expressed within ACT that if the travellers are given good standards of serviced sites, then some, particularly those in the younger age group, having experienced an intermediate form of 'settled' living, might decide to give up travelling. There is, as yet, no evidence of the likelihood of that trend but with the on-going development of serviced sites, it might eventually happen when those sites are well established and become familiar to the travellers. On the face of it, the travellers intend to continue as travellers.

The NICTP and Travellers Support Groups have campaigned for a number of years for statutory responsibility for provision of all types of accommodation to be taken from local councils and given to the NIHE and that legislation to effect this should be introduced if necessary. As the provider of public sector accommodation, it has the technical expertise and experience lacking in councils. The measure would also have the effect of taking the Travellers' sites issue out of the party political arena (see Chapter 2) and would allow the development of a co-ordinated long-term strategy and the implementation of improved standards of provision (including both group housing and transit site provision) throughout Northern Ireland. The Paris Report recommends this as one of two alternative future policy options for dealing with the accommodation issue. The other is that a financial penalty should be imposed on councils that do not make site provision. However, voluntary sector groups believe that this measure may not be effectively applied and that councils could find alternative ways of resisting site provision. Irrespective of which agency is ultimately responsible, it would clearly, as Liégeois (1994:185) suggests, 'be less costly from every point of view to respond to the needs and demands of Travellers than to go on building infrastructures that they do not want. After so many disasters and some successes, this much should be obvious, but in fact it is far from being generally recognised.'

Education

In Northern Ireland, Traveller children attend 'mainstream' schools with the exception of the Traveller-only primary school in Belfast. The Paris Report, however, noted the lack of comprehensive official data on the numbers of Travellers attending primary or secondary school and called on the Department of Education (Northern Ireland) (DENI) and the local education and library boards to establish statistical monitors of attendance and attainment by Travellers. In 1993, DENI produced a circular entitled *Policy and Guidelines on the Education of Children from Traveller Families* (DENI 1993). The initiative followed a European Union (EU) resolution by the Council of Ministers and the Ministers for Education requesting member states to improve access to schooling for Gypsy and Traveller children. The document states that Travellers are entitled to the same rights as (settled) parents and children in accordance with the Education Reform (NI) Order 1989. The second part of the circular contains a number of guidelines for ensuring equality of opportunity for Traveller children. Reference is made to the value of pre-school provision, school record transfer systems, designated teaching staff to co-ordinate Traveller matters, the function of the Youth Service, the role of Education and Welfare Officers and the development of teaching resource materials. Criticism from some voluntary sector groups has focused on the largely permissive nature of the guidelines which fail to commit specific agencies to concrete actions. Nevertheless, the policy circular has led to the development of a Travellers' Education Forum, which provides some in-service teacher training; establishment of a working group to draft appropriate curricular materials reflecting Travellers' life and culture; and the appointment of Traveller Liaison Teachers by three of the education and library boards. A Travellers Support Group has been grant-aided by the Belfast Education and Library Board to pilot a two-year culturally specific youth project, which will seek to engage the mainstream Youth Service in meeting the needs of young Travellers.

The number of Traveller children transferring to secondary school remains very low. Indeed, significant secondary transfer from the segregated primary school for Travellers in Belfast only commenced in 1997. Voluntary groups provide pre-school playgroups on three sites in Derry and Belfast, but no long-term statutory resourcing of these is available to develop this provision. After-school groups run by voluntary groups exist in Belfast and Derry but similarly have no guarantee of medium- or long-term statutory funding. The Department of Education (NI) will be required (as are all other government departments) to review the effectiveness of its policy after five years. This review is due to take place in 1998 and the outcome will be thoroughly scrutinised by those concerned with Travellers' rights for concrete evidence of improvement in the achievement of access to the various levels of provision and, crucially, in the key outcome of standards of attainment by Travellers.

In its 1989 report, the ACT highlighted a variety of obstacles for Travellers wishing to access mainstream training opportunities: 'Both young and adult Travellers have considerable anxieties at the prospect of attending mainstream courses, arising from low self-esteem and their feeling of rejection by, and the hostility from, the settled community. Without the support of their peer group, those few Travellers who have taken up existing provision have great difficulty in completing courses' (ACT 1989:12). The ACT recommended the development of training schemes specifically for Travellers. However, the historic policy of the state agencies responsible for overseeing provision of training has been to pursue an 'open door' arrangement, based on the assumption that there is equality of access to all potential user groups. The Report of the Northern Ireland Working Party on Site Provision for Travelling People (DOE 1984:4) commented therefore: 'DED [Department of Economic Development] does not make special sorties to travellers' communities to invite up-take of jobs or training. However, Employment Services Office staff are mindful to encourage travelling people in use of the full range of facilities of DED. DED makes special efforts within its current framework to help individual travellers.' Paris *et al.* (1995a:102), however, point to low levels of Traveller participation here.

Irwin (1996:54, 80) confirmed this pattern, pointing out that although 62 per cent of Traveller males are unemployed, there was a negligible level of take-up of government training programmes. Noonan (1994) has argued that the failure of the 'open door' policy can be explained by the cultural inappropriateness of mainstream training and consequently that the Training and Employment Agency (TEA) should resource culturally appropriate training projects. In 1993/94, the Belfast Travellers' Education and Development Group ran a pilot project along these lines, with support from an EU programme (Horizon) targeting the long-term unemployed. Although an external evaluation of the project deemed it successful and recommended the resourcing of further and more intensive training, the response of the TEA has been disappointing. Despite a recognition of the need for culturally specific training, two years of negotiation between BTEDG and TEA (following on from the Horizon project) failed to elicit any firm commitment to tangible support. In contrast, state training agencies in the Republic of Ireland have provided financial support for Traveller-specific training since the early 1970s.

Health

It is only relatively recently that any research at all into Travellers' health status has been undertaken for Northern Ireland. These were Dr M. Gordon's 1989 study, 'The health of Travellers' children in Northern Ireland' (Gordon *et al*. 1991) and the Director of Public Health's report on the health of Travellers in Belfast (EHSSB 1989). These reports showed a level of ill health among Travellers which was significantly above that of the majority population. In particular, adult life expectancy was between 11 and 15 years below that of the settled community, levels of childhood immunisation were poor, the death rate for Traveller children up to 10 years of age was 10 times that of non-Traveller children and hospital admission rates for preventable childhood illnesses were very high. A number of recent studies have agreed that there are three main factors responsible for these deficiencies: poor environmental conditions on illegal sites, inaccessibility of the National Health Service and the lack of access to appropriate health education.

Neither the Department of Health and Social Services (DHSS) nor the various area health boards have specific policies on Travellers, preferring a universal policy approach. Many of the detailed policy recommendations contained in Pauline Ginnety's (1993) comprehensive EHSSB report, *The Health of Travellers*, have not been implemented. The DHSS's *Regional Strategy for Northern Ireland 1992–97* (DHSS 1991) identified Travellers as a group which may require particular attention. The area health boards have been subsequently directed by the DHSS through this strategy to identify vulnerable groups and focus resources on them accordingly. Also, a number of initiatives have been developed in the Eastern and Southern Health Board areas. These include the establishment of multidisciplinary teams to address the health problems of Travellers, a client-held child health record system, training on Traveller culture for some staff and the provision of on-site baby clinics. The Western Health and Social Services Board has provided some grant-aid and support in kind to the Derry Travellers Support Group. Significantly, the Paris Report (1995a:83) drew attention to the failure of the DHSS and the area health boards to collate routine health statistics on Travellers and concluded that 'consequently, the absence of longitudinal data on the health status of Travellers has made it almost impossible to quantify the effects of health policy on Travellers in Northern Ireland'.

Travellers and Race Relations Legislation

In August 1996, the government finally published the Draft Race Relations (Northern Ireland) Order 1996, following, and largely as a result of, a lengthy campaign by a coalition of minority ethnic groups, Travellers Support Groups, civil liberties bodies, voluntary sector agencies and trades unions. The Order is almost identical to the Race Relations Act 1976 and, therefore, shares its many shortcomings as identified in the Commission for Racial Equality's *Second Review* (1992). One significant addition, though, is the specific naming of Travellers as a group which will be protected within its ambit. The Order has also authorised the establishment of a Commission for Racial Equality for Northern Ireland (CRENI). However, there is a danger that some of the potential gains here for Travellers via the Race Relations Order may be affected by a strong lobby from local council officials to have new additional powers introduced to Northern Ireland to deal with illegal camping. In June 1996, an ACT-organised conference on 'Traveller Traders' provided a platform for various district council officials and councillors to bemoan the inadequacy of existing legal provisions for containing Travellers and the likely further dilution of these via the Race Relations Order and to call for new legal measures which will circumvent any protection given to Travellers by the Order. In response, the DOE proposed the Local Government (Miscellaneous Provisions) (Northern Ireland) Order 1997, which will repeal the provision for designation contained in Articles 9 and 10 of the Local Government (Miscellaneous Provisions) (Northern Ireland) Order 1985, but substitute general powers to remove unauthorised campers, based on those contained in Sections 77/79 of the Criminal Justice and Public Order Act 1994 (extant in Britain). Directly discriminatory legislation applicable only in selected districts will be replaced by indirectly discriminatory legislation applicable in all districts leading to *de facto* designation throughout Northern Ireland. SACHR has given an opinion that the powers proposed in Articles 3 and 4 of the Draft Order are likely to place the government in breach of Article 8 of the European Convention of Human Rights – which guarantees respect for private family life and home (Jones 1997).

The NICTP has organised a campaign against the proposed legislation arguing that it will impact differentially on the Traveller community, given the lack of sufficient legal serviced sites available and that it is therefore in breach of the government's Policy Appraisal and Fair Treatment (PAFT) guidelines. PAFT (see Chapter 4) is meant to apply to government departments, Next Step Agencies and non-departmental public bodies, although district councils are not included. PAFT guidelines require these bodies to consider the practice of fair treatment alongside issues of economy, efficiency and effectiveness for all new policy proposals; for service delivery and whenever existing policies are reviewed. Following the publication of the government's first annual report on PAFT (CCRU 1995), concerns have been expressed about the rigorousness of its application by departments. Subsequently, a case for removing the discretionary basis of PAFT and replacing it with a legal one has been advanced (McCrudden 1996). The Paris Report (1995a:47) concluded that a PAFT appraisal of recent policy initiatives was almost impossible because of the lack of baseline data available from government departments. This finding suggests that government has not been particularly concerned with the application of PAFT to the Traveller community. In this context, the fate of the proposed new anti-camping measures will provide a test case for the relevance of PAFT to the Traveller community.

The Advisory Committee on Travellers

The Advisory Committee on Travellers was granted a fourth term of office (1996–99) by the Minister of the Environment (NI) and it is perhaps now opportune to assess its role, a decade after its establishment. It is worth pointing out that SACHR, which has been proactive in supporting the case for legislative protection for Travellers, declined to nominate a representative to the ACT when government rejected its suggestions that the DOE should have reserve powers available to ensure site provision for Travellers in the event of a reluctance by district councils to provide such facilities and that the ACT's terms of reference be 'strengthened to enable it to play a role in the payment of grants to secure any improvement in the living conditions of Travellers' (SACHR 1987:28). Recent research implicitly recognises the ACT's impotence, recommending that 'removing disadvantage for the Travelling community may be best achieved through a co-ordinated effort influenced by the new CRE for Northern Ireland' (Irwin 1996:83).

These issues of lack of power have indeed been exposed as a key shortcoming of the ACT. The completion of the programme of provision of serviced Traveller sites by district councils was established as 'the major policy priority' during the ACT's first term of office (1986–89). To date, ten sites have been completed (although at least three of these were either constructed or under construction when the ACT came into being). However, the layout and design of most of these sites have resulted in bleak high-density concrete environments. There is little provision for family privacy, safe areas for children to play or workspace to enable residents to store scrap or generate other means of income to sustain the Traveller economy. To many Travellers, these serviced sites resemble little more than reservations. Neither do the sites – typically comprising a two-room amenity unit (a toilet/bathroom and, in some cases, a kitchen) and a pitch (a concrete square on which caravans are parked) – provide value for money. The average cost per amenity unit/pitch was identified by Paris *et al.* (1995a:64) as £36,000, as opposed to the cost of £35,000 for an NIHE four-bedroom house, whilst the latter offered comparably higher levels of health and safety due to building quality and design specifications. A survey of district councils by Paris *et al.* (1995a:63) indicated that the majority of local authorities which had provided sites for Travellers considered the amenity unit version (and this constitutes the bulk of currently available serviced sites) to represent low value for money.

In 1997, construction of a serviced site for 20 families at Monagh Wood, Belfast, was suspended after it was discovered that the gradient of the pitches was such as to prevent the safe parking of caravans. An independent assessment, commissioned by Belfast City Council, revealed that virtually the entire site (on which £1 million has been spent to date) would have to be demolished and rebuilt at additional cost. Ten years on, the ACT has been unable to ensure that even the accommodation needs of the hundred or so Traveller families living in Belfast have been met. Outside Belfast, a number of councils have continued to ostentatiously prevaricate on making provision, despite numerous attempts by the ACT to persuade them to do so. In several instances, the ACT has recommended the setting up of interagency committees at district council level to address the accommodation issue, but these have usually been largely relegated to the status of talking shops by the local councils. Elsewhere, the ACT has often merely reacted to initiatives from other sources, such as its *post facto* endorsement of educational initiatives by DENI, the education and library boards and voluntary agencies or its belated support for race relations legislation.

Significantly, the ACT has been actively hostile to Travellers Support Groups. The preconditions for the NICTP's representation on the ACT have been changed on a number of occasions, effectively obstructing participation for long periods, and there is no representation from the NICTP on the DOE Working Party on Accommodation for Travellers (1996/97). Of note, too, the relationship between district councils and Travellers Support Groups is on the ACT's agenda for its fourth term of office during 1996–99 (following complaints by council representatives about the active advocacy role of the Groups). Perhaps unsurprisingly, virtually all the Traveller representatives on the ACT have voted with their feet, whilst the Committee is held in low regard by members of Travellers Support Groups, who believe it to be unrepresentative of Travellers' views, antipathetic to nomadism, lacking specialist knowledge and skills (particularly regarding cultural issues) and failing to assert the need for stronger terms of reference.

Towards a Political Accommodation of the Ethnic Identity of Travellers

Erikson (1993:2) has pointed out that despite the forecasts of many social theorists in the early twentieth century that ethnicity would decrease in importance and eventually vanish, as a result of modernisation, industrialisation and individualisation, there has been a resurgence in the political importance of ethnicity since 1945. Berger (cited by Sibley 1987:87) further suggests that the type of economic practices pursued by indigenous peoples, peasants and Gypsies 'enable them to maintain a degree of autonomy within the capitalist mode of production and [they] are able to adapt to external changes. They change in order to stay the same.' Glazer and Moynihan (1963:8), examining the accommodation of ethnic difference in the USA, a country often cited as one of the most successful examples of the effectiveness of the assimilation process, comment that 'the most important point about the American melting pot is that it never occurred'. The authors contend that, rather than eradicating ethnic differences, modern American society has actually created in individuals a new form of self-awareness, which is expressed in a concern about roots and origins. Moreover, in a global context, it has been argued that in the post-Cold War era, ethnic conflicts have largely taken over from ideological conflicts. Erikson (1993:2) estimated that of 37 armed conflicts taking place across the world in 1991, most could plausibly be considered as ethnic conflicts.

Parallel to the resurgent profile of ethnicity as a structuring factor in social relations have been attempts, at national and more particularly at international level, to devise means to regulate ethnic conflict and accommodate difference. The non-discrimination principle, therefore, has been firmly embedded and elaborated in international law through such instruments as the United Nations' Charter, the Universal Declaration of Human Rights and the International Covenant on the Elimination of all Forms of Racial Discrimination. The conceptions of human rights within these documents have a bias towards individualism, resulting from traditional Western liberal political philosophy. As Anaya (1995:326) notes, this perspective 'acknowledges the rights of the individual on the one hand and the sovereignty of the total social collective on the other, but it is not alive to the rich variety of intermediate or alternative associational groupings actually found in human culture, nor is it prepared to ascribe to such groupings any rights not reducible to the liberties of the citizen or the prerogatives of the state'. Thornberry (1991a:16), too, points out that while 'non-discrimination must be a requirement of any regime to protect minorities, it does not go far enough in the direction of accepting or cherishing differences between human beings; it does not commit the state to a high valuation of its minorities'.

The Race Relations (Northern Ireland) Order 1997 provides for measures to prevent discrimination within the parameters of individual rights. If the assumption is made that individual Travellers will act to claim their rights, the Order may to a limited extent vindicate these. It is questionable, though, whether the problem of group disadvantage as, for example, instanced in the low level of educational achievement, poor health status or the erosion of rights to enjoy Traveller culture (particularly nomadism) – which has accrued as the legacy of past discrimination – can be solved by legislation focused on individual rights. A growing body of opinion concerned with human rights has supported the right to cultural survival and the granting or recognition of the right of groups to self-determination within established state boundaries. This right may generally be understood to encompass the right of ethnic, religious or linguistic minorities to enjoy their own culture, to profess and practise their religion or to use their own language.

Articles 13, 55, 57 and 73 of the United Nations' Charter affirm cultural co-operation and development as among the purposes of the UN Article 27 of the International Covenant on Civil and Political Rights, to which the United Kingdom is a signatory (see Chapter 3), recognises the right of members of 'ethnic, religious or linguistic minorities ... in community with the other members of their group, to enjoy their own culture, to profess and practise their own religion, or to use their own language'. The UNESCO Declaration of Principles of Cultural Co-operation affirms a right and duty of all peoples to protect and develop the cultures throughout human kind. Article 2 of the UN Draft Declaration on the Rights of Persons Belonging to National, Ethnic, Religious and Linguistic Minorities (Thornberry 1991a:4) also requires that: 'States shall protect the existence and the national or ethnic, cultural, religious and linguistic identity of minorities, within their respective territories and shall encourage conditions for the promotion of that identity.' The UN Draft Declaration on Indigenous Rights utilises the language of respect for indigenous identity and institutions, the cultural contributions of the indigenous groups to the common heritage of human kind, their collective right to existence and to be protected against ethnocide, positive action by states to contribute to the maintenance of indigenous identity, self-management by groups and 'ethno-development' (Thornberry 1991a:18). Ethno-development is here defined as 'strengthening and consolidating a culturally distinct society's own culture by increasing it's independent decision-making capacity to govern its own development'.

Critics of the concept of group rights, for example Hartney (1995: 220–3), have pointed to the diminution of individual rights as an inevitable consequence of proactive legal safeguards for minority groups. In contrast, Glazer (1995:136) argues that individual rights are without meaning if they do not lead to a measurable improvement in the social and material well-being of an oppressed group. Glazer cites the judgment of Justice Krishna Iyer (considering the case for special preferences to be given to certain 'backward' castes), in the Indian Supreme Court, as a formula for deciding on the granting of group rights: 'The social disparity must be so grim and substantial as to serve as a basis for benign discrimination.' As indicated already, report after report by a wide range of statutory and voluntary agencies have drawn attention to the prominence of the Traveller community in the indices of social deprivation. The extent of the differential is such that there can be no doubt that it should be considered 'grim and substantial'.

SACHR (1990) has suggested, in a discussion of the applicability of group rights to Northern Ireland, that the rights of the two main communities (British/Irish, Catholic/Protestant) be included within a Northern Ireland Constitution Act. Moreover, the draft Bill of Rights for Northern Ireland prepared by the Committee on the Administration of Justice (CAJ 1993b) provides (in Article 16) for persons belonging to ethnic, religious or linguistic groups (including Travellers) to have the right 'to enjoy their own culture'. The Secretary of State for Northern Ireland, Mo Mowlam, has indicated that she is prepared to re-examine the case for a Bill of Rights. Perhaps the time is now appropriate for the Travellers' rights movement to begin to consider whether it is worthwhile to campaign for Travellers' nomadism to be protected within such measures. The legal recognition of nomadism would provide a broader underpinning of Travellers' rights and challenge the sedentarist assumptions which inform anti-Traveller prejudice and discrimination.

O'Connell (1994a:11–15) has categorised perceptions of Travellers held by the dominant population as falling within the framework of five models: liberal humanist, social pathology, sub-culture of poverty, idealist, and human rights. He points out that 'sometimes these perceptions are held explicitly and consciously, at other times they are implicit in what people say or write about Travellers. They also become visible in the relations between sedentary people and Travellers or in the interventions of the state.' The liberal humanist model posits that Travellers have the same needs and rights as other citizens of the state, but also implies that they have no distinct identity or culture. The denial of difference may arise from a monocultural perspective on society or from the equation of difference with deviance. The model disregards social structuring factors such as gender, class, 'race' or ethnicity. As a consequence, Travellers are expected to live within the norms of sedentary society and failure to do so is viewed as a problem. The model tends to focus on individual membership and fails to take account of structural patterns of group privilege and oppression.

The social pathology model views as problematical individuals and groups who deviate from what is assumed to be a mainstream society, which is considered to be essentially just. Travellers are characterised as drop-outs and misfits. From this perspective, Travellers are seen as a pathology requiring treatment. By defining Travellers as the problem, the model does not address structural inequality or the prejudice and racism of sedentary society. Interventions based on this model utilise techniques of social control such as evictions or forced settlement with a view to assimilation. Rehabilitation techniques, often informed by a charitable ethos, can also be deployed in service provision. These have a tendency to perpetuate dependency and promote assimilation. The social pathology model does not take account of Travellers' ethnic identity, which is located in their separate historical development, cultural traditions, values, nomadism and resilience as a group.

The sub-culture of poverty model recognises that Travellers pursue a distinct lifestyle but locates it within the context of an explanation of intergenerational poverty as a function of inherited dysfunctional characteristics which are peculiar to the long-term poor. McCarthy (1994:122–3) identifies a number of fatal flaws in this model. In the first instance, it does not take account of the wealth of some Travellers. Second, the model fails to recognise Traveller culture as having more in common with those of Gypsies and other economic nomads worldwide, than with (as a sub-culture) Irish society. Third, the sub-culture of poverty theory does not address the issue of nomadism as the key to understanding Travellers, their way of life and relationship with the sedentary community. Finally, the model does not take account of the separate cultural norms and values and the language of the Traveller community. Interventions based on this model tend to be similar to those of the social pathology model.

The idealist model is a variant of the 'noble savage' theme: 'Travellers are 'special'; they are an exotic group who come from some idyllic and carefree past. At its most simplistic and naive this portrays all Travellers as having 'special' innate positive qualities' (O'Connell 1994b:14). This model ignores Travellers' oppression; in particular, the internal oppression is seen as unnecessary or even misguided. The human rights model acknowledges that Travellers are a distinct minority ethnic group and situates them within the context of the social relations engendered by the interaction between dominant and subordinate ethnic groups. Using an amalgam of anthropological, legal and sociological criteria, Travellers can be identified as a minority ethnic group since they regard themselves and are regarded by others as people with distinct characteristics: they have a long, shared history; values; customs, lifestyle and traditions associated with nomadism; a distinct language (Gammon or Cant); an identity expressed in a range of arts and crafts and work practices; and they adhere to a popular form of religion in the Catholic tradition. Furthermore, Travellers constitute a small minority group who share a history of oppression and discrimination (O'Connell 1994b:15).

Simpson and Yinger (1972:17) provide a typology of policies applied to minorities by dominant groups as follows: Assimilation (forced or permitted); Pluralism; Legal Protection of Minorities; Population Transfer (peaceful or forced); Continued Subjugation; Extermination. An examination of the policies historically pursued by the Northern Ireland state must lead to the conclusion that forced assimilation, forced population transfer and continued subjugation have been (not necessarily discretely) and are currently being applied. The population transfer option can be identified as being pursued through the policy of harassment by police and local councils during the period from the 1940s through to the 1980s. With the introduction of the legal provision for designation since 1985 it has been given institutional status. Furthermore, an ex-Deputy Lord Mayor of Belfast has even promoted extermination when he declared that 'itinerants are rubbish who should be sent to an incinerator' (*Belfast Telegraph*, 2 August 1982).

The assimilation option has been pursued through the various measures taken to inhibit nomadism, including the panoply of legislative means deployed against illegal camping on unserviced sites, the bouldering and blocking-off of such sites, the failure to provide serviced transit sites and the deplorable condition of most official sites. The continued resistance by the state to provide group housing or allow for the NIHE to assume responsibility for Traveller-specific provision, instead of insisting that it can only allocate individual families to individual houses within its general housing stock, is indicative of an underlying intention to disperse the Traveller population. It is only recently, as noted above, that any effort has been made to mention Travellers in a positive light within the school curriculum. The previous absence of reference to Travellers and their way of life implied that sedentarism was the norm to be aspired to. Further, most statutory services' providers have not ensured equality of access to Travellers. In some cases, nomadism and its consequences – insecurity of tenure and sub-standard living conditions – have been cited as an obstacle to effective service delivery. Barth (1996:312) draws attention to the obstacle to the process of assimilation posed by the pariah status of Gypsies, which 'imposed a definition in social situations which gave very little scope for interaction with persons from the majority population and simultaneously as an imperative status represented an inescapable disability that prevented them from assuming the normal status involved in other definitions of the situation of interaction'.

The predominant theoretical model informing the actions of the Northern Ireland state has been the social pathology one. The focus of the Itinerant Settlement Movement in its attempt to persuade the state to reform its policies towards Travellers, has been that of the culture of poverty. Essentially, both state and Itinerant Settlement Movement approaches have been based on the ethos of assimilation. The emphasis in the state's response has been to attempt to eradicate nomadism and force settlement, whereas that of the Itinerant Settlement Committees was on the 'humane' solution of alleviating living conditions through the provision of sites as a halfway stage *en route* to assimilation. These two agendas fused together to provide the basis of the current arrangements for settlement of Travellers following from the 1984 Working Party report on site provision for Travellers in Northern Ireland. Whilst the implementation of race relations legislation, itself a consequence of the campaign for Travellers' rights pursued from the mid-1980s onward, will introduce an element of legal protection, this measure continues to co-exist alongside those of assimilation and population transfer.

Hechter's theorisation of internal colonialism (1975:349–50) focused on an uneven pattern of development between core economic and cultural groups and those on the periphery. Although developed within the context of the British state and its relationship with its 'Celtic fringe', Hechter cites its applicability elsewhere to the situation of indigenous minority groups such as Amerindians in their relationship with the dominant Mestizos. He suggests three key variables by which an internal colony can be identified. First, there is the degree of administrative integration, the degree to which laws passed for the core apply to the periphery. Second, there is the extensiveness of citizenship in the periphery (including civil, political and social rights). Finally, there is the degree of geographical contiguity. A key characteristic of internal colonies is the existence of a cultural division of labour involving the assignation of individuals to specific types of occupations or other social roles on the basis of observable cultural traits or markers.

To what extent do the characteristics of the relationship between the Traveller community and sedentary society in Northern Ireland fit within the parameters of Hechter's model? Clearly, the balance of legal and administrative practice has been weighted in favour of the sedentary core communities. Travellers have not been provided with any legal rights which served to validate their way of life or, until the recent of race relations legislation, with even the most limited redress against discrimination. As noted above, administrative practice in relation to service provision was not historically concerned with including the Traveller community. Likewise, the rights of citizenship enjoyed by Travellers are clearly not as extensive as those taken for granted by the sedentary population. A prerequisite for the exercise of the right to vote is the possession of a fixed address. The discretionary nature of the legal powers concerning accommodation provision for Travellers and the limitations imposed by low levels of educational attainment on the ability of Travellers to participate in the political process are two further examples of the differential nature of citizenship. The distribution of the Traveller population throughout Northern Ireland is, generally speaking, contiguous with that of the sedentary population. Commercial nomads have a symbiotic relationship with the sedentary population, occupying an economic niche provided by opportunities to exploit occasional demands for goods and services by the majority population. However, the contiguous distribution of the Traveller population has been effected by the enforcement of designation which has led to the creation of nomad-free zones. A further factor concerning access to land also falls within the colonial paradigm. The expropriation of traditional camping sites used by Travellers, in the context of the more intensive use of both rural and urban land, has been implemented without any consideration of its effects on Travellers' way of life or examination of compensatory measures.

Ó Rian (1995:15–16) identifies the symptoms of colonisation in the existence of low self-worth and internalised oppression which can manifest itself in delinquency and lead to the breakdown of the fabric of Traveller society. He points to the similarities with overt colonialism: the enactment of legislation to prevent Travellers using their traditional land; the definition of Travellers themselves as the problem; the depiction of Travellers as an obstacle to progress and who can, at best, only be 'tolerated'; and the denial of their cultural identity or its characterisation as primitive, uncivilised or archaic. He suggests that the process of colonisation was probably not a premeditated, one-off act; rather, more likely, it is a gradual, seeping, cultural domination. The coloniser may not have come from a foreign land but transgressed instead across the border between nomadism and sedentarism.

Hawes and Perez examine the applicability of the term 'ethnic cleansing' to describe state policy in respect of the Gypsy and Traveller population, defining it as meaning 'the forced and wholesale removal of people, by reason of ethnicity, nationality or religion, from one place to another'. Whereas the phrase gained currency in the context of the Balkan civil war of the 1990s, the British variant is not pursued at the point of a gun, but through the enforcement of the law. Thus, through:

> mechanisms such as designation and the planning laws, through the failure of successive ministers to use the powers given them by parliament and through pressures to be assimilated set out in the Criminal Justice and Public Order Act 1994, a people who claim a common ethnicity are legally unable to pursue their way of life in vast tracts of Great Britain ... underlying British policy is an understated and somewhat ambiguous proposition that Gypsies should, in due course, become something other than nomadic ...
> (Hawes and Perez 1995:141)

The authors maintain that this is a new form of ethnic cleansing not previously envisaged. The cogency of this proposition is demonstrated in the access which it affords to rights which are basic to citizenship such as education, health care and social welfare. Such access is unattainable or at best precarious for Travellers without a site on which to stop legally.

Conclusion

Whilst the introduction of legal measures such as the Race Relations Order to provide protection against discrimination represents a starting point for reform, a more fundamental and far-reaching change is required. Following Davion's comments on black/white power relationships (in Anthias and Yuval-Davis 1992:135), this must involve the recognition that there is a contingent link between being a member of the sedentary community and promoting the superiority of sedentarism. Thus, it is not sufficient to simply believe in racial equality or even to consciously promote racial equality. What is required is a thorough scrutiny of and changes in those behaviours which may not appear on the surface to promote sedentary superiority but in fact keep a system of sedentarist supremacy in place.

A number of key initiatives have the potential to address the reproduction of the ideology and practice of sedentarist dominance. These are also broadly applicable to the prevention of racism and the reproduction of racist ideology generally. In the first instance, there is a need for the strengthening of race relations legislation along the lines suggested by the CRE's *Second Review* (1992). Second, the adoption of unequivocal anti-racist policies and the naming of Travellers within these by the full range of statutory agencies is imperative, followed by the implementation of affirmative action strategies whose progress should be measured against baseline data. The role of the education system is also vital, both to improve access for the Traveller community at all levels and to develop an intercultural approach which promotes an understanding of an respect for difference amongst all children, the citizens of the future. Closely associated with these measures is the development of equality proofing mechanisms, which will assess institutional policy making and practice for their potential to promote equality or generate further inequalities. In this context, it was suggested that the uneven implementation of the PAFT guidelines could be addressed by placing them on a statutory basis.

In this chapter, I have concentrated on the structural analysis of anti-Traveller racism and the campaign to assert rights. However, Kenny (1994:186) warns that an emphasis on undoing structural injustice and racism must also be accompanied by a celebration of identity. Whilst statements of victimage are useful and necessary strategic tools, they do not alone provide a healthy basis for a sense of identity for Travellers. There are some signs that the imperative of celebration of identity is beginning to be addressed: the path-breaking wall mural painted in 1996 by young Travellers in Andersonstown; participation of Travellers in the 1996 and 1997 West Belfast *Féile an Phobail* (Community Festival); cultural awareness days organised by Travellers' Support Groups in Armagh, Craigavon and Derry; the Belfast-based studio, Northern Visions' television documentary *Travelling People* – devoted almost entirely to the opinions of Travellers themselves and shown on Channel 4/RTE (1991) – and the DENI initiative on the development of intercultural curricular materials. More of this type of contribution needs to be resourced.

Finally, the above account has been an account from a non-Traveller perspective. While it may serve to provide some challenge to the hegemony of sedentarist analysis, it is not a substitute for the voice of the Traveller community. The crucial task for all those concerned with the present and future rights of the Traveller community must be to afford them the means to become actors in their own liberation. In the first instance, this means listening, as Kenny (1994:185) points out, and providing 'opportunities to undo internal and internalised colonialism, we must return to them [Travellers] the space to come to terms with their experience and to find their voice'. Second, this process of ethno-development does not just imply the legal restriction of anti-Traveller discrimination, but also the positive resourcing of Traveller culture and values, particularly nomadism. The development of the Irish Travellers' Movement in the Republic has taken place against a background of over 20 years of state-funded culturally specific training provision. The equivalent provision in Northern Ireland is notable by its absence. In conclusion, it is evident that the widespread practice of exclusion and assimilation against Gypsies and Travellers over some 500 years of European history has proved fruitless. As Liégeois (1994:122) comments: 'The multiplication of rules and regulations over five centuries is proof of the entirely relative effectiveness of such measures: Gypsies and Travellers have not, despite being ordered by decree to do so, disappeared.' Surely, it is time to pursue a more constructive approach which, in the succinct slogan of the recent Council of Europe campaign against racism, recognises that we are 'all different, all equal'.

Note

1   In March 1998, the NICTP changed its name to Traveller Movement (Northern Ireland).

9 The Indian Community in Northern Ireland

Greg Irwin

At present, assessing the demographic status of ethnic minorities living in Northern Ireland is problematic. There was no question on ethnic status in the Census of Population for Northern Ireland in 1991. Against this background, Irwin and Dunn (1997), in two major surveys of the main ethnic minority groups in Northern Ireland in 1995–96, presented a range of information which gave an insight into their demographic, social and economic status. Unless otherwise stated, this chapter is based on the information derived from these surveys of ethnic minorities in Northern Ireland.

One of the initial difficulties in conducting research based on the position of ethnic groups in a Northern Ireland context is the use of the term 'ethnic'. There is much dispute as to the use of the label 'ethnic' and to whom it applies. Common indicators of ethnicity include attributes such as a common culture, complex relations of kinship and shared territorial attachments. Based on these attributes alone one could classify, as many have done, the Protestant and Catholic communities in Northern Ireland as groups engaged in ethnic conflict. Yet, whilst the arguments will continue about the use of the word 'ethnic', there is no disputing the point that the term is usually applied to those who are non-white in a UK context. The development of the term 'ethnic' has been linked to the redundancy of 'race' as a concept with its biological and ideological stereotypes. Even so, the claims for 'ethnicity' grounded in self-definition of a collectivity's members have been undermined by what Mason sees as the 'tendency for the term "ethnic" to refer only to those who are thought of as different from some assumed indigenous norm' (1995:13).

It should be stressed, from the outset, that the use of the term 'ethnic minority' in this chapter is important and deliberate. First, the chapter refers to 'ethnic minorities' rather than 'racial minorities', in recognition of the aforesaid redundancy of 'race' as a concept (Barry and Tischler 1978; Miles 1989). Second, the concept of ethnicity seeks here to challenge the assimilationist assumptions connected with

184

'race', and accepts the permanence of the ethnic groups in question (Mason 1995). Finally, the use of ethnic minority is important as a flexible construct which also allows self-definition. In this way, it has positive ramifications for ethnic groups and, as Michael Banton (1983:103) comments, 'the former (ethnic group) reflects the positive tendencies of identification and inclusion where the latter (race) reflects the negative tendencies of dissociation and exclusion'.

It is important to state also that, although this chapter will refer to the Indian community in Northern Ireland, the use of the term 'community' is not without its shortcomings. Central to these shortcomings are attributes concerned with having a common habitat, a common interest and sense of belonging, and a degree of social interaction. It is accepted that there may be Indians living in Northern Ireland who do not conform to these elements of what is termed a 'community'. The term 'Indian community' is, therefore, used here as a generic label to denote those who have classified themselves as being of Indian ethnic status.

The Indian Community in Britain

The mass migration of Indians to Britain occurred in the 1950s and 1960s. Robinson (1996:95) has pointed out the key reasons for this migration: the attraction of higher wage levels and job vacancies in the British manufacturing industry being synchronised with the availability of cheaper travel from India, population pressure within the subcontinent, and the 'development of a powerful localised social momentum in certain villages, which saw peasants leaving simply because they felt everyone else was'. Thereafter, population growth was through the process of 'chain migration', which was subsequently replicated in the movement of Indians from Britain to Northern Ireland (Kapur 1997).

Yet, in the 1960s and 1970s, Indian immigration into Britain entered a new phase. Not only was the difference quantitative – successive legislative changes after 1962 applied the brakes on immigration from the New Commonwealth – but also there were qualitative differences. There is no doubt that those Indians participating in the initial mass migration were diverse in terms of social and economic status; for instance, Smith (1977) points out that many Indians were not highly educated and some had a poor grasp of English. The effect of successive restrictive legislation, added to economic recession in Britain in the 1970s, was to gradually professionalise Indian immigration (Robinson 1996:96). This had an effect on the social and economic status of those migrating to Northern Ireland, since Britain was the initial entry point for Indians coming to the UK. The net outcome of this professionalisation of the Indian community, in tandem with the existing entre-preneurial orientation of many, but not all, members of this ethnic group, has been a rise in their overall social and economic status. Peach (1996) suggests that the rising fortunes of Britain's Indian community are consistent with a 'Jewish' model of development, with a strong white-collar and self-employed bias, and owner occupier status. In a Northern Ireland context, as Marger (1989) points out, the shortage of unskilled jobs during the 1970s and 1980s prevented the migration of non-bourgeois Indians from other cities in the UK. Political violence also affected migration of Indians into Northern Ireland, while members of the Indian community left the region at the height of the political unrest in the 1970s (Kapur 1997).

The profile of the Indian community today reflects its well-established presence in Britain. The status of Indians in Britain as members of an ethnic minority is borne out by demographic characteristics such as the higher average household size and age profile, which is younger than that of the white population. There are, however, signs that Indians are moving away from characteristics which some commen-tators have associated with their ethnic minority status. The spatial distribution of Indians is now more diffuse, the large gender differ-entials that characterised their immigrant status are now more balanced (Robinson 1996:98), and Indian families have a mean number of dependent children which is closer to figures for the white population than to other ethnic minorities, such as Pakistanis or Bangladeshis (Owen 1994:9). Economic success by many Indians further demonstrates the unique progress of Indians living in Britain, which may yet have impli-cations for their cultural identities (Modood *et al.* 1994).

The Indian Community in Northern Ireland: Historical Development and Characteristics

The contrast between the development of the Indian communities in Northern Ireland and in Britain is significant. There were 295 households and just over 1,000 members of the Indian community living in Northern Ireland in 1995. In Britain, the Indian community is the largest ethnic minority group with 840,000 members, according to the 1991 Census. This relatively large population base and factors such as strong entrepreneurial instincts have seen the Indian community make a significant impact in social, economic and cultural areas of British society. The economic success story of some members of the Indian community in Britain is well documented (Owen 1994; Robinson 1996) in this respect, and the economic profile of Indians living in Northern Ireland is similar to the experience in the rest of the UK. Noticeably, though, the occupational status of Indians living in Britain is much more diverse than is the case with the same ethnic group living in Northern Ireland.

Unlike most other ethnic minority groups living in Northern Ireland, a historical overview of the development of the Indian community shows its relative longevity in the region. There are Indians living in Northern Ireland who have been there for over 60 years. Also, the patterns of settlement of the Indian community reflect the strong ties that have been built up in specific areas of Northern Ireland, such as in the north-west, and emphasise the high level of integration with the general population. Indians have a social and economic profile which points simultaneously to attributes that are similar to other ethnic minority groups, such as family type and country of birth, and characteristics such as age, which reflect – on the other hand – the degree of longevity and relative integration. Some economic indicators show that the Indian community may be regarded as among one of the more prosperous sections of the population in Northern Ireland. Some members of the Indian community are well-established leaders in various professions in Northern Ireland. Running parallel to this has been a growing awareness of the race relations issue in the region. Indians are concerned about the need to eradicate racial discrimination but recent research has reflected a scepticism about attempts to check this bias, and many members of the community are worried that the introduction of race relations legislation will actually lead to a rise in racial prejudice.

Kapur (1997) traces the historical development of the Indian community in Northern Ireland. The closely knit structure of the community has been significant. Many of the immigrants came from the same village and, ironically, many came to Northern Ireland to escape the communal conflict in India, and what was to later become Pakistan (after 1947). Most of the original Indian settlers in Northern Ireland came from northern India, from the states of Punjab and Gujarat, with a minority originating from southern India, and urban areas in other parts of the subcontinent (MCRC 1996).

Many of the early Indian immigrants were involved in door-to-door selling of goods, and, as Kapur points out, the success of this enterprise was based on the mobility of the salesmen, the credit facilities offered, and the market for the clothes. This tendency to concentrate in a specific occupational area was largely due to the chain migration process (Marger 1989), wherein members of the Indian community would follow friends or family and migrate to a new home. The first Indian high street retailer opened in Londonderry, in 1943, starting a trend which led to the opening of other outlets, particularly in the north-west region. The emphasis on the clothing trade is still a characteristic of the Indian community in Northern Ireland, but other types of retail provision – such as catering – have seen substantial growth. As in Britain, a proportion of the restaurants are owned and staffed by Bangladeshis. The recent growth of Indian catering outlets in towns throughout Northern Ireland has demonstrated both the entrepreneurial nature of the Indian community, and the more cosmopolitan eating habits of the local populace.

Members of the Indian community today figure prominently in a number of professions. The traditional association with the medical profession continues with Indians working as general practitioners, house doctors and consultants throughout the region. An Overseas Doctors Association has been recently formed as a networking facility for Asian doctors throughout Northern Ireland. In commerce too, Indians have risen to prominence and, in 1992, a well-known and economically very successful member of the community, Diljit Rana, was elected President of the Belfast Chamber of Commerce.

Like the general population, the Indian community has been exposed to political violence in Northern Ireland. In the early 1970s, for instance, two restaurants – belonging to Diljit Rana – were destroyed in terrorist bombings (in 1974) and a young Indian, Asha Chopra, was killed by crossfire between security forces and the Irish Republican Army (IRA) in Londonderry. Kapur estimates that as many as six Indian families left Northern Ireland at this time. More recently, an analysis of immigration into Northern Ireland (Irwin and Dunn 1997) reveals that there was a significant drop-off in the numbers of Indians coming to the region in 1986, when political violence in the aftermath of the Anglo-Irish Agreement was at its height. Nevertheless, there is no doubt that the overall profile of the Indian community has risen within Northern Ireland over the years, and its cultural presence was symbolised by the opening of the Indian Community Centre in Belfast in 1982. Whilst the Indian Community Centre is used for religious worship by the majority Hindu Indians (see Table 9.1), an Islamic centre was opened in 1986 catering for Muslims. In the early 1990s, moreover, members of the Sikh community purchased a former primary school in Londonderry and converted it into a temple or 'gurdwara'.

Table 9.1: Religious affiliation of the Indian community in Northern Ireland (%)

Hindu	78
Sikh	7
Islam	5
Christian	3
Other	1
None	6

N = 134

The Demography of the Indian Community in Northern Ireland

A lack of official demographic information has prevented policy makers and statutory bodies in Northern Ireland from being able to make informed policy decisions and plan resource allocation for ethnic groups living in the region. Work by Irwin and Dunn in 1995–96 elicited important information on the position of the main ethnic minorities in Northern Ireland – the Chinese, Indian, Pakistani and Traveller. These surveys concluded that ethnic minorities make up to 1 per cent of the total population of the region, and that these groups have significant demographic attributes which make them different from the general population. Ethnic minorities in Northern Ireland have relatively large households, are younger, have significant numbers born outside the region, are geographically concentrated, and have a greater rate of population growth compared to the general population.

The surveys (Irwin and Dunn 1997) revealed two perhaps contradictory features about the Indian community in Northern Ireland: first, the Indian community is more like other ethnic minorities in the region than like the general population; second, contrary to this, is the impression from the data that the Indian community in Northern Ireland is also more distinct from other ethnic groups in the region than like them. This is not only in terms of quantifiable findings, as will be shown below, but it is also from the views of the Indian community, which seem frequently at variance with the opinions of other ethnic groups.

Table 9.2: Persons per household by ethnic group (%)

	General population	Ethnic groups[1]	Indian
1 Person	25	9	10
2 Persons	27	14	21
3 Persons	16	17	18
4 Persons	17	24	25
5 Persons	9	16	16
6 persons	6	20	10

Note: [1] Chinese, Indian, Pakistani and Traveller communities combined.

Source: General population: PPRU (1995).

Indians do have a larger average household size than the general population. This is largely explained by the high incidence of extended families within households and, to a lesser extent, by factors such as higher fertility rates, and the temporary hosting by Indian homes of recent migrants into Northern Ireland. Although Indian households are larger than the general population and are less likely to contain only one person, other ethnic groups living in Northern Ireland have bigger households again. Table 9.2 shows that, compared to other ethnic minorities in Northern Ireland, Indian households are more likely to contain only two persons also, and are less likely to have over six persons.

One of the key variables differentiating the Indian community from other ethnic minorities in Northern Ireland, and which points to their relative longevity in the region, is age. Like other ethnic minorities, Indians tend to have a larger proportion of their population in the prime working age (16–44 years) category (Table 9.3). Aside from this category, however, the age profile of the Indian community in Northern Ireland is closer to that of the general population than to that of other ethnic minorities. Table 9.3 shows that Indians living in Northern Ireland have a smaller proportion of members in the youngest age category than do the general population, while the comparison is exact for the school age (5–15 years) category. What is perhaps most significant of all, is the finding which shows that Indians have a much greater proportion of members in the three oldest age categories than do the other ethnic groups. As with Britain (Owen 1994), the Indian community in Northern Ireland has a relatively higher proportion of pensioners than is the case with the other ethnic minorities, and Robinson (1996) has pointed to the comparable age profile as an indicator of the narrowing of differences between Indians and the white population.

Table 9.3: Age category comparisons by ethnic group (%)*

	General population	Ethnic groups[1]	Indian
0–4 years	8	11	6
5–15 years	18	25	18
16–44 years	42	50	49
45–59 years (female); 45–64 years (male)	18	12	22
60–79 years (female) 65–79 years (male)	12	3	5
Over 80 years	3	**	1

Notes: [1] Chinese, Indian, Pakistani and Traveller communities combined.
  * Column percentages may not add up to 100 due to rounding.
  ** Indicates less than 1 per cent.

Source: General Population: OPCS (1995).

Analysing age by country of birth further illustrates the relative longevity of the Indian community in Northern Ireland. The greatest proportion of those Indians born elsewhere (that is, those born outside the UK or the Republic of Ireland) are now in the 45–64 years age category, which is unlike the profile of any of the other ethnic minorities studied. At one end of the spectrum, 49 per cent of the Chinese community born in Northern Ireland are now in the school-age category, compared to the 34 per cent of Indians at the other extremity of the range.

Compared to Britain, the country of birth of those Indians living in Northern Ireland is less diverse. A much greater proportion of Indians in Northern Ireland were born in the UK, Pakistan and India. By contrast, the proportion of Indians born in the 'Other' category – that is born *outside* either the UK, India or Pakistan – is much greater in Britain. In Britain, whilst 17 per cent of Indians, for instance, were born in East Africa, there are only 4 per cent of the Indian community in Northern Ireland whose birthplace is classified as 'Other'. The family structure of the Indian community reflects the older age profile when compared to other ethnic minorities in Northern Ireland. Indian households are more likely to contain three or more adults, which is explained mostly by the higher incidence of non-dependent children compared to other ethnic groups. Only a third of Indian households in Northern Ireland are categorised as containing a 'married-couple family with dependent children' compared with as many as 65 per cent of Traveller homes.

What is distinctive about the settlement patterns of the Indian community in Northern Ireland, compared to other ethnic minorities, is the bimodal distribution. Indians are concentrated in the north-west and the Belfast areas of Northern Ireland. Table 9.4 divides Northern Ireland into three areas and emphasises the difference between the Indian community and other ethnic minorities, particularly when the Traveller community is excluded from the comparison. Over seven in ten Indians lived in the Belfast and west Northern Ireland areas, compared to just over half of Chinese and less than half of the Pakistani community.

Table 9.4: Distribution of ethnic groups by area (%)[*]

	Chinese	Indian	Pakistani	Traveller
East Northern Ireland[1]	45	28	59	5
Belfast	41	36	34	35
West Northern Ireland	14	35	7	61

Notes: [1] 'East Northern Ireland' refers to all of the district councils east of the river Bann, except Moyle and Newry and Mourne; 'Belfast' is the Belfast City council area; and 'West Northern Ireland' consists of the other district councils.
[*] Column percentages may not add up to 100 due to rounding.

Although Northern Ireland still has a low proportion of its population from ethnic minority groups, due to factors such as barriers on immigration – including political violence and the physical separation between the region and the rest of the UK – the population of the Indian community, like other ethnic minorities, is growing at a rate in excess of the general population. Between 1984 and 1992, the annual average growth for the total population of Northern Ireland was 0.6 per cent (PPRU 1995); in the same period, the Indian community in the region had a yearly growth of 3.4 per cent. In the 1950s and early 1960s, the Indian community was the largest ethnic minority in Northern Ireland, but around the mid-1960s the Chinese community became the largest ethnic minority in the region. Table 9.5 analyses the year of entry of those ethnic minorities born outside Northern Ireland, and shows the considerable and consistent growth of the Chinese community. Over half of the Chinese community born elsewhere have come to live in Northern Ireland in the past decade. What is interesting about the immigration patterns of the Indian community, in the past four years, is the arresting of a 20-year decline in the number of Indian immigrants coming to Northern Ireland. Analysis of the occupational class, for instance, of those entering Northern Ireland in the past four years provides no clues as to reasons for the increase in the number of Indian immigrants, and it is a matter of speculation regarding an explanation of this phenomenon. Marger (1989) argued that restrictive immigration practices and concentration in specific roles by the Indian community would hinder future population growth. Any future growth, Marger continued, would only come from migration to Northern Ireland from other parts of the UK. Social disruption and the economic decline associated with deindustrialisation in Northern Ireland, it was further contended, would prevent population growth. While the data do not allow analysis of the migration of Indians from Britain to

Table 9.5: Years living in Northern Ireland by ethnic group (respondents born elsewhere) (%)[*]

Years in Northern Ireland	Chinese	Indian	Pakistani
0–4 years	29	21	15
5–10 years	22	7	17
11–15 years	17	9	16
16–20 years	15	9	18
21–25 years	7	17	15
26–30 years	7	12	7
Over 31 years	2	25	12

Note: [*] Column percentages may not add up to 100 due to rounding.

Northern Ireland, the relatively significant numbers of this community entering the region in the past five years conflicts with Marger's predictions. It seems possible that the onset of recession in Britain in the late 1980s, the continuing shortage of skilled professionals (in medicine, for instance), the relatively low house prices (until very recently) and rising investment in business may have been economic factors in attracting Indians to Northern Ireland.

The Economic Success of Indians in Northern Ireland

Most Indians have prospered economically living in Northern Ireland. Many of the factors which mark the success of the Indian community in Britain explain this ethnic group's advancement in Northern Ireland. Indians have exploited gaps in the market in areas such as textile retailing and catering, and the bias towards professionally qualified immigrants entering the UK in the 1970s, which has been noted as an outcome of more restrictive immigration legislation, would have affected those entering Northern Ireland. This entrepreneurial orientation and professional achievement means that the Indian community in Northern Ireland is characterised by economic success – high levels of home ownership, high rates of employment, a dispro-portionate number of members in the upper occupational classes and relative educational success.

As in Britain, rates of home ownership amongst the Indian community in Northern Ireland are higher than the general population. In Britain, two-thirds of the white population own their homes, compared to 82 per cent of Indians (Owen 1994:9). The Indian community in Northern Ireland has a higher rate of home ownership again, with 84 per cent in this category. Undoubtedly, most Indians are materially wealthy, and have the necessary purchasing power to buy their own homes but, as in Britain (Owen 1994), the Indian community is less likely to rent property compared to other ethnic groups. Only 3 per cent of Indian households in Northern Ireland, for instance, are resident in public rented accommodation.

One indicator of housing quality, concerned with overcrowding – defined in terms of one or more persons per room – further points to the economic wealth of the Indian community. Table 9.6 reflects the degree of overcrowding in homes amongst particularly the Chinese and Traveller communities. Indian households are less likely than any other group to experience overcrowding, and the feedback from survey interviews used by Irwin and Dunn (1997) emphasised the large and frequently prosperous homes in which members of this community live.

Table 9.6: Density of occupation (persons per room) by ethnic group (%)*

	General population	Ethnic groups	Chinese	Indian	Pakistani	Traveller
>1.5 persons	2	29	31	2	3	61
1 to 1.5 persons	9	30	39	11	41	25
0.75 to 1 person	27	13	10	13	30	5
0.5 to 0.75 persons	37	18	15	41	14	7
< 0.5 persons	26	10	4	33	12	2
N	1554538	694	259	136	116	183

Note: *Column percentages may not add up to 100 due to rounding.
Source: General population: DHSS (1992).

Although the economic success of the Indian community is demonstrated by a series of indicators, the area of employment reflects the achievements of Asians as a whole in Northern Ireland. Like the Chinese and Pakistani communities, Indians in Northern Ireland have high proportions in employment, are more likely than the general population to be self-employed, and are less likely to be in part-time employment. One of the key determinants with regard to labour market participation – particularly in terms of pointing to evidence of structural inequalities – is the rate of economic activity, which is divided into two categories: the economically active (those in employment or actively seeking employment), and the economically inactive (such as students, retired people, the long-term sick and those looking after the home). In comparison with the general population, the proportion of economically active Indians – and Chinese and Pakistanis – is favourable (Table 9.7).

Table 9.7: Economic activity by ethnic group (%)

	General population	Ethnic groups	Chinese	Indian	Pakistani	Traveller
Economically active	58	64	80	62	59	47
Economically inactive	42	36	20	38	41	53
N	1167938	719	262	142	122	193

Source: General population: DHSS (1992).

Two further key economic indicators demonstrate the distinct success of the Indian community in Northern Ireland compared to both the general population and other ethnic minorities. First, the educational attainment of Indians is superior with 37 per cent of Indians questioned having achieved a degree qualification (Table 9.8). Interestingly, although the numbers are quite small, a quarter of those Indians interviewed who were born in Northern Ireland had also attained an educational qualification to degree level.

Table 9.8: Educational level by highest qualification by ethnic category (%)*

	General population	Ethnic groups	Chinese	Indian	Pakistani	Traveller
Degree level or higher	6	14	11	37	17	1
BTEC (Higher), HND, HNC	2	2	1	5	3	–
GCE A-Level	6	7	7	13	8	1
BTEC (National), ONC, OND	2	1	1	4	2	–
GCSE, GCE O-Level	16	12	11	14	21	6
CSE (other than grade 1)	3	2	1	1	7	1
No formal qualification	65	27	14	19	27	50
Other formal qualifications	–	35	54	8	15	42
N	1167938	722	264	142	122	194

Note:* Column percentages may not add up to 100 due to rounding.
Source: General population: DHSS (1992).

Table 9.9: Occupational class for the economically active population by ethnic group (%)*

	General population	Ethnic groups	Chinese	Indian	Pakistani	Traveller
Professional	3	5	1	16	11	–
Managerial/technical	19	24	24	49	22	1
Skilled (non-manual)	17	10	2	23	28	1
Skilled (manual)	17	19	35	3	7	7
Partly skilled	13	9	16	1	4	1
Unskilled	6	2	1	–	1	6
Other[1]	4	15	18	5	19	13
No paid job within last ten years	21	16	2	3	7	70
N	1167938	483	223	91	72	97

Note: [1] 'Other' in this classification includes those who are unemployed seeking work who have had a job in the last ten years, those on government employment or training schemes, and those with not enough information to classify in the other categories. This does not include those classified as retired.
    * Column percentage may not add up to 100 due to rounding.
Source: General population: DHSS (1992).

Related to the variable of educational attainment, is undoubtedly that of occupational status. Indians in Northern Ireland are disproportionately concentrated in the highest occupational classes (Table 9.9). This finding is very much in accordance with the class profile of Indians in Britain, unlike in the rest of the UK, but there is not a disproportionate number of Indians in the skilled manual category. Undoubtedly, this finding points to the unique professional and merchant bias that was discussed earlier, and also reflects the relatively small numbers of Indians working in service provision when compared to Britain. This state of affairs may well change with increasing numbers of Indians entering Northern Ireland in recent years. Also, the significant rise in the number of catering outlets providing Indian food, for instance, may contribute to an increase in the number of skilled manual workers within this community.

Conclusion

The Indian community is probably one of the more economically successful sections of society living in Northern Ireland. The relative economic success of many of its members is undoubtedly similar to that experienced by Indians living in Britain, although the occupational class profile is even more skewed to the professional and managerial classes. Indians do have similarities with other ethnic groups in Northern Ireland, not least to do with employment characteristics and certain demographic attributes. Yet there is evidence to suggest that the Indian community is in some way – as in Britain – losing its shared characteristics with other ethnic minorities. In Britain, this has been demonstrated in terms of spatial diffusion and decreasing family size as well as economic advancement, and these factors and others are becoming apparent with regard to the Indian community in Northern Ireland.

Developments with regard to race relations legislation in Northern Ireland may have further effects on the demography of the Indian community in the region. It is clear, however, from the work completed by Irwin and Dunn (1997), that Indians are sceptical about the positive effect of race relations legislation, and some Indians expressed fears that, in highlighting the whole issue of racism, there was a danger of increasing racial bigotry.

10 'Because you Stick out, you Stand out': Perceptions of Prejudice Among Northern Ireland's Pakistanis[1]

Hastings Donnan and Mairead O'Brien

I was with a friend, a Pakistani guy and he told me how this fella asked him, 'Are you Catholic or Protestant?' He said: 'Neither, I'm Muslim.' 'But are you a Catholic or Protestant Muslim?' You hear that type of thing as a joke, but you don't really believe that people say those things, you think they're only jokes.

Like its template, this variant of the old 'joke' about the Catholic Jew/Protestant Jew is unlikely to elicit more than a tired groan, but as evidence of a local sensitivity (even if not explicitly articulated) to the plight of a minority group in a society pervasively divided between Catholic and Protestant, it is still suggestive. Jews have a much longer association with Northern Ireland (see Chapter 11) than the Pakistani Muslims who are the subject of this chapter, although as the quotation above indicates the 'joke' has apparently retained its appeal, albeit in an updated form where 'Jew' is variously substituted by 'Muslim', 'Sikh' or 'Hindu'. Moreover, and whatever we think about the value of its wit, the joke does draw attention to the particularity of the circumstances in which ethnic minorities in Northern Ireland must live their lives. It would seem to raise questions about where and how ethnic minorities 'fit' into a deeply divided society, and even about whether or not they can be fitted in at all.

To what extent do these circumstances really make a difference? How far do they differentiate the experiences of Pakistanis in Northern Ireland from those of Pakistanis elsewhere in the United Kingdom? Do they have a bearing on the kinds of occupations which local Pakistanis enter, on where they are educated and, in particular, on their experiences of prejudice? By considering some of the similarities and differences between Pakistanis in Northern Ireland and those in Britain,

197

we suggest that the experiences of the former, as an ethnic minority, are as much shaped by their comparatively small numbers and geographical and occupational dispersal as by the challenges of living in a divided society. While Pakistanis in Northern Ireland must clearly adapt and respond to wider political circumstances, as must everyone else in the Province, to put too much emphasis on these circumstances would risk attributing to Northern Irish Pakistanis a uniqueness and specificity within the UK's Pakistani population which, at least from our material, it is not clear they possess. Such an emphasis is likely to overlook the fact that Northern Ireland is an area of secondary settlement for this population, most of whom migrated to Northern Ireland from Britain and who remain in close contact with South Asians still living there. So although the conflict in the wider society does affect them in ways we indicate below, we should not over-emphasise its influence on their lives and thus obscure the continuities and commonalities and indeed, the other sorts of difference, with Pakistanis in Britain.

Throughout the 1970s and 1980s, social researchers began to take a greater interest in Britain's growing Pakistani population, and a body of literature directed towards understanding Pakistani culture and society began to emerge. This did not happen in Northern Ireland, where the attentions of local and foreign researchers and media were understandably drawn to the dramatic political events of the day and where, in contrast to the rest of the UK, Pakistanis were anyway small in number and residentially dispersed. Thus, amidst the voluminous writings on Northern Ireland's 'troubles', scarcely a mention is made of the Pakistanis who live there. This marginalisation and virtual invisibility of Pakistanis in local academic and journalistic discourse led to their being referred to, where they were mentioned at all, somewhat uncritically as the Pakistani 'community', a term with implications of common identification, values, associations, perspective, and patterns of interaction, and one which continues to (mis)inform popular understandings of local ethnicities. The diversity and heterogeneity of backgrounds and interests of Northern Ireland's Pakistani Muslims that we describe below have seemed to militate against the development of any well-defined commonality of interest, and so question the value of such a description.[2] We suggest in this chapter that Pakistani ethnicity, and by implication other local ethnicities, must be understood from within as well as from beyond the ethnic category, for it is in the interaction between internal differentiation and outside domination that the specific form of an ethnic identity is forged. We begin by sketching the context and historical background of Pakistani migration to Northern Ireland.

History of Migration

Pakistani Muslims are but one component of a wider South Asian population in Northern Ireland which includes Sikh and Hindu migrants from Pakistan, India and Bangladesh, as well as Muslim migrants from these countries. While estimates vary as to the size of these populations, there appears to be approximately 1,000–1,500 Hindus and Sikhs, and approximately 600–700 Pakistani Muslims in addition to the small number of other locally resident Muslims from outside the Indian subcontinent (Marger 1989:205; O'Leary 1990:4; Irwin 1996:21–2; Ryan n.d.:100, 113). Northern Ireland's Muslims thus constitute a heterogeneous population in terms of country of origin, not to mention urban or rural background, migratory experience, religious sect, gender, age, geographical location within the Province, occupation, educational qualifications and language. Labels such as 'South Asian' and 'Muslim' therefore always require qualification to reflect this diversity.

South Asian migration to Northern Ireland cannot be understood in isolation. One integral component of contemporary local South Asian identity is a history of diaspora. Few South Asians came to the Province directly from the subcontinent. Some first migrated within the Indian subcontinent prior to migration to Britain, while others left East Africa (from where they were expelled as a result of post-independence policies of Africanisation) for Britain before subsequently migrating to Ireland.[3] Many locally resident Pakistanis have thus had a previous migratory experience in Britain, and their internal migration within the UK must be seen against this backdrop. Mass migration to Britain from the Indian subcontinent began after the Second World War, when migrants were employed to replace the upwardly mobile indigenous population in the manufacturing industries as part of Britain's economic restructuring. Some came to escape political conflict and instability, particularly following the partition of India in 1947 (Allen 1971; Jeffery 1976; Anwar 1979). Migrants arrived in Britain from all over Pakistan, though chiefly from the Punjab, Azad Kashmir and, to a lesser extent, from the North West Frontier Province. These areas had strong colonial links with Britain and historically had provided recruits for the Merchant Navy and the British Army.

Changes to the structure of employment from the 1970s onwards and subsequent economic recession led to the closure of many manufacturing industries and to high levels of unemployment among Pakistanis in Britain. While Northern Ireland was not immune from these forces, increasing numbers began to cross the Irish Sea in search of work, encouraged by the handful of Pakistanis already employed there and by the fact that, as part of the United Kingdom, entry was unrestricted. As with the earlier migration to Britain, the men arrived

first, and were joined by their families only once employment and accommodation had been found. Northern Ireland's limited and declining
industrial base and the migrants' earlier negative experiences of working
in heavy industry stimulated self-employment, particularly in jobs for
which they could draw on contacts in Britain, such as the 'rag trade'.
Some migrants became very successful, and this encouraged further
movement to the Province. Economic motives for migration were
reinforced by kinship ties, as families sought to reunite and as parents
sought spouses for their children in Pakistan, encouraged by a cultural
preference for marriage between cousins (cf. Ballard 1987:27).

Professionals have migrated to Northern Ireland in somewhat
smaller numbers, and estimates suggest that they constitute not much
more than about a quarter of the local Pakistani population. In certain
respects, the migration of professionals has followed a rather different
pattern to that described above in so far as most of them came directly
from Pakistan and only rarely had existing kin ties in the Province on
which they could draw for support. Moreover, they came initially not
to find employment, but to obtain qualifications (mainly as doctors,
engineers or teachers), attracted by high educational standards or the
promise of a university or college scholarship. While some returned
to Pakistan on completion of their studies, the eventual offer of a job
and the promise of a higher standard of living encouraged others to
stay and have their families join them.

Pakistanis in Northern Ireland

The varied history of migration already suggests that to refer to
Northern Irish Pakistanis as a 'community' risks a sociological reduc-
tionism which flattens out their many differences. Not only did they
bring with them the varied cultural and regional backgrounds and
migratory experiences alluded to above but, as one would expect,
occupation, education, and socio-economic position have all affected
in different ways their involvement in Northern Irish society. Here we
offer a brief sketch of such diversity and its implications.

The majority of Pakistanis in Northern Ireland are involved in the
clothing, grocery or catering business. As in Britain, where reliance
on ethnic bonds as a source of cheap labour facilitated the development
of small businesses and a 'culture of entrepreneurship' (Werbner
1984) among South Asians – particularly in the garment trade – so in
Northern Ireland such employment was also based initially on these
ties. Self-employment was attractive for many reasons: educational qualifications were unnecessary; it was thought to enhance upward social
mobility; and it was believed to offer protection against the kinds of
racial discrimination which many had experienced in factories in

Britain. Moreover, employment in a family business made it easier to realise the cultural ideal of establishing and maintaining an extended household, since all household members could potentially be offered work and so contribute to the household's economic viability.

In the 1970s and early 1980s, settlement in Northern Ireland was characterised by residential and occupational clustering, as newly arrived migrants drew on kin and ethnic bonds for support. Encouraged by the apparent economic success of kin, by the comparatively low financial risks, and by the fact that little start-up capital was necessary, the market trade quickly became an important source of employment. Early migrant families, many but not all from villages in the Punjab, settled in Legahory in Craigavon, approximately 18 miles from Belfast and close to some of the Province's main market towns. It was, moreover, an area with a surplus of inexpensive housing. As these families grew in size and began to establish themselves, they increasingly sought other kinds of work. This occupational diversification was accompanied by geographical dispersal and, of the approximately 50 families (80 adults and 300 children) who had settled in Legahory, most have now moved out to the countryside or to the suburbs of Portadown, Bleary, Waringstown and Lurgan. This pattern was replicated right across the Province and, as in Legahory, was prompted partly by increasing commercial competition from other Pakistanis and the large high street chain stores, especially in the rag trade. As a result, some moved out of market trading into sectors with which they had not been previously associated, such as property development and the retail trade in ornaments and jewellery. Others expanded into catering, opening restaurants or fast food outlets. The residential dispersal of local Pakistanis can thus be understood partly as a means of pioneering new economic opportunities in the face of increased competition and partly as a means of upward mobility. To some extent, it parallels the experiences of Pakistanis in Britain where, as Werbner (1990a) explains, upward social mobility has similarly been associated with movement into self-employment and dispersal from the inner cities to the suburbs.

However, it would be misleading to imply that self-employment has been a fail-safe path to upward social mobility. Even among the small number of Pakistanis in Northern Ireland there are many variations in the size and viability of their businesses, which range from mobile kebab stalls to the ownership of a fashionable clothes store or sophisticated restaurant. As Cashmore and Troyna (1983:86–92) suggest for Britain, the apparent scale and success of Asian business can be deceptive, its seeming prosperity but a hollow façade, something certainly true of a number of local South Asian businesses forced to close their doors shortly after opening. While some local businesses have remained family based in an effort to deal with economic uncertainty, others have become major employers in the wider labour

market, maintaining wide-ranging economic and social contacts with
the majority population. Similarly, some suburban residences are
more sought after by the upwardly mobile than others, and a few local
Pakistani entrepreneurs have purchased homes which for most will only
ever be a dream. Divergent interests, social as well as economic, thus
characterise self-employed Pakistanis, and cannot always be readily
subsumed by a common ethnic bond, however things may look when
viewed from the 'outside'. Furthermore, not all local Pakistanis are
self-employed. We mentioned earlier that some are salaried professionals,
an occupational grouping likely to increase and diversify as second-
generation Pakistanis receive their education locally, and as they reject
the long hours required by work in family businesses. As salaried
employees, they have a different set of interests from those in self-
employment.[4]

The different interests and backgrounds of local Pakistanis, and the
difficulty of establishing a common project solely on the basis of
shared ethnic origin, is evident from the activities and composition of
their mosques and cultural centres, one in Belfast and another in
Craigavon. At the risk of over-simplification, the membership of the
Belfast Mosque and Islamic Centre might be described as being predominantly composed of professionals and shopkeepers/wholesalers
with large businesses in the Belfast area; in contrast, the Craigavon
Mosque and South Asian Women's and Children's Centre depends
chiefly for its members on market traders bound by bonds of kinship.
Although, overtly, a common identity as Muslims is foremost in both
places, and although all express a belief in the Muslim *umma*
('community of believers'), this conceals certain internal differences.

The Belfast Centre serves all Muslims in the Province of whatever
ethnic background, and emphasises their common Muslim faith rather
than the particular cultural traditions of each. Pakistani professionals,
many of whom live in South Belfast where the Centre is situated, occupy
a prominent role in the Centre's organisation and social networks. As
a result, some less well-educated local Pakistanis have felt excluded
and attempts to involve them by forming a committee with members
from different ethnic groups and occupations, as well as from each
gender, have had limited success since those elected are still predominantly professionals. This highlights the difficulties of ensuring
that the needs of different sections of the population are adequately
represented.

In contrast, the South Asian Women's and Children's Community
Centre in Craigavon, which despite its name has only Pakistani
members, is both more community focused and more closely oriented
to the particular welfare and cultural needs of the localised Pakistani
population, providing English-language courses and encouraging
contact with other non-Pakistani women's organisations. But even here

internal differences have led to disagreements. Unlike the Belfast Centre, which is self-financed through donations and so can determine its own programme, the Craigavon Centre depends on external funders, who since 1997 have appointed a Development Officer to oversee its affairs. Prior to this, a local Pakistani woman, who was externally funded as a lay health worker, acted as *de facto* organiser of the Centre's affairs. Attempts by this woman to politicise the membership by drawing public attention to racism in the area met with resistance from members, and led to questions about her ability to represent the other women. Similarly, her efforts to improve (as she saw it) the position of Pakistani women were resisted by both men and women for the challenge it was thought to pose to the culturally legitimated patriarchal authority embedded in the kinship system. Recent suggestions by some members that another mosque and centre be established closer to where they now live might thus be seen as a thinly veiled guise for justifying a split stemming from such internal dissension.

The ability of these two organisations to act as a potential focus for ethnic mobilisation would thus seem to be compromised to varying degrees by a number of factors ultimately rooted in the diverse characteristics of their memberships. Since not all local Muslims are Pakistanis, ethnic origin and religion do not neatly coincide. Moreover, differences in socio-economic position, as well as in attitudes about how Pakistanis should accommodate to their new surroundings, ensure that even the interests of the Pakistani Muslims in the Province rarely correspond.

Visibility and Vulnerability

As we have seen, the Pakistani population in Northern Ireland differs in certain important respects from that of Pakistanis in the rest of the UK. Northern Ireland Pakistanis do not constitute a residentially discrete and geographically bounded community, and so have no large ethnically identifiable neighbourhoods like those found in Britain in cities such as Bradford and Birmingham. Nor have Pakistanis clustered in occupations historically associated in Britain with a migrant Pakistani workforce, who found work mainly in the steel mills and other heavy engineering plants, industries largely absent in the Province. Furthermore, while the cultural and religious associations to which many local Pakistanis belong obviously encourage contact with other Pakistanis and with co-religionists, they usually mobilise only in relation to some major cultural or religious event and have not become the political pressure groups with the highly visible public presence which such associations have so often become in Britain. In these respects at least, Pakistanis in Northern Ireland have been less visible as an ethnically distinct element of the local population, and though apparently less encapsulated by the wider society than other ethnic minority populations in the Province, such as the Chinese (see Chapter 7), they have for the most part tried to keep themselves to themselves. Indeed, they have seemed to pursue this course almost as a matter of strategy, as many of the comments cited later suggest.

One consequence of attempting to maintain a low profile has been the tendency to remain silent about prejudice and racist abuse, partly for fear that the reporting of such experiences will only increase their frequency. This can be illustrated by reactions to a prime-time television programme which set out to describe racist attacks on ethnic minorities in Northern Ireland (*East*, BBC2, 17 April 1996). Local Pakistani response to the screening of the programme was generally negative, partly out of concern that it could lead to further recriminations and damage relations with the wider population upon which so many local Pakistani businesses depend, and partly on the grounds that it presented an unremittingly bleak picture of local Pakistani life. According to one young man, 'It was all bad things, negative things about it. It didn't say anything positive about the community in Northern Ireland.' In fact, another young Pakistani man even went so far as to suggest that the apparently forced removal of a Pakistani family from a local housing estate was not the result of racist attack as the programme claimed, but the planned departure of a household now financially in a position to build its own home. That the interpretation of such incidents can be contested in this way is a useful reminder that the labelling of a particular incident as 'racist' is itself a political act, one moreover which those most closely involved may not necessarily consider to be in their own best interests. Indeed, we have been acutely conscious of this fact when selecting the material to include in this chapter.

But even where the racist nature of a particular incident is not in dispute, it may pass unreported. As the following remarks made by three Pakistani men indicate, there is a feeling, especially among those Pakistanis living in Northern Ireland but born in Pakistan, that such experiences are a 'normal' and expected part of being a member of a minority ethnic group, an integral and inevitable element of the migrant experience, and thus not something which can be effectively addressed or dealt with. Such a view is reaffirmed by comparing experiences with friends and kin in Britain.

You'd expect it because you're different like you know, you're not the same as them. You really expect it ...

Sometimes, when you are coming out of a pub, someone will call out to you 'nigger'. Racism is within people and you will find that racism is here just as it is in England; it is rife here.

It's like you know, when you're growing up with it [racism] all your life you sort of get used to it, you get habituated to it. When you're asking someone they just consider that as normal, people's attitudes, so we say we don't experience any racism, whereas you would probably put a comment that we just brushed aside, you'd put that down as being racism.

Although such opinions are also sometimes expressed by the younger generation, they are not so widely held by them, and we shall see later that Pakistanis born in Northern Ireland, or who grew up in Britain before moving there, less readily acquiesce to this 'normalisation' of prejudice than do their elders.

Structural factors also tend to inhibit the reporting of prejudice. Residential dispersal has meant that there have not been the neighbourhood watch schemes or vigilante groups set up to protect localities from racist abuse as there have been in Britain. Nor has there been the political organisation necessary to publicise such abuse, and to recruit concerted support against it. This absence of a collective and organised response to combating racism again demonstrates the limited and contested sense of community among Pakistanis and reflects the difficulties of establishing communal structures and agreeing on individuals who can represent the interests of this small but diverse population.[5] Thus many local Pakistanis were sceptical of the motives of those individuals who took part in the television programme mentioned above, questioning their right to present themselves as somehow representative of the majority of Pakistanis living in Northern Ireland.

The tendency to under-report racist abuse has also been related to the absence of protective legislation in Northern Ireland and to a perceived lack of support from the police, either because of the latter's powerlessness to deal effectively with complaints or because, in some instances, of a lack of trust in the local constabulary and a disbelief in their willingness to help (cf. Irwin 1996:63–4). The introduction of race relations legislation into Northern Ireland in 1997 is set to change this state of affairs. Much of the Draft Order approved in 1996 mirrors the Race Relations Act (1976) in Britain, and under Article 3 refers to 'racial discrimination' as a special category of offence (Race Relations (NI) Order 1996:7–8). It has also enabled the creation of a Commission for Racial Equality for Northern Ireland, charged with enforcing the legislation, and which should assist in bringing cases to court (see Chapter 4). While this new legislation might make it easier to pursue matters through the courts, by encouraging disclosure of racially prejudiced behaviour where this is an element in a specific offence, it is something about which many local Pakistanis feel sceptical and ambivalent. Thus they refer to the existence of widespread racism in Britain which, they point out, race relations legislation has done little to curb. Moreover, once again the fear is of drawing unwanted attention to themselves; by politicising race, and by creating a heightened awareness of ethnic minority issues, such legislation might only succeed in aggravating that which it is intended to address. Paradoxically, then, legislation enacted to protect them is felt by some local Pakistanis to be likely to increase their vulnerability, at least in the short term, though these same individuals sometimes recognise that the need for such legislation may grow in the future. The following remarks, one made by a first-generation Pakistani man and the other by a first-generation Pakistani woman, illustrate these ambiguities:

> There is no need for it at the moment, so why stir things up? But it may become useful in the future.

> Not yet, but maybe in the future. If numbers get bigger ... the Chinese suffer a lot of discrimination, so maybe the ethnic groups need to work together.

It is not only the introduction of race relations legislation which Pakistanis fear will have an adverse effect on their visibility and thus, potentially, on their vulnerability. Life in a divided society such as Northern Ireland is thought by some to have had its beneficial effects for local ethnic minorities, by diverting antagonisms along other more deeply entrenched and historically sedimented channels. Thus according to one man, who reflected the views of many, 'the troubles mean that ethnic minorities don't experience much racism', at least when compared to Britain. However, in the eyes of some, this seems set to change (cf. Irwin 1996:66–7). Since 1994, with the faltering attempts to reorient Northern Ireland politics towards a democratic resolution to its sectarian conflict and away from the violence and military campaigning of the last three decades, representatives of different ethnic minorities have expressed increasing concern that aggression will now be redirected at them. One anxiety is that locally resident ethnic groups will become the new victims of those individuals, on both sides of Northern Ireland's sectarian divide, who had previously directed their antagonism at one another. To some extent, this is a view shared by the Royal Ulster Constabulary, who began to monitor racially motivated attacks after the introduction of the paramilitary ceasefires in autumn 1994, in recognition that the 'end' of the political conflict which had hitherto hidden the true volume of such attacks might now result in more widespread discrimination.

Other anxieties are also generated by the prospect of peace, namely that the relative quiescence of sectarian antagonisms will result in an increased influx of Pakistanis from Britain. One woman remarked:

I think that because there was war on there were fewer immigrants. If the peace is still like this, maybe more people will start emigrating here. If there's more people here, there might be the same situation as in England. It might be to the future that we need to look, not at the moment. There's hardly two houses together here. If you go to England its streets are full of Pakistani and Indian people. That's the main reason we don't have those type of things here.

A peaceful Northern Ireland, so the argument goes, would have its attractions for Pakistanis in Britain with their rising levels of unemployment. After all, those already in Northern Ireland maintain that, at least when compared to Britain, it remains – in the words of one Pakistani man – 'a gold-mine from a business point of view', even if profits are not as great as they once were. But any such influx would obviously contribute to a growth in numbers, with a consequent increase in visibility and the likelihood of racial attacks.

Such fears highlight how local Pakistanis believe that they have evolved a *modus vivendi* rooted in the desire and ability to keep out of the public eye, a strategy which has in part depended on the continuation of sectarian conflict. The price has been a silence about their experiences of prejudice, which so far have passed largely unremarked in the wider society, where images of exotic festivities and business successes have tended to dominate the public face of local Pakistani life. In the following sections, we try to go some way towards redressing this skewed image by examining the everyday experiences of prejudice in the words of the ordinary Pakistani men and women who must deal with prejudice as a matter of routine.

Perceptions and Contexts of Prejudice

Social scientists have generally understood prejudice as an 'inflexible attitude towards specific groups of others based on unreliable, possibly distorted, stereotyped images of them' (Cashmore and Troyna 1983:36). Prejudice may be 'racial', based on the idea that people can be distinguished by physical differences which are genetically transmitted, or 'cultural', based on people's different ideas and beliefs about the world. While rarely distinguished by those who experience them, both types of prejudice are evident in the everyday lives of Pakistanis in Northern Ireland.[6]

Although it is difficult to say just how widespread prejudice is, it is possible to provide a qualitative account of the kinds of experiences reported by the wide range of Pakistanis with whom we talked, and seemingly shared by them largely irrespective of differences in age, gender, and occupation (see also Irwin 1996:65–76). Moreover, and significantly, many of these experiences are also shared by Pakistanis in Britain (see, for example, Shaw 1988:139–40; Werbner 1990b:342–3; Modood *et al.* 1994:95–100). It is only in relatively well-defined contexts and fairly predictable ways that living in a divided society differentiates the experience of being a Pakistani in Northern Ireland, and almost all their talk about prejudice in this regard centres on the political constraints imposed by circumstances there.

Thus most interviewees stressed that they have attempted to cope as a minority population within a divided society by emphasising their political neutrality, and by not drawing attention to themselves, as we mentioned earlier. This has discouraged active involvement in local politics, resulting in a low level of participation in elections, as several Pakistani men and women indicated to us in comments which suggest an ambivalent attachment to Northern Ireland:

> Here it's not really politics, it's mostly local tribal differences and I think [for] someone who has come from another country or culture, that it is foolish to take sides.

> We want to stay neutral so we try not to vote here, we don't want to be seen for one party and not for the other party ... But if the policies were made by these people then I would vote, I would vote on the criteria of what the policy is offering, not on the basis of [religion].

Such views were reiterated again and again in our conversations with local Pakistanis, with the sectarian nature of local politics reportedly reinforcing a feeling of 'outsider' status as a migrant minority, and frustrating an apparent desire to be politically active were circumstances different. For some Pakistanis the 1996 Forum Elections, organised to establish an all-party body with a broad-based brief to consider Northern Ireland's future, seemed to create just such an opportunity for wider political involvement. This encouraged some Pakistanis to vote, in the belief that their voice would not only have something novel to contribute but might at last be heard.

Yet it has been the recurrent failure of elected politicians to address the broader social and economic issues underlying Northern Ireland's 'troubles' which some Pakistanis believe has had a direct bearing on their own experiences of prejudice, and has led them to identify more closely with the local Catholic rather than the local Protestant population. Both Catholics and Pakistanis, the latter point out, share experiences common to minority groups. Somewhat paradoxically, given this identification, though perhaps in part explanation of it, most Pakistanis live in mainly Protestant areas and attend state schools (which are mainly Protestant) and, as a result, they claim to have experienced most antagonism from this quarter.[7] In pointing this out, however, local Pakistanis are quick to add that social class and socio-economic disadvantage are important factors in explaining antagonism towards them, since where there have been assaults on their property or person, these have occurred in neighbourhoods of high unemployment and rising levels of crime and vandalism. In other words, they recognise that it may be difficult to disentangle racially motivated attacks from a more general pattern of crime and delinquency. As one middle-aged male respondent indicated:

> I don't believe in [housing] estates because that is where a lot of trouble is, because it's mostly young families, they have very little to do other than to bring grief to their next-door neighbour or to anyone else. That may be white to white, black to black, it doesn't make any difference.

Despite efforts to remain neutral, most Pakistanis with whom we talked claimed to have experienced some form of harassment, most frequently verbal abuse (cf. Irwin 1996:80). However, in only two instances – both involving young second-generation Pakistanis; one male and one female – did we record conversations where living in a divided society was said to give a specifically local inflection to the nature of this abuse:

> I reckon there's a bit of racist abuse from British troops. I've experienced that a lot. Shouting, you know, general harassment, pulling you over, searching your car, and the police as well to a certain extent. You get some racist police and some who are dead on [that is, congenial and personable].

> One time I was in the shop and I was wearing a green and white outfit, and someone yelled out 'You're lacking the orange.' They always reduce everything to Catholics and Protestants. I haven't worn the outfit since, and it was a lovely outfit.

In all our other conversations about racism the content of abusive remarks which local Pakistanis reported would be immediately recognisable to Pakistanis in Britain. For reasons of space we include only some of the more common examples.

Like Pakistanis in Britain, Pakistanis in Northern Ireland identify certain key and obvious attributes as contributing to their visibility, such as skin colour, dress and language. Such features make them distinctive and noticeable, they say, prompting one young man to quip: 'because you stick out, you stand out, everybody looks at you'. The majority of Pakistanis in our study report that their physical visibility has attracted verbal abuse and racist remarks at some point in their lives. A rather smaller number claim to have suffered other forms of abuse, though as already mentioned they are ambivalent about whether this was the result of racism or of more 'ordinary' crime. Some have had their property vandalised or burgled, while others have had their homes or businesses maliciously set on fire, or have been deterred from attending the mosque out of fear for their safety after one mosque was attacked in 1995.

As in Britain, stereotypical assumptions about the Muslim faith are widely reported by Northern Ireland Pakistanis, something which they believe the representation of Islam in the Western media has encouraged. According to a young Pakistani man:

There is a need for education to broaden the understanding about different colours, race, religions ... Northern Ireland people are ignorant – not all, some – about Islam. They always portray Muslims as debauched, as people having nothing else to do but getting married every week, having multiple wives, slashing people's hands off for minor offences, killing people, stoning people.

Not surprisingly, it is the more visible physical signs of difference such as dress and skin colour which Pakistanis report as most likely to attract attention. The women mentioned how they felt vulnerable when wearing Pakistani dress (shalwar-kamiz), something which they repeatedly reported as attracting abusive comment:

At the start, my husband didn't want me to wear English clothes, and then we went out and everybody was looking at me in these clothes [that is, shalwar-kamiz]. And then he says to me, no way are you wearing them.

As one woman lamented, wearing shalwar-kamiz in Northern Ireland has the opposite effect to that intended, since the objective of this dress is to detract attention from women, not increase their visibility. As a result, many Pakistani women have ceased to wear the shalwar-kamiz, except when in the company of other Muslims, thereby modifying their behaviour in the public domain in an effort to avoid abuse, a strategy clearly in keeping with the aim of trying not to draw attention to themselves. However, not all local Pakistani women have altered their behaviour in this way, for reasons we shall consider later.

For Pakistani men, who in Britain and Ireland routinely dress in Western clothes except when relaxing at home, it is skin colour which is usually reported as attracting unwanted comment. Two young men recalled for us the kinds of comment made to them:

You walk through town and people stare at you, you walk through university and people stare at you ... we were in the library ... and we walked out and they were all standing on the stairs. They were staring at us walking along. That's at a university where they're supposed to be educated. They were staring at us as if we were going to attack them.

... if the sun comes out, they say 'it's like being back home again, isn't it?' or 'I'm nearly the same colour as you.'

Even a casual remark about cold weather risks attracting a potentially abusive reply: 'Aye, it must be cold coming from a hotter climate. Do you feel it more?' While comments such as these are experienced by local Pakistanis with small regard to age, gender and occupation, some Pakistanis seem more likely to encounter prejudice than others. As one might expect, given the heterogeneity outlined earlier, the kind, intensity and frequency of relationships with the wider population vary; while some come into regular contact with non-Pakistanis, others more rarely encounter anyone outside a closed circle of kin defined in ethnic terms.

Perhaps because of the nature of the work in which each is involved, Pakistani men were quicker than women to point out to us how they felt discriminated against in the workplace. Although to a lesser extent than in Britain, local Pakistani women are mainly engaged in work which requires limited contact with the wider public, in preparing food for restaurants and take-aways, or in backroom work in retail businesses. Men, on the other hand, are largely responsible for serving the customers in such businesses, in which capacity they can be the targets of verbal abuse. Prejudice is also more likely to be encountered in some occupations than in others. The professionals to whom we talked – mainly academics and doctors – were less able (or less willing) to offer examples of prejudice than were those Pakistanis who worked as market traders or in other small businesses which serve the public sector (cf. Irwin 1996:71). Where discrimination was reported in the professions, it was thought to be based on factors such as gender and lifestyle, rather than on ethnic identification, as one doctor indicated:

Women doctors are discriminated against ... In medicine there is more cultural discrimination rather than racial discrimination. It is a closed society so that if you don't belong to their little club you won't progress as quickly. There are, for example, some [male] Asians who have assimilated completely and they don't experience any discrimination, so it's more cultural than racial.

Comments such as these are suggestive, indicating that the experience of prejudice by Pakistanis in Northern Ireland is inflected by gender and socio-economic position, but in complex ways which only further research will uncover. What does seem clear, however, is that whatever the incidence and distribution of prejudice towards Pakistanis in Northern Ireland, its everyday content, while less extensive, is not so very different to that in Britain, with local Pakistanis in all walks of life dismissing instances of which they know as insignificant, and attributing them to a lack of experiential contact with ethnic minority populations. If this apparently benign and resigned acceptance of discriminatory practice, to which we have already alluded, is a view held by those of different socio-economic class and gender, this is true only of the older generation. It is not a view shared by younger Pakistanis for whom, though the content and contexts of prejudice may be much the same as for all local Pakistanis, the *response* to it differs, as we now consider.

Prejudice, Identity and the Second Generation

There is some evidence to suggest that attitudes and responses to racism differ between the generations, particularly between Pakistanis born in Northern Ireland (or raised there from an early age) and those born elsewhere. Some 75 second-generation Pakistanis were interviewed, either individually or as members of focus groups set up as part of our research. Both young men and young women were interviewed, most of them over 14 years of age. Some of those interviewed were in secondary school or higher education, but others were already in employment and/or had families of their own. It is hardly surprising that the views of these second-generation Pakistanis should differ from those of the senior generation. We might expect those born, educated and raised in the Province to feel differently about their sense of local attachment than an earlier generation with memories and experiences of living in Pakistan, though it is a difference always constrained by the perceptions of the wider society, as one young hospital worker reported:

People would ask me where do you come from, and sometimes that gets me very angry, and I say 'Belfast.' 'No, no where do you come from?' 'Belfast!' 'But where were you born?' 'Belfast!' And then I try and go, 'Well do you want to ask where my parents came from?' And I go, 'Pakistan, but I was born and bred in Belfast!' Sometimes it makes me really angry that people just don't accept you as a British citizen. They still expect that if you're coloured that you come from another country. People at work ... would go, 'You're foreign.' And I go, 'No, I just spent two weeks in Greece and this is just a suntan!'

Such remarks are clearly predicated on a perceived migrant origin, and can take a number of forms, referring variously to skin colour, language and accent: 'Where are you from?'; 'Were you born here?'; 'You've got a lovely accent'; 'You're not like the normal Asian'; 'You have a Belfast accent.' Remarks like these are not dissimilar to those reported in the preceding section, but far from being passively absorbed as we described above, such comments, according to one young man, 'do your head in'.

In our conversations it was second-generation Pakistanis who most readily admitted to having had experiences of racism and who most freely expressed their anger at them. Many of them felt that, because of the colour of their skin, they were being denied full membership of the society into which they had been born or in which they had spent most of their lives, and they resented the external imposition of a migrant status with its associations of a host–guest relationship. Their supposed foreign origins also created difficulties at school, where pupils and even teachers sometimes made stereotypical remarks, as one young Pakistani woman recalled:

One day [the schoolteacher] came down to me during class and said, 'What's wrong, you can speak and understand English can't you?' And this guy in the class shouted out, 'Well she wouldn't be studying English A-level if she couldn't, would she?' The teacher was really embarrassed after that, she realised it was a stupid thing to say ... I'll never forget that.

Despite some variation in the work and social experiences of young Pakistani men and women, both sexes relate very similar personal stories of prejudice, and share the same feelings of irritation, frustration and anger, as the following examples illustrate. We begin by citing the experiences of two young male market traders:

The thing that really got me was when we used to go to the markets. They think you're stupid. That really irritated me that, but [my friend] can take it as long as they're buying. But with me and my brother it got to the stage that if they're saying too much I just put the clothes back. And you catch on afterwards, God I shouldn't have done that. But then you just sort of think, well you've been patronised for the day, that's enough, they can keep it. [The friend] tried to explain the principles, take the money and let them call you whatever they want. Pretend you don't understand.

The phrase that got us was when they said 'you boys'. That's the ultimate, that just sort of sets you going, and you say, 'Bugger off, I don't want to bother with you.' I found it more that it was the markets where you got it ... it's the lower classes. The middle classes, the more educated you àre, the more tolerant you are. If you go up ... to the Shankill or the Falls, the customers, the people who live there, they give you very little respect because they have very little understanding, they think you've just come off the boat.

Young women may experience prejudice in slightly different contexts, but their response is the same as the following account illustrates:

There was one time, I'll never forget it. One guy said to me one time, 'Do you go home often, love?' I said, 'Yes, I go home every day.' 'Oh', he says, 'you're crafty. I mean do you go back to where you're originally from?' I said to him, 'You mean to Rochdale?' He says, 'Do you go home to where your parents are from then?' I said, 'You mean back home to Belfast?'

These accounts of prejudice differ in certain respects from those described in the preceding section. To begin with, they suggest that younger Pakistanis detect an almost paternalistic condescension in the attitudes of those around them, as reflected in terms of address such as 'you boys'. But they also differ in more important ways. While such patronising remarks may be allowed to pass by other Pakistanis – in the interests of business, as noted above – young Pakistanis are more likely to confront those who make them. This resistance can take a number of forms. In some cases, wit and humour may be used to parry persistent inquiry like that in the final quotation above. In other cases, those making prejudicial remarks may be confronted with their own ignorance: one young woman described how when a white youth was making derogatory comments about her and calling her an Indian, she contradicted him by telling him she was a Pakistani, a response which left him speechless. In a similar vein, a young man indicated how he copes with racist attitudes:

Sometimes they are talking and don't expect you to understand and you just go, 'No understand', you just wind them up a bit, let them feel they are superior to us ... Sometimes it can annoy you; other times you'll play along, you enjoy it, just winding them up back [that is, in return]. Because they think they're laughing at you. They'll be talking to their friends saying he hasn't a clue or whatever, slagging you off and you know exactly what it is they're saying, so you're having the other laugh, you're getting back at them.

These types of verbal resistance are occasionally accompanied by other forms of opposition. We mentioned earlier how Pakistani women are reluctant to wear *shalwar-kamiz* because it attracts unwanted attention. Some young local Pakistani women, however, have begun to wear this dress precisely because of its ability to indicate difference. Viewed externally, such actions might seem like a sentimental attachment to tradition, but this would miss the point that they are primarily a response to contemporary circumstances, serving as one means to construct a space in the majority society in which young Pakistanis can restore their sense of moral and social distinctiveness. Local women have not yet adopted the veil as a sign of political revolt, as have some Pakistani women in Britain (cf. Watson 1994), but the less radical act of wearing *shalwar-kamiz* is nevertheless driven by a similar need to manage competing cultural values and personal aspirations.

Unlike their parents, therefore, these young Pakistanis do not have the preconceived notions associated with diaspora which could make sense of prejudicial experiences, or which encourage their passive accommodation, but come to them with a different set of expectations and emergent attachments which reflect the many ambivalences they face, particularly over the issue of identity. Young Pakistanis explicitly recognise that their identity is a composite made up of a number of elements. Continuing ties to Pakistan, the maintenance of ties to Britain and birth and residence in Northern Ireland are all elements incorporated in the self-ascriptions of some. According to one view, therefore: 'I would identify myself as a British Pakistani with an Irish identity'. Some see these different elements as ranked in a hierarchy of nesting identities, with their faith as Muslims being the stable and transcendent core (cf. Joly 1995), as in the case of the young Pakistani man who remarked:

[I am] a Muslim first, Pakistani second and British third. I will not compromise my Muslim identity ... For some it's a conflict between assimilation and their identity. Nationality comes second because in the Mosque you find people of all different nationalities and there is no difference between them, they are Muslims first.

Of course, such self-ascriptions are always constrained by the perceptions of others, and however these Pakistanis might see themselves they must contend with a racial and cultural exclusionism in the wider society, which too often insists on an identity as 'Pakis'. One young man, married to a woman from Northern Ireland, thus remarked to us that while he himself 'felt Irish', his skin colour forever prevented him from being more widely recognised as such; a predicament succinctly expressed by a young Pakistani woman who referred to herself as 'too Western to be Pakistani and too different to be Western'.

According to another Pakistani youth, when combined with the kin ties and endogamous marriage practices that reinforce ethnic and religious boundaries, such feelings of exclusion may create the sense of having to choose between being Pakistani and being Irish:

> I would identify myself in terms of dual nationality. I live here, I practise most of my tradition over here and I still think about my native country ... So in that way I would consider myself to be a dual national rather than one-sided. I find myself caught between the two, that's about the hard and fast of it really.

Such comments recall, and indeed may perhaps ultimately derive from, a view widespread among those such as social workers and youth leaders who regularly deal with South Asians in their work (Ballard 1994:30). This view maintains that the relationships of British-born members of migrant minorities are characterised by 'culture conflict'; they are caught 'between two cultures' and, as a result of having to conform to the competing value systems of minority and majority cultures, suffer from an almost pathological 'crisis of identity'. It is certainly true, as we have tried to indicate, that second-generation Pakistanis are more likely than their parents to move regularly through a variety of contexts where different cultural rules apply. As Ballard (1994:31) points out, should 'culture' determine behaviour in some fixed and immutable way, therefore, their experiences would indeed be unmanageable. However, what this view ignores is the situational fluidity of identities and the ability of local young people to switch between different cultural codes. It is not so much that they are caught between two cultures, belonging to neither one nor the other, as that they have developed skills which enable them to move between the two as the situation requires, constructing new and varied lifestyles of their own and claiming identities according to context (thus one man jokingly recalled how, when visiting Britain, he refers to himself as 'a browned-off paddy'). While to be wholly successful this may require some degree of audience segregation – such as keeping from parents details of what they do beyond the home – it avoids many of the more dramatic dilemmas sometimes reported in the press as typical of South Asian youth. Moreover, it is this which makes behaviour such as wearing *shalwar-kamiz* in public – or switching from English to Punjabi – so effective (see Ballard 1994): by transferring behaviour considered appropriate in one context to another, the taken-for-granted boundaries are subverted.

A striking but not unusual example of the situational manipulation of identities is provided by the case of a young Northern Ireland-born man visiting the Punjab on holiday. Though familiar from photographs and parental descriptions, the rural setting with its lack of amenities and strict separation of male and female still came as something of a shock. While in Belfast he had emphasised his Pakistani origins, in a Punjabi village he stressed that he was from Belfast and insisted that he was British. Although meeting him for the first time, he threw his arms around one of the authors (who was conducting research in Pakistan at the time), declaring to the other villagers: 'It's great to see someone from home. We are both from Belfast'. His experience is not untypical, as the remarks of another young man recently returned from Pakistan suggest:[8]

> You're stuck in the middle because you're not truly Irish, you're never going to be accepted. The first thing that people are going to see is the colour of your skin before anything else. So you're not one of them and you're not a Pakistani either. Even over there [Pakistan] you're seen as a stranger as well. So you can't win, you're stuck in the middle.

The identities of these young people thus depend to some extent on where they are not, with 'home' that fixed point which is forever beyond and so subject to a perpetual process of imagining. However, as the above quotation indicates, it is an imagining unavoidably limited in Northern Ireland by the colour of their skin, which makes complete acceptance improbable. In this sense, then, the identities of these young British-born Pakistanis will always be articulated in the space between the racial exclusionism of the dominant white culture and the fact that their everyday point of reference is Northern Ireland.

Conclusion

We have tried to show in this chapter that while the Pakistani population in Northern Ireland cannot be viewed in isolation from wider political circumstances, it is not these circumstances alone which have resulted in their being thrown back on their own cultural and social resources, and which distinguish them from Pakistanis in Britain. Relatively small numbers and geographical dispersal have also played their part in keeping local Pakistanis invisible in the wider society, except within a narrow range of contexts: the exotic, the contribution to business, the owner of a high street restaurant or take-away. Beyond these limited points of contact, the lived realities of people's daily lives, including their internal differences, have gone largely unremarked, something we have tried to rectify on the grounds that 'a study of the wider context in which immigrant groups interact must necessarily examine, not only the interface between different groups but the internal structures that motivate their actions' (Werbner 1991:141).

More insidiously, however, it has been racist attitudes in the dominant white culture which have persuaded some, mainly first-generation, Pakistanis to attempt to insulate themselves from what they perceive to be the morally corrosive influence of the wider society, a position and response which appears to have diminishing appeal to the second generation who are actively seeking to establish new forms of identity for themselves in response to, or in spite of, these same racist attitudes. In these respects at least, Pakistanis in Northern Ireland, of whatever generation, appear to be little different to those in Britain, despite evidence from a survey of perceptions of racism in Northern Ireland which might lead us to expect otherwise (Brewer and Dowds 1996).

In a helpful summary of data from the recent Social Attitudes Survey, Brewer and Dowds (1996:97) report that 'six times as many people in Great Britain than in Northern Ireland think that there is a lot of prejudice against Asians', with only 10 per cent of Northern Ireland respondents, compared to 59 per cent of respondents in Britain, believing that there is extensive prejudice against Asians. This apparent belief in a tolerant society may be comforting, but it is potentially misleading when set beside the comments of the Pakistanis themselves which, as we have seen, suggest a widespread and broad-ranging experience of prejudice. What can explain this seeming lack of fit between the reported perceptions of tolerance on the part of the mainly white respondents in the Survey and the perceptions of prejudice expressed by our Pakistani informants; and, more importantly, what might be its consequences?

Brewer and Dowds suggest that the low level of perceived prejudice towards ethnic minorities in Northern Ireland is related to experiential contact with members of these groups. Since only a relatively few people in Northern Ireland come into direct contact with ethnic minorities, because these groups are so small, they are likely to witness little or no prejudice. Pakistanis, on the other hand, are likely to perceive somewhat different levels of prejudice, since they are its victims. While not intended as a criticism, it is worth pointing out that this seems to favour a relatively benign interpretation of the Survey's results. After all, low levels of reported prejudice in the white population could be a result of many different factors: an unwillingness to admit to prejudice, an effort to enhance one's image in a society otherwise viewed by the world as intolerant, a paternalistic and self-congratulatory attitude towards minorities, or a deliberate effort to play down yet another local problem. While Brewer and Dowds briefly consider such possibilities, they nevertheless discount them in favour of the explanation mentioned. They are probably right. It may indeed be the case that because people do not directly encounter prejudice themselves, they do not believe it exists. However, other factors also seem to be at work, and with certain consequences.

Low levels of perceived prejudice are not in any sense an indication of the absence of prejudice in Northern Ireland, as Brewer and Dowds recognise, though the risk must be that this is what the unwary could easily conclude. This would be unfortunate, for it would underestimate the extent to which actual experiences of prejudice and fear of it have helped to shape the lives of local Pakistanis in the ways that we have indicated. Moreover, if the wider society is unaware of this fact, this can be the result not just of limited direct experiential contact with minority populations, but of the comparative absence in Northern Ireland of any sensitising wider discourse – in the media or in politics, for instance – which would generate an awareness of 'race' as a local issue. For all its failings, the television programme mentioned earlier tried to do just this, its very title – 'The *Hidden* Troubles' – indicative of this omission. Indeed, in Britain, it has been just such public exposures that have helped to heighten awareness of race as an issue for large segments of the population, many of whom have also had no direct experience of ethnic minorities, given the latter's residential clustering in particular neighbourhoods and parts of the country. Racist attitudes may have been diffused to Northern Ireland from Britain, especially among those with closer contacts there (as Brewer and Dowds point out), but associated critiques and alternatives, such as anti-racism and multiculturalism, have been slower to follow, having only recently emerged among a small number of concerned and engaged professionals and voluntary workers.[9]

We like to think that our material complements the findings of the Social Attitudes Survey by adding a voice which is largely missing there: that of the Pakistanis themselves. As we have shown, this voice presents a different view, one which suggests that Northern Ireland is far from being the tolerant haven for ethnic minorities that the Survey indicates many in the wider society suppose. Denial that racism is an issue in Northern Ireland, for whatever reason, can only result in a failure to grasp the many and different ways in which it shapes the lives of local minorities. The result is likely both to compromise our intellectual understanding of ethnic relations in the local context, and perpetuate the current lack of provision for minority needs.

Notes

1   This chapter draws on research carried out by Hastings Donnan from 1989–91 among Pakistanis in Belfast, though the material presented derives mainly from Mairead O'Brien's research with Pakistanis in Belfast and Craigavon from October 1995 to June 1998. Most of the quotations cited in the text derive from this latter research unless indicated otherwise. Material was collected through in-

depth interviewing and observation. Mairead O'Brien interviewed 140 Pakistani men and women living throughout Northern Ireland, with particular emphasis on Greater Belfast and Craigavon. Both first- and second-generation Pakistanis were among those interviewed. Observation was facilitated by attending social and religious events in the Islamic Centre (Belfast), the South Asian Women's and Children's Community Centre (Craigavon), and in people's homes.

2   One might further wonder about the moral and political significance of this association between ethnic minorities and the term 'community', especially when the dominant white population is not referred to in the same way.

3   A qualification is necessary here, since it would be misleading to characterise the whole local South Asian population as 'immigrants', and not only because of the pejorative connotations of this term. Many locally resident South Asians were born in Northern Ireland and are second- and third-, and even fourth-generation descendants of those who first came from the subcontinent. Even the term 'migrant' must be used with care – while it does not have the same negative connotations as 'immigrant', it clearly does not apply to these descendants, whatever the perceptions of the wider society.

4   This concentration of Northern Ireland Pakistanis in professional and entrepreneurial occupations distinguishes them from the Pakistani population in Britain, where most have remained in manual employment. In this respect at least, Northern Irish Pakistanis bear closer comparison to South Asians in North America, where merchants and professionals have predominated from the outset (Marger 1989; see also Ballard 1994).

5   Race and ethnic issues are currently dealt with in Northern Ireland by the Northern Ireland Council for Ethnic Minorities (NICEM) and the Northern Ireland Council for Ethnic Equality (NICEE). The former was established in 1994 and the latter a year later. The diverse interests of the local Pakistani population have sometimes undermined the extent to which it considers its representatives on these bodies to be truly representative. Far from being actively involved in these organisations, many of the Pakistanis to whom we talked were unaware of their existence.

6   Everyday experiences of prejudice obviously take place against a wider institutional background, which in Northern Ireland seems less responsive to the needs of ethnic minorities than is the case in Britain. For instance, interpreters are rarely available when dealing with public sector services. Although such institutional inadequacies do not affect all local Pakistanis to the same extent, they aggravate the kinds of difficulties all are likely to encounter, and

constitute an unsupportive backdrop for the individual accounts of prejudice considered here.

7   Take-up of integrated schooling (which in Northern Ireland refers to the integration of Catholic and Protestant pupils) appears to be slight, and we recorded only one instance among those to whom we talked. Geographical proximity appears to be the main factor influencing choice of school.

8   Elsewhere, a young Pakistani woman explained why her brother had not enjoyed a recent trip to Pakistan by suggesting that 'he really did belong in Belfast [but] he would not admit this' (Kilfeather 1988:54–5). Young British Bangladeshis are similarly ambivalent about visits to Bangladesh (see Gardner and Shukur 1994).

9   Things may be beginning to change. Since the mid-1990s, the Multi-Cultural Resource Centre has published material on, and become actively involved in, anti-racist training, particularly for social workers (see O'Leary 1990), and the Northern Ireland Council for Ethnic Minorities has organised conferences and workshops to highlight ethnic minority issues. The media's racial awareness week in December 1996, and the introduction of an ethnic minorities slot on local radio, are further instances of recent developments in this area.

11   The Jews of Northern Ireland

David D. Warm

The material used as a basis for this chapter is the product of a research project, 'The Northern Ireland Jewish Oral and Documentary History Project', which the author has been undertaking since 1994. Two types of data have been drawn upon: first, oral in-depth history interviews; and, second, documents originating from within the Jewish community. A description of the research design and the theoretical perspective underpinning the presentation of data is provided and a historical account of the community is given, from its early origins to the present day. The material has been organised to present patterns of formal and informal social life and events. The substantive part of the chapter is an account of the Jewish community illustrated with perceptions by Jews of their own community. Less well-known Hebrew or Yiddish terms/works appear in italics in the first instance. A glossary is provided at the end of the chapter.

The data upon which this chapter is based is drawn from a series of oral interviews with Jews who are presently resident in Northern Ireland and others who, whilst having lived a significant period of their lives in the Province, now live elsewhere, mainly in England or Israel. This approach emphasises the importance of folk memories as a source of historical and sociological information. Documentary material has been treated in the same way and has been used to give a context and framework in which to present the illustrative subjective experiences of Jews, which are reported as direct quotes in the body of the chapter. However, the individual names and identities have not been revealed due to a commitment to maintain confidentiality and anonymity.

Respondents were recruited on an ongoing *ad hoc* basis and were not selected through any random sampling procedure. Some 60 interviews were undertaken in the period 1994–97; these were conducted using an in-depth open interview format and were tape-recorded with the permission of the respondents. The content of the interviews was organised around the personal biographical experiences of the interviewees through which their life history was traced, and shared collective experiences explored. A number of themes were concentrated on:

family of origin, religiosity, community, significant others, education, occupation, social life, marriage, the community, and relations with the wider world. The approach taken during the interviews was to consider the respondents as being at the epicentre of the social world they inhabited, and significant others and events – whether personal, family, or communal – were looked at from their point of view. Thus, as a result of the set of interviews undertaken, a multidimensional understanding of the Jewish community is constructed.

The theoretical viewpoint adopted in this chapter is based broadly around a social interactionist perspective. The subjective meanings held by the respondents are the building blocks used in constructing an understanding of individual personal histories and emerging social patterns. In data analysis the emphasis is on identifying commonly held subjective meanings and understandings of life experiences within, and without, of the Jewish community of Northern Ireland. These meanings and understandings are not deconstructed to identify underlying social norms or rules of behaviour but are accepted as they are presented as reliable descriptions of social life.

The Jewish Community

The chapter seeks to outline the pattern of settlement and development of the Jewish community of Northern Ireland. Throughout it, the designation 'Northern Ireland Jewish community' will be used to refer to the collectively of Jews who live in the Province. However, whilst there was some dispersion of Jews throughout the Province, the major centre of settlement was in Belfast and its surrounding areas. Smaller pockets of Jewish settlement could be found outside of Belfast, the largest being in Londonderry, but this Jewish community had ceased to exist by 1946.

The use of the term 'community' to describe the social organisation of Jewish life in Northern Ireland is not merely the application of a well used, and often abused, sociological concept, but moreover represents how Jews themselves perceive their own social organisation. As one Jew said in an interview: 'The Jews of Northern Ireland have a collective sense of identity ... we felt part of something larger than just our immediate family.' The Jewish community of Northern Ireland displays the features of a functioning organic entity providing a wide range of formal and informal 'services' to its members delivered through a range of formal institutional structures. One respondent commented that: 'The Jewish way of doing things seems to be by committees. I've sat on committees to do with the synagogue, charity work and tennis games! If something has to be done then we form a committee or an organisation to do it.' Another suggested that:

Jewish communities had to develop their own organisations because they were often excluded anyway from those in the wider world and, even if they weren't, the religious requirements of Jews is such that it was necessary to have organisations to provide for these special needs. Burial, kosher food and charity giving are examples of aspects of Jewish life that without an organisation to provide for them they simply could not happen. Individuals on their own would not have been able to provide for themselves.

Whilst the Jewish community of Northern Ireland developed a range of formal organisations it did, and still does, manifest self-help and voluntarism in practice. An informant said that: 'We prided ourselves on the fact that we looked after our members. Only rarely did Jews look outside of the community for help. I think we had a welfare state long before the wider world had one.' The Jewish community functions as a source of personal and sub-cultural identity. According to one interviewee: 'My social, family and personal life was spent amongst Jews. I knew I was Jewish and was proud of it, but it didn't stop me from feeling Northern Irish either.' It also serves as a focal or reference point for its members, as well as for others from outside of the community. Thus: 'There were many non-Jews who supported us and gave donations to our causes ... a lot of them had a real respect for the Jewish community.'

The Jews are a minority culture existing and interacting with an even larger heterogeneous cultural whole. While many distinctive cultural features have been retained, the overwhelming impression is of an ethnic minority which has integrated and assimilated with its host society: 'When my grandparents arrived from Russia they could speak only Yiddish, wore clothes which made them stand out and carried on more or less as they had done when living in the *shteitel* ... My parents learnt English and went to school in the local elementary school ... eventually they had ambitions for me to go to university.' It would be doubtful if what remains today of that cultural heritage would be recognisable by the Jews who founded the community at the beginning of the twentieth century. 'After the pogroms and ghetto life which our grandparents knew it's no wonder that when they came to a country in which there were few, if any, restrictions placed on Jews that they wanted to participate as much as they could within it, but it was at a cost of a way of life which they brought with them.'

Jewish Settlement in Northern Ireland

The first Jews to emigrate to England came after the Norman Conquest, but they were to be expelled later by Edward I in 1290, only to be readmitted by Cromwell in 1656. Similarly, the settlement of Jews in Ireland can be traced to the early Norman period. However, they only came in substantive numbers from 1690 onwards. Similar settlement of Jews into what is now Northern Ireland can be traced to the same seventeenth-century period.

Earlier references to individual Jewish immigrants have been chronicled in 1623, 1652, 1690, 1754, 1771 and 1846. By 1861, the Census records show nearly 400 Jews living in Ireland, the vast majority of whom were resident in Dublin with, it was thought, between 50 and 60 Jews resident in the north of Ireland, mainly in Belfast. Over the next decade, the Jewish community of Northern Ireland grew slowly, such that by 1871 there were approximately 70 Jews resident in the north. The year 1864 was a significant one in the history of the Jewish community in Northern Ireland, for it was during that year that the Jewish community in Belfast was formally inaugurated. The official name of the synagogue is the Belfast Hebrew Congregation, whose purpose is defined in its constitution of 1932 as to 'provide members and seat holders with seats in the synagogue, a *Mohel*, a *Mikvah* and also *Schochetim*, and arrange with victuallers for the supply of Kosher meat' (Belfast Hebrew Congregation 1932). A mohel was needed for the performance of circumcision, a mikvah provided for ritual immersion and Schochetim provided for the slaughter of meat in accordance with Jewish law.

By the 1890s, Shachter (1945) suggests that there were 'barely two hundred souls in all, and two-thirds of these consisted of recent arrivals from Russia'. Such were the differences, stemming from social class divisions as well as from language and cultures, between the original German Jewish settlers and the Russian Jews, that the latter established their own places of worship, often in rented houses. This social separation lasted until the time that the synagogue in Annesley Street was opened in 1904, when the community was united, at least for purpose of religious worship, under one roof.

The documentary history of the early Jewish settlement in Northern Ireland is sparse, to say the least. The first Jewish immigrants to Northern Ireland were financially secure linen merchants from Hamburg, Germany, seeking to establish trading links with the flax industry. Sufficient numbers settled so that by 1871, a synagogue was established in the city centre of Belfast. Later in the nineteenth century, Jewish immigration came mainly from Russia and Lithuania and other parts of Eastern Europe. These immigrants were distinct from their German co-religionists in culture, social and economic standing, religious orthodoxy and education. Eventually, these immigrants became the dominant group in size and influence within the Jewish community.

By 1904, the first city synagogue was replaced with one built by Sir Otto Jaffe, who became the only Jewish Lord Mayor of Belfast. At this stage, the community was centred on the working-class districts of the lower Crumlin Road and adjacent streets, and it was into this area that the synagogue moved from its original city-centre location. The majority of the community lived within a one-mile radius of the synagogue. This physical proximity to the synagogue was typical of an orthodox Jewish community. These early Jewish immigrants to Northern Ireland were predominantly orthodox in their religious observance. This orthodoxy prevented them from using public or, even if they possessed it, private transport to attend the synagogue on the Sabbath or other important days in the Jewish calendar. This necessitated living within easy walking distance of the synagogue.

As the community grew and became established, it became an increasingly attractive place to settle for Jews from other parts of Ireland and the UK. By the end of the Second World War, it offered economic and social opportunities – especially for marriage. Thus, according to one interviewee: 'I was here in the Army during the war and liked what I saw. The people were friendly, the community was very hospitable to me and I met my future wife to be at one of the dances at the club. It seemed to me a good place to come and live ... so when the war finished and I was demobbed, I left England for Belfast.'

The growth of the community was sustained as much by this 'inward investment' of people as it was by internal renewal and stability. Jews did leave Northern Ireland to emigrate to other places of settlement but this was more than compensated for by both internal growth and immigration from outside. The net result was that the community expanded in size up to the early 1970s. It will be seen that much of the decline can be attributed to the reversal of this process of demographic and social change.

An unforeseen factor, influencing the decline of the community, was the advent of the state of social unrest, 'the troubles' as they are often referred to, which has been in existence since 1968 to the present. In the view of one respondent: 'It was clear that by 1974 business opportunities were going to be very limited given the continued level of violence and disruption. I had an opportunity to sell my business and set up another one in London. I took the opportunity whilst I could.' Another reported that: 'Most of my friends were leaving for England to go to university and this really had a big impact on my social life. It wasn't that my friends in Belfast weren't nice or anything like that but I wanted to find new relationships and have different experiences. Belfast was no longer the place for me, especially if I wanted to marry another Jew.'

Immigration of Jews from other parts of Ireland, the continent and the mainland continued through the life of the community up to the end of the early 1950s. The community grew at a steady pace over the first 100 years of its existence to reach its peak in the late 1960s when it numbered 365 households, estimated at approximately 1,500 individuals of all ages in total. From then onwards the community steadily contracted in size so that, by 1997, the community had been reduced to 140 households, consisting of 230 individuals of all ages.

The community became geographically and socially mobile with its increased social, political and economic integration. The process of immigration, settlement and development occurred in a number of stages. This is reflected in institutional developments, population growth and social changes within the Jewish community. Jewish immigration and settlement in Northern Ireland has been in progress for 130 years, and Jews are one of the most established minority groups within the Province, even though the size of the community has varied over time.

The Institutional Structure of the Jewish Community

Throughout its life, the institutional infrastructure of the community developed to meet the religious and social needs of the Jewish population. Welfare, social, burial, loan, education, benevolent and Zionist societies were established and supported. One of the main factors which has impacted upon the institutional development of the community is its physical distance from other large Jewish centres. Dublin is the nearest Jewish community of any size and a great deal of social interaction has taken place between the two, but a more formal relationship between the two communities was not established. This was simply because it was in another independent state, falling outside of the brief of the United Kingdom Chief Rabbinate based in London. On the other hand, London was for all intents and purposes divorced from the everyday needs of the Northern Ireland Jewish community. This isolation is a major reason why the Jewish community of Northern Ireland adopted, to a large extent, an independent attitude towards its own self-government. Many organised groups came into existence to service the community and contributed to its growth and stability over time. These formal structures covered almost all, if not all, aspects of life – as intimated in one of the above quotations, a welfare state in miniature, from the cradle to the grave. This can be illustrated with reference to some of the key institutions which were established.

The Synagogue

The foundation stone of the first purpose-built synagogue was laid in Belfast in 1869. It remained in existence until 1904 when the second purpose-built synagogue was opened. The third and present purpose-built synagogue was opened in 1964 on a site in North Belfast. The synagogue plays a central role in the life of a Jewish community. In the context of geographical isolation from the mainstream of Jewish life, civil unrest and the fact that there is only one synagogue to which Jews can affiliate, this role becomes exaggerated, as illustrated in the comment from one interviewee: 'The synagogue was not just a place of worship. Certainly once we moved to Somerton Road and everything was under one roof it was easier to see how important it became. Everything took place there and really it was a big help, let alone being sensible to bring everything together.'

The place of the synagogue in everyday life can also be seen from these quotes taken from interviews with some senior members of the community. Looking back on their childhood and youth, they commented:

When we were young everyone attended the synagogue on *Shabbat*. It wasn't something you could not do.'

I remember walking with my parents to *shul* and meeting my friends with their parents as they walked down the Antrim Road to Annesley Street.

Very few people worked on Shabbat. Most attended the synagogue. In those days we attended on other days as well. In the evening people would meet to study and learn *Gemorah*.

The importance of the synagogue was not restricted to religious matters but to the social life of the community as well:

It was where you met your friends, talked to people and made your arrangements to go to.

People came to meet and talk to their friends, have a laugh and generally enjoy themselves. I am not saying that is all they did – of course, they came to take part in the service, but it was not just to do that.

This distinction between the religious and social aspects of Jewish experience should not be too severely drawn. The religious and the secular systems are often indistinct, which heightens the importance of the religious and lay leadership within the community. The offices of communal Rabbi and President of the community made for a powerful alliance when the office holders worked in harmony, but in times of dispute it could cause tensions within the community. As the community diminished, so the importance of these offices diminished. Social change has also made its mark in this area. As democratic principles and leadership became more widely practised in all areas of social life, the use of arbitrary authority was replaced with more collective and shared responsibility. This change in attitude and practice can be seen in the elevation of women of the community onto the synagogue council. The importance of the synagogue in maintaining the essential core of Jewish life in Belfast has increased with time, not diminished. If anything it has become the vital heart of the community, serving a group with a wide spectrum of personal religious practice. This has not been an easy role to fulfil and the overt policy of maintaining an umbrella facility remains the formal policy of the synagogue council, despite the problems this creates in everyday life.

It was only at the beginning of the twentieth century that the community manifested in its institutional arrangements, differences in its social structure. Several small places of worship existed in various houses, reflecting the distinctive social composition of the community. However, this period of differentiation was short-lived and by 1904 the new synagogue in Annesley Street served all sections. This has been the pattern to date. On the positive side, it has meant that a monolithic religious structure helped to preserve the unity of the community. On the other hand, tension between those holding different degrees of religious orthodoxy and ideology has led to conflict and at times an uneasy harmony. Maintaining unity has been a primary policy goal within the government of the community. The 'umbrella' concept of a synagogue, orthodox in practice but seeking to serve a spectrum of personal religious practice and commitment, has been largely achieved.

Education

Throughout Jewish history, the importance of *Torah* study has always been a part of the fabric of everyday life. Without such educational provision, the observance and practice of Judaism would have been impossible. The study of the Torah was both an end in itself, a positive commandment which had no other purpose than the fulfilment of a religious obligation and, on the other hand, education was a necessary condition and prerequisite for practice. This applied at all ages and was an expression of, what we understand today as, the concept of life-long education. Learning is something integral to all Jewish communities, and it is no different in this respect for the Jews of Northern Ireland.

Beth Hasepher, literally translated as 'The House of the Book', or its other more usual name, *chedar*, is the name given to the Hebrew education school established to provide Jewish education and instruction for the children and youth of the community. Its origins can be traced to the early days of the community but certainly the main impetus to create a formal institution dedicated to the education of the young can be traced to 1908. A respondent observed that: 'We attended chedar every night after school and on Sunday mornings as well. I learnt to *daven* and many other things which I wouldn't have got at home.' Another said:

At one time there were as many as three full-time teachers in the chedar. We went to chedar every day straight from school and again on a Sunday morning. Some children had private tuition at home, but most went to chedar. The Jaffe school at the bottom of Clifton Park Avenue was where we went to chedar. Later on it moved to Northleigh on the site of the present synagogue. When the Wolfson Centre was built the chedar transferred there.

The *Chevra Gemorah* was established in 1895 to provide for the study of the Talmud, the codified oral law. Study sessions took place, in the evenings, in the Beth Hamidrash within the synagogue. The Chevra Gemorah continued to provide a forum for adult study for nearly 75 years. Shachter (1945) wrote that the Chevra Gemorah, certainly in its early days, provided an escape for many Jews: 'There were Jews who, during the day, were hard pressed in their pursuit of a living, and yet in the evening went to the *Beth Hamidrash* where they spent a happy hour that helped them to forget the misery of their material lot.' The inspiration for the creation of a Chevra Gemorah came from Lithuanian Jews, whose background was in Yeshiva study and life-long experience of Torah learning. The Yeshiva system of education developed in countries like Poland and provided an intense Torah education, in particular but not exclusively for children and young adults. This experience of learning was carried into adult life and was taken with Jews to wherever they emigrated.

The Belfast Jewish Institute

The Belfast Jewish Institute, or the 'club' as it was generally known, was established in 1926. It was, next to the synagogue, the most important social institution in the life of the community. It acted as a focal point for social events, meetings and organised activities. It played a prominent part in the cohesiveness of the community by providing a common ground in which people joined together, irrespective of religious orthodoxy or social status. This can be seen from one respondent's comments: 'I never once felt that I was looked down upon. My parents weren't rich and I know that many of my friends' parents were a lot wealthier than mine, but it didn't matter. Once we were in

the club it was as if we were all equal. I was never made to feel inferior.'
The bond and web of social relationships it engendered left its mark
on people's lives. Many friendships – and indeed, marriages – were
the product of the Institute:

> We met in the Institute. Eventually we got married. Many of my
> friends met their future partners at the Institute.

> It was an amazing place. Many visitors to Belfast were envious of
> the Institute – they hadn't seen anything like it. It was certainly as
> good as anything that the bigger Jewish communities in Manchester
> and London had to offer.

For the adolescents of the community, it is clear that the Institute
functioned on many levels but, in particular, it provided a wide range
of informal educational experiences which were to remain with them
throughout their lives:

> All of my age group in their early teens attended the Junior Forum.
> It was where we gained confidence. I never thought that I could speak
> in public, but it was through the Junior Forum that I was able to
> overcome my shyness.

> I suppose there were some people who didn't go to the Forum. Most
> went along to its meetings, even if it was just to hear the debates.
> It really provided everyone with an experience which remained with
> them for a long time. At least it did for me.

The Institute provided kosher meals and a place to celebrate
important events such as marriages and engagements, or communal
functions:

> I think I spent nearly every Sunday for almost 25 years at the
> Institute. I'd get there about 12 o'clock and stay until about 11 at
> night. You could get a meal and there were always people to talk
> to. I had a regular card game with three other people.

> There was a regular poker-school in the club on a Sunday. People
> queued to get into it, but if you weren't part of that regular crowd
> you had no chance of getting a place. It was very popular.

Religious festivals were often a reason for having a communal function,
which almost all members of the community attended:

Simchat Torah and *Purim* were the most enjoyable events held at the Institute. The whole community attended the dinners that were held after the shul service. Children, parents, friends, old and young attended – everyone came.

The Institute was also an important place for providing hospitality for many Jewish servicemen during the war years:

During the war I remember that hundreds of Jewish servicemen, British and American, attended the *Seder* night as well as on Sunday evenings during the year. The Belfast Jewish community had a worthy reputation for showing hospitality to servicemen. Many invited them for meals to their home, but the Institute was the main place they went to. Even though it was the war years, the Institute was a great place to be, with so many people about and enjoying themselves.

Welfare Organisations and Family Life

The Belfast Jewish Ladies Benevolent Society (1962) which collected and dispersed monies to needy families was founded in 1896 and continued functioning up to the early 1970s. Similar in function was the Belfast Board of Guardians which provided financial help for Jews in distress, whether they were living in the community or were transient Jews passing through Belfast. This commitment to welfare was a concrete expression of the religious obligation of Jews to provide charity for less fortunate members of the Jewish community.

The *Chevra Kadisha*, or burial society, is one of the oldest institutions within the Northern Ireland Jewish community. It has been in existence since the early days of the community and is still today a functioning organisation. It is essentially a co-operative friendly society, owned by its members, designed to provide for the ritual burial of Jews in consecrated ground. Families contribute a small yearly fee, generally paid on a weekly or monthly basis, for membership (Belfast Chevra Kadisha 1957–77). The chevra, as they are known, who carry out the task of burial are normally given high status within a Jewish community. This is because it is considered as a particularly kind act, which one Jew can do for a fellow Jew, to ensure that a person is buried according to all the requirements of Jewish law.

The importance of family life and the extended family system within Jewish communities is well-documented, and it was no less true of the Jewish community in Belfast as it was elsewhere:

If I think back to my childhood I can remember the many times that our house was a meeting place for the family. My mother's two sisters used to come over with their husbands and my cousins to spend *Yom Tov* and, very often, for Sunday lunch. We were a close family. In particular my grandmother, who moved from Manchester to live with us, was important to me. She and I were very close. I could talk to her and I always valued her advice.

The home often provided not just an informal meeting place for family members, but the family acted as a system of informal care and support in times of crises, need, or simply in facing the demands of life:

My father used to support nearly all the family. He was good to his brothers and sisters and never let them go without.

When we first came to Belfast just after the war, Mr—, who was a distant cousin, came to us in our rented apartment and offered to help us to buy a house. We lived in that house until my husband's death.

My father became ill and could no longer manage to live on his own after my mother's death. At first he didn't want to come to us ... he was very independent, but in the end he agreed. He's no trouble and we enjoy having him with us. Our own children are long married and we have the space ... it's not a problem, in fact its a *mitzvah*.

The Refugee Settlement Farm at Millisle

A significant wave of Jewish immigration into Northern Ireland consisted of those Jews who entered the UK prior to 1939, in an effort to flee the Nazi Holocaust. By 1939, refuges in Belfast and Millisle had been established and functioned until the end the Second World War. Prior to the outbreak of war in 1939, the Jewish community in Northern Ireland established a refuge for Jews fleeing Nazi Germany and other countries on the continent, such as Austria, Hungary and Czechoslovakia. 'The farm', as it was colloquially known, was at Millisle, County Down. Sugar (1990), who was nine years old when he arrived at the farm, states that its official title was the Refugee Settlement Farm, Millisle, Northern Ireland. It was leased to the Belfast Jewish community by a local businessman and provided a home a place of refuge from the Holocaust for Jews fleeing continental Europe. During its life some 70 refugees came to the farm, the first of whom arrived there at the beginning of May 1939. The refugees arrived in England first of all, before being helped to make their way

to Northern Ireland. Their age range was wide, but most seem to have
been young people – children, teenagers, and young adults. The
children attended local schools whilst the others worked the farm as
an ongoing concern. Once there, they contributed to the life of the
farm doing either domestic or agricultural work. Apparently, the agricultural methods used on the farm seemed strange to the local farmers
and were described by some of the refugees as being, at best, unorthodox.

In this way, many learnt agricultural skills and, although it operated
as a kibbutz, growing agricultural produce which was later sold on the
open market, the farm's primary function was to provide a place of
safety and security for the refugees. Local farmers helped the farm to
operate and, in return, the young people living there contributed
labour and equipment to help the locals at different times. Contact
with the local Jewish community seems to have been minimal, even
though the farm was run under the auspices of a committee of Belfast
Jews. The Rabbi to the community visited from time to time, as did
some Jewish individuals, but the overwhelming impression was of a
certain social distance between the local Jews and the refugees. Most
of the refugees left the farm at the end of 1945, and by 1948 it no longer
existed. The destination of its inhabitants is not clear, but it would
appear that most went to England or to what was then Palestine, and
some settled in Northern Ireland.

Decline

From the early to mid-1970s, the community began its decline. It is
often argued that this was associated with 'the troubles' and sectarianism between the Catholic and Protestant communities in the
Province. Whilst there is some evidence to indicate that it was a contributing factor, it would be too simplistic to credit it with being the
sufficient condition causing Jews to emigrate from Northern Ireland.
'The troubles' perhaps played more of a role in dissuading Jews from
looking towards the Jewish community in Northern Ireland as a place
to establish a family or find employment. Fear of the conflict was
probably the underlying reason here as well as the knowledge that the
community was not as viable as it had been previously.

Interviews with respondents reveal that a number of complex reasons
underpinned their decision to emigrate. Many factors played some part
in the decisions of Jews to leave Northern Ireland. Ideological
commitment to Zionism prompted some to leave or else not to return
after they had completed their higher education. This can be illustrated
as follows:

Once I completed my higher education I decided to settle in Israel. It was always in the back of my mind that I might do that rather than return to Belfast to make my life. I was a *madrich* in *Bnei Akiva* and so the idea of making *aliyah* was always there.

For others, it was because they wanted to be near adult children and their families who had previously left Belfast:

Both my children had left Belfast to settle in England after they got married. It wasn't unusual for the boy to move to be near his wife's family. Both my sons married English girls and so settled in England after their marriage. During the first few years it didn't matter too much that they were living in London, but once grandchildren came along it was a great loss to us that we weren't near to them. We decided that, once H— retired, we should move to England. 1974 was when we went and we have been here since.

Retirement also played its part as the above and the following quote suggest:

As I said to you previously, we had made a decision to move to England after we retired from our business. It was difficult to leave before because we didn't want to start our business again in England as all our contacts were in Northern Ireland. We were tied to Belfast, not like many professional people who could more easily pack up and leave. The community had shrunk ... people had left and our social life wasn't the same any more. The friends that we had said we would be mad to move away from Belfast, but, whilst we love to go back to visit and see the Cavehill again, our lives are here now.

It is also the case that many young people left Northern Ireland to attend higher education institutions in Britain, and they remained to establish careers and their own families. Other young people left because their social life had diminished in quality:

I really enjoyed my life in Belfast, but it was becoming restricted because of 'the troubles'. Not only were there fewer young Jewish people of my or similar age but within my social group we knew each other so well that people were looking for new faces and relationships, to meet new people. Three of us decided to go to London and find somewhere to live and get ourselves jobs ... this was after *Rosh Hashana* in 1973.

It is obvious that a complex set of reasons intertwined in the decisions that Jews took to leave Belfast, as can be seen from this quote:

Going to university in England gave me the chance to be independent of my parents. I wasn't really financially independent but I lived in a flat with some other students and going back home to live didn't appeal to me. Belfast wasn't that attractive any more. 'The troubles' didn't look as if they were going to go away. I thought my job prospects would be better if I stayed in England. When I left university I got a job easily enough and I've lived here ever since.

A hidden and important factor in the decline was the reduction in immigration of Jews into the community. Since 1978, only three Jewish families are known to have settled in Belfast and associated themselves with the community. All three families moved to Northern Ireland for career and employment purposes. In the previous periods of immigration and settlement into Northern Ireland, economic and security concerns were probably the main reasons for the emigration of Jews from their place of origin. Economic considerations are always likely to be important for almost all immigrants, and no doubt this factor continued to exert its influence. Safety and security were undoubtedly less prominent motives for immigration after the Second World War, compared to the desire to seek marriage partners and establish businesses. Reduction in average family size, consistent with economic and social security, together with relaxation of religious orthodoxy, meant that the community did not renew itself as in previous generations. The dearth of young married families deprived the community of its future nucleus. The social and demographic processes which had sustained the community for over 100 years had waned in their potency. Added to 'the troubles' factor, it is not surprising that the present Jewish community is at its lowest level since the last century.

Relations with the Wider Community

The interviews undertaken with Jews from Northern Ireland produced little, if any, substantive evidence of anti-Semitism. In this context, typical responses were:

Anti-Semitism wasn't something you experienced. Not of any consequence. At school you might be called names, but it was nothing really.

Not to my memory. We had good relations with our neighbours. In fact, Rabbi Shachter was so respected that even the non-Jews took off their hats when he passed by.

No, it was not a problem. Others might have had some [experiences of anti-Semitism] but not me. Northern Ireland was a good place to live.

However, simply to suggest that Jews are not conscious of anti-Semitism as a real possibility would be very simplistic. That is not to say that it has not been a reality, but it has been very infrequent, mild and held to be an aberration. Good intercommunity relations seem to have been both fostered and established throughout the life of the community. A cynical viewpoint would be that the two main Christian groups have been too busy with each other to have given much thought to the relatively small numbers of Jews living in Northern Ireland. A more positive and generous viewpoint is that the Jews of Northern Ireland have broadly speaking been well accepted and integrated into the wider cultural, social and economic structures. There is a strong link between Christian fundamentalism and its emphasis on both Old and New Testaments as a source of religious belief and truth to provide an obvious linkage with the Jewish community. The events of the Second World War and the continued fight for the survival of the State of Israel have further cemented the position of the Jewish community in the life of Northern Ireland, especially within the Protestant tradition. In reciprocation, the Jewish community – through its individual members and as a collective – for the most part, has maintained a social distance, particularly from the political process. Jewish values have emphasised the importance of loyalty to the host society within which any particular group of Jews find themselves. In this instance, loyalty has gone hand in hand with good citizenship and a sense of gratitude for the hospitality afforded Jews in times of crises.

The concern to establish an appropriate social distance from the political process has been fuelled by three factors: first, a concern not to be seen to be taking sides in a civil dispute in which they are not directly involved; second, a desire not to relinquish wider social ties which cut across religious divisions; and, third, as a response to an underlying psychological feeling of insecurity. This latter factor has played a remarkable role in forming the attitudes of Jews regarding the civil unrest. This has been brought about through literally thousands of years of persecution, expulsion and social discrimination which has been etched into the social consciousness of most Jews. The striving towards integration and the social acceptance that this implies can be seen to be the outcome of feelings of insecurity and rejection. This is in spite of the absence of overt or substantive anti-Semitism within the society. No external threat has ever been voiced at the Jewish community; nevertheless, a concern for communal security has been prominent. This concern with security has also had its origins in the actions of Middle East terrorists who have used the weapon of terror against Jewish communal organisations throughout the world. This has sensitised Jews to their vulnerability in such a situation and prompted the need to maintain a less than prominent public profile.

Undoubtedly, the relationship between a host community and a minority community within it can be problematic for both. This can be no more clearly seen than in the domain of integration. Integration represents the willingness of the host society to incorporate minority group members into its social structure and is clearly important in the realms of good community relations and principles of democracy and equal opportunity. Both groups can benefit from such a social process. From the minority group's point of view, though, it holds potential dangers. Integration in the form of assimilation means loss of cultural identity and traditions held onto and passed on over generations, and replacement by cultural features prominent within the host society. These new cultural features represent a threat to continuity. An inherent tension exists between the need for acceptance and participation and the need for cultural independence (cf. *Belfast Jewish Record* 1962–97).

Conclusion

The contemporary situation within the Jewish community in Northern Ireland can best be described as being essentially concerned with maintenance of the *status quo*. As numbers have decreased, so there has been a corresponding diminishment in the ability of the community to provide the basics for a full Jewish life. Correspondingly, this has given rise to an increasing need to rationalise services and provision. Increasing reliance is placed upon self-help and voluntarism. A smaller community means a diminishment in the pool of potential informal and formal leadership. Little can be done to stem the process of social change, but much has to be done, and is done, to support and maintain the basic fabric of community life.

For those who remain, the community can be a vital source of social cohesion, and a continuance of historical and cultural traditions and values. Tradition is a major force within Jewish life, and this continues to be so for Jews of Northern Ireland. These traditions are communicated primarily through the religious practices and services within the synagogue, but are also transmitted through the remnants of independent organisations which now are integrated into the synagogue structure. The burial society, Hebrew school and social centre are just some of the structures which continue to function in the present, and which represent continuity with the past. Many members look back with nostalgia to the past, to the sense of communal confidence and self assurance, and contrast it with the present climate of uncertainty and doubt. Inevitably perhaps, memories of the community, as it was in the past, have become distorted in the face of present difficulties. Decline and change have been difficult processes for the community to adjust to and deal with. The community has tried to face up to them by looking to the future and not dwelling too much on the past.

Glossary

aliyah	Emigration to Israel.
Beth Hamidrash	Study House, where the study of the Torah is undertaken.
Beth Hasepher	House of the Book, another name for Hebrew School.
Bnei Akiva	Religious youth movement.
daven	To pray.
chedar	Part-time religious school, normally for children up to the age of 13 years.
Chevra Gemorah	Adult study group established for the study of religious texts, in particular the Talmud.
Chevra Kadisha	Burial society.
Gemorah	The Talmud consists of two essential parts – Mishnah and Gemorah. Gemorah is the commentary on the Mishnah (law).
madrich	Youth leader.
mikvah	Bath for ritual immersion.
mitzvah	Religious commandment or obligation.
mohel	The person who carries out circumcision according to Jewish law.
Purim	Jewish festival celebrating events which took place in Babylonia after the destruction of the first Temple.
Rosh Hashana	Jewish New Year.
Schochetim	Plural of Schochet. Men who slaughter cattle and poultry according to Jewish law.
Seder	Religious service performed on the first and second nights of Passover.
Shabbat	Jewish Sabbath.
shteitel	Small Jewish rural settlements found in Eastern Europe.
shul	Synagogue.
Simchat Torah	Jewish festival celebrating the completion of the annual cycle of the reading of the Five Books of Moses.
Torah	Specifically the Five Books of Moses, but can also refer to the whole of Jewish theological literature. It is translated as 'The Law'.
Yom Tov	Collective name for religious days other than the Shabbat.

Bibliography

Aanchawan, A. (1996) 'Room at the Top', *Health Service Journal*, 7 March, 26–8.

Advisory Committee on Travellers (ACT) (NI) (1986) Minutes, 25 September.

—— (1988) 'Interim Findings on a Survey of Travellers in Northern Ireland' (unpublished).

—— (1989) *Final Report 1986–89* (Belfast: HMSO).

—— (1992) *'With Not For' Conference Report* (Belfast: ACT).

—— (1993) *Final Report 1990–93* (Belfast: HMSO).

—— (1996) *Final Report 1993–96* (Belfast: HMSO).

Ahmad, W. (1993) 'Making Black People Sick: "Race", Ideology and Health Research', in Ahmad, W., *'Race' and Health in Contemporary Britain* (Buckingham: Open University Press).

Alfredsson, G. and de Zayas, A. (1993) 'Minority Rights: Protection by the United Nations', *Human Rights Law Journal*, vol. 14, 1–9.

Ali, R. (1996) Asian Women and Children's Centre representative, speaking at conference, *'Speaking Out*, Identifying and Addressing the Health and Social Needs of Ethnic Minorities in Northern Ireland', Belfast, November.

Allen, S. (1971) *New minorities and old conflicts: Asian and West Indian migrants in Britain* (New York: Random House).

Alliance Party of Northern Ireland (1997) *Agenda for Change: The Alliance Manifesto*, General Election, 1 May.

Anaya, J.S. (1995) 'The Capacity of International Law to Advance Ethnic or Nationality Rights Claims', in Kymlicka, W. (ed.) *The Rights of Minority Cultures* (Oxford: Oxford University Press).

Andrews, A. and Jewson, N. (1993) 'Ethnicity and Infant Deaths: the Implications of Recent Statistical Evidence for Materialist Explanations', *Sociology of Health and Illness*, vol. 15, no. 2, 137–56.

Anthias, F. and Yuval-Davis, N. (1992) *Racialised Boundaries: Race, Nation, Gender, Colour and Class and the Anti-Racist Struggle* (London: Routledge).

Anwar, M. (1979) *The myth of return: Pakistanis in Britain* (London: Heinemann).

Assisi Fellowship (1966) *Committee to Investigate and Make Recommendations regarding Itinerants in Northern Ireland* (Belfast: Assisi Fellowship).

—— (1967) Minutes of Working Party on Itinerants (Belfast: Assisi Fellowship).

Asylum and Immigration Act 1996 (UK) (London: HMSO).

Baiden, F. (1994) *Cultural Awareness in Northern Ireland: Are student midwives prepared for practice in multi-cultural society?*, unpublished MSc dissertation in Nursing, Queen's University of Belfast.

Balarajan, R. and Soni Raleigh, V. (1993) *Ethnicity and Health: A Guide for the NHS* (London: DOH).

Baldwin, R. (1995) *Rules and Government* (Oxford: Clarendon Press).

Ballard, R. (1987) 'The political economy of migration: Pakistan, Britain, and the Middle East', in Eades, J. (ed.) *Migrants, workers, and the social order* (London: Tavistock).

—— (ed.) (1994) 'Introduction: The emergence of Desh Pardesh', in Ballard, R. (ed.) *Desh Pardesh: The South Asian presence in Britain* (London: C. Hurst).

Banton, M. (1983) *Racial and Ethnic Competition* (Cambridge: Cambridge University Press).

Barnardos (1995) *Barnardos Chinese Lay Health Project* (Belfast: Barnardos).

Barry, B. and Tischler, H.L. (1978) *Race and Ethnic Matters*, 4th edition (Boston, MA: Houghton Mifflin).

Barry, J., Herity, B. and Solan, J. (1989) *The Traveller Health Status Study: Vital Statistics of Travelling People 1987* (Dublin: Health Research Board).

Barth, F. (1996) 'Ethnic Groups and Boundaries', in Sollos, E. (ed.) *Theories of Ethnicity* (London: Macmillan).

BBC Radio Northern Ireland (1996) 'Racism Awareness Week', interviews, December.

Beirne, M. (1998) 'PAFT on the March', *Just News*, vol. 13, no. 2, February.

Beishon, S., Virdee, S. and Hagell, A. (1995) *Nursing in a Multi-ethnic NHS* (London: PSI).

Belfast Chevra Kadisha (1957–77) *Statement of Accounts*.

Belfast Hebrew Congregation (1932) *Complete Amendment of Rules*.

—— (1945–97) *Reports and Accounts*.

Belfast Jewish Ladies Benevolent Society (1962) *Financial Statement and Report*.

Belfast Jewish Record (1962–97) *Belfast Jewish Record – The Journal of the Jewish Community in Northern Ireland*.

Belfast Law Centre (1993) 'Travellers win case against Belfast City Council', *Frontline Social Welfare Law Quarterly*, No. 9, July.

Belfast News Letter (1954) 'Gypsy Nuisance in Ulster', 4 October.

—— (1956) 'Control of Gypsies', 9 March.

Belfast Telegraph (1982) '"Nazi" charge as itinerants are attacked', 2 August.

—— (1993), 24 May.

Belfast Travellers' Education and Development Group (BTEDG) (1997) *Submission to the United Nations Committee on Economic, Social and Cultural Rights,* 9 May (Belfast: BTEDG).

Benedict, R. (1943) *Race and Racism* (London: Routledge and Kegan Paul).

Betz, F. (1996) 'Cultural Production and the Politics of Identity: On the Strategic Use of "Multiculturalism" in Two Austrian Cities', *Innovation*, vol. 9, no. 1, 105–17.

Bhopal, R. and Donaldson, L. (1988) 'Health Education for Ethnic Minorities: Current Provision and Future Directions', *Health Education Journal*, vol. 47, 137–40.

Bindman, G. (1996) 'When Will Europe Act Against Racism?', *European Human Rights Law Review*, vol. 1, 143–9.

Birmingham City Council Housing Department (1993) *Housing Needs of Black Elders* Seminar report, 28 July (Birmingham: Birmingham City Council Housing Department).

Boerefijn, I. (1995) 'Towards a Strong System of Supervision: The Human Rights Committee's Role in Reforming the Reporting Procedure under Article 40 of the Covenant on Civil and Political Rights', *Human Rights Quarterly*, vol. 17, 766–93.

Borchardt, K. (1995) *European Integration – the origins and growth of the European Union* (Luxembourg: OOPEC).

Boyd, A. (1969) *Holy War in Belfast* (Belfast: Anvil).

Boyd, A. (1994) *Broadcast Journalism: Techniques of Radio and TV News,* 3rd edition (Oxford: Focal Press).

Breitenmoser, S. and Richter, D. (1991) 'Proposal for an Additional Protocol to the European Convention on Human Rights concerning the protection of minorities in the participating states of the CSCE', *Human Rights Law Journal*, vol. 12, 262–73.

Brett, R. (1996) 'Human Rights and the OSCE', *Human Rights Quarterly*, vol. 18, 668–93.

Brewer, J. and Dowds, L. (1996) 'Race, ethnicity and prejudice in Northern Ireland', in Breen, R., Devine, P. and Dowds, L. (eds) *Social attitudes in Northern Ireland* (Fifth Report, 1995–1996) (Belfast: Appletree Press).

Brewer, J.D. (1992) 'Sectarianism and racism, and their parallels and differences', *Ethnic and Racial Studies*, vol. 15, no. 3, July, 352–64.

Burke, A.W. (1976) 'Attempted Suicide Among Asian Immigrants in Birmingham', *British Journal of Psychiatry*, vol. 128, 528–33.

Butler, C. (1985) *Travelling People in Derry and Tyrone* (Derry: World Development Group).

Cameron, F. C. (1995) 'Promoting Multi-culturalism', *CRC News*, vol. 18, 6.

—— (1996) 'Issues Pertaining to Ethnic Minority Elders in Northern Ireland', Press Release, 30 September.

Campbell, R. and Stevenson, G. (1993) *Community Differentials in Health in Northern Ireland* (Belfast: DHSS).

Cant, B. and Kelly, E. (1995) 'Why is there a need for racial equality activity in Scotland', *Scottish Affairs*, no. 12, summer.

Cape, E. with Luqmani, J. (1995) *Defending suspects at police stations: the practitioners' guide to advice and representation* (London: Legal Action Group).

Carr-Hill, R. and Rudat, K. (1995) 'Unsound Barrier', *Health Service Journal*, 9 February.

Cashmore, E. and Troyna, B. (1983) *Introduction to race relations* (London: Routledge and Kegan Paul).

Causeway (1998) 'Editorial', vol. 5, no. 1, spring.

Central Community Relations Unit (CCRU) (1992) *Race Relations in Northern Ireland* (Belfast: CCRU).

—— (1995) *Policy Appraisal and Fair Treatment, Annual Report 1994* (Belfast: CCRU).

—— (1996) *Policy Appraisal and Fair Treatment, Annual Report 1995* (Belfast: CCRU).

—— (1997) *Policy Appraisal and Fair Treatment, Annual Report 1996* (Belfast: CCRU).

Chan, C. (1994) 'Chinese Have Special Needs', *Nursing Times*, vol. 90, no. 15, 7.

Chan, M. (1994) 'Breaking Down Barriers', *Healthlines*, November, 10.

—— (1996) Director, NHS Ethnic Health Unit, speaking at conference, '*Speaking Out*, Identifying and Addressing the Health and Social Needs of Ethnic Minorities in Northern Ireland', Belfast, November.

ChildCare NI/SHSSB (1994) *Assessment of Need for Services for Children and Families in Need in the SHSSB* (Belfast: ChildCare NI).

Chinese Welfare Association (CWA) (1996) *Development Plan 1996–2001* (Belfast: CWA).

—— (1997a) *Chinese Welfare Association (NI): Housing Survey Report* (Belfast: CWA).

—— (1997b) *Annual Report 1996–1997*.

—— and Central Council for Education and Training in Social Work (1987) I like the way I am (video) (Belfast: CWA/CCETSW).

——, Committee on the Administration of Justice (CAJ) and Northern Ireland Council for Travelling People (NICTP) (1993) *Combating Racism in Northern Ireland*. Joint submission to the Home Affairs Committee inquiry into 'Racial Attacks and Harassment' (Belfast: CAJ).

—— and Ethnic Minorities Working Party on Health (1997) *Speaking Out*, Conference Report in Health and Social Needs of Ethnic Minorities in Northern Ireland (Belfast: CWA/EMWPH).

Cochrane, R. and Bal, S.S. (1989) 'Mental Hospital Admission Rates of Immigrants to England: a Comparison of 1971 and 1981', *Social Psychiatry and Psychiatric Epidemiology*, vol. 24, 2–11.

Commission of the European Communities (CEC) (1989) Communication from the Commission concerning its action programme relating to implementation of the Community Charter of Fundamental Social Rights for Workers, COM (89) 586, 29 November.

—— (1990) Community Charter on the Fundamental Social Rights of Workers, *Social Europe*, 1/90, 46–50.

—— (1994) European Social Policy – A Way Forward for the Union: a White Paper, COM (94) 333.

—— (1995) Communication from the Commission on racism, xenophobia and anti-semitism, and Proposal for a Council Decision designating 1997 as European Year against Racism, COM (95) 653, 13 December.

—— (1997) *Newsletter for the European Year against Racism*, 30 January.

Commission for Racial Equality (CRE) (1992) *Second Review of the Race Relations Act 1976* (London: CRE).

—— (1997) *The Irish in Britain* (London: CRE).

—— and National Association of Community Relations Council (1986) *Immigration Control Procedures* (London: CRE).

Commission on Itinerancy (1963) *Report of the Commission on Itinerancy* (Dublin: Stationery Office).

Committee on the Administration of Justice (CAJ) (1992) *Racism in Northern Ireland: The need for legislation to combat racial discrimination in Northern Ireland* (Report of a CAJ Conference) (Belfast: CAJ).

—— (1993a) *Combating Racism in Northern Ireland: A submission by the racism sub-group of the CAJ in response to the consultative document 'Race Relations In Northern Ireland'*, March (Belfast: CAJ).

—— (1993b) *A Bill of Rights for Northern Ireland* (Belfast: CAJ).

—— (1994) *Submission to the United Nations Committee on the Rights of the Child*, 1 August (Belfast: CAJ).

—— (1996) *Fair Employment for all – a submission by CAJ to the Standing Advisory Commission on Human Rights Employment Equality Review* (Belfast: CAJ).

—— (1997) *Submission to the United Nations Committee on the Elimination of Racial Discrimination*, 3 March (Belfast: CAJ).

—— and the Northern Ireland Council for Ethnic Minorities (1996) *Submission to the United Nations Committee on the Elimination of Racial Discrimination*, 4 March (Belfast: CAJ).

Committee on the Elimination of Racial Discrimination (CERD) (1996) *Report of the Committee on the Elimination of Racial Discrimination*, UN Document A/51/18, paras. 229–35.

Commons Debates (NI) (1956) Official Report of Debates, Parliament of Northern Ireland, Commons, 2041–2.

—— (1965) Official Report of Debates, Parliament of Northern Ireland, Commons, 1016.

Consultative Commission (1995*) Final Report of the Consultative Commission on Racism and Xenophobia*, Ref. 6906/1/95 Rev 1 Limite RAXEN 24 (Brussels: General Secretariat of the Council of the European Union).

Council of Europe (1993) 'Vienna Declaration of the Heads of State and Government of the Member States of the Council of Europe on the Reform Mechanisms of the ECHR, on National Minorities, and on a Plan of Action against Racism', *Human Rights Law Journal*, vol. 14, 373–6.

Craigavon Travellers' Support Committee (CTSC) (1993) *Addressing the needs of the Traveller community* (Craigavon: CTSC).

Creaney, I. (1977) *The Chinese Community in Northern Ireland*, unpublished Social Anthropology dissertation, Queen's University of Belfast.

Criminal Justice and Public Order Act 1994 (London: HMSO).

Critcher, C., Parker, M. and Sondhi, R. (1977) 'Race in the Provincial Press: A Case Study of Five West Midlands Newspapers', in UNESCO, *Ethnicity and the Media: An Analysis of Media Reporting in the United Kingdom, Canada and Ireland* (Paris: UNESCO).

Crowley, N. (1993) 'Racism and the Travellers', *Anti-Racist Law and the Travellers* (Dublin: DTEDG, ICCL and ITM).

Cruickshank, J.K. and Beevers, D. (1991) *Ethnic Factors in Health and Disease* (Oxford: Butterworth Heinemann).

Dean, G., Walsh, D., Downing, H. and Shelley, E. (1981) 'First Admissions of Native-Born and Immigrants to Psychiatric Hospitals in South-East England', *British Journal of Psychiatry*, vol. 139, 506–12.

Delors, J. (1989) *Debates of the European Parliament*, no. 2-380/94, 13 September.

Democratic Left (1996a) *Election Communication* (leaflet), 30 May.

—— (1996b) *Rebuilding Politics: Setting the Agenda for Conciliation*, A Democratic Left Proposal.

Department of Education (NI) (DENI) (1993) *Policy and Guidelines for the Education of Children from Travelling Families*, Circular 37 (Belfast: HMSO).

Department of Education and Science (DES) (1983a) Education Act 1981 and Education Act 1981 (Commencement no: 2) Order (London: HMSO).

—— (1983b) *Assessments and Statements of Special Educational Needs*, Circular 1/83 (London: HMSO).

Department of Health (DOH) (1992a) *The Patient's Charter* (London: HMSO).

—— (1992b) *The Health of the Nation: A Strategy for Health in England* (London: HMSO).

Department of Health and Social Services (DHSS) (NI) (1991) *A Regional Strategy for Northern Ireland 1992–97* (Belfast: HMSO).

—— (1996a) *Regional Strategy for Health and Social Wellbeing 1997–2002. Health and Wellbeing into the Next Millennium* (Belfast: DHSS).

—— (1996b) *A Strategy for Nursing, Midwifery and Health Visiting in Northern Ireland* (Belfast: DHSS).

—— (1996c) *The Children (NI) Order* (Belfast: HMSO).

Department of Health and Social Services Inspectorate (DHSS) (1995) *Promoting Social Welfare* (Belfast: DHSS).

Department of Health and Social Services Registrar General Northern Ireland (1992) *The Northern Ireland Census 1991 Summary Report* (Belfast: HMSO).

Department of the Environment for Northern Ireland (DOE) (NI) (1984) *Report of the Northern Ireland Working Party on Site Provision For Travelling People* (Belfast: HMSO).

—— (1993) *Northern Ireland Travellers Census 1993* (Belfast: HMSO).

—— (1994) *Regional Development Strategy for the Provision of Sites for Travellers over the period 1994–2000* (Belfast: HMSO).

—— (1996) *Government Response To Recommendations Contained In 'A Review Of Policies Affecting Travellers In NI'*, November (Belfast: DOE).

de Zayas, A. (1993) 'The International Judicial Protection of Peoples and Minorities', in Brölmann, C., Lefeber, R. and Zieck, M. (eds) *Peoples and Minorities in International Law* (Dordrecht: Martinus Nijhoff), 253–87.

Dickson, B. (1995) 'The United Nations and Freedom of Religion', *International and Comparative Law Quarterly*, vol. 44, 327–357.

—— (1997a) 'Complaints against the Police', in Dickson, B. (ed.) *Civil Liberties in Northern Ireland*, 3rd edition (Belfast: CAJ).

—— (1997b) 'Meetings and Demonstrations', in Dickson, B. (ed.) *Civil Liberties in Northern Ireland*, 3rd edition (Belfast: CAJ).

Donaldson, L.J. and Taylor, J.B. (1993) 'Patterns of Asians and Non Asians Morbidity in Hospitals', *British Medical Journal*, vol. 286, 949–51.

Donovan, J.L. (1986) *We Don't Buy Sickness, It Just Comes: Health, Illness and Health Care in the Lives of Black People in London* (Aldershot: Gower).

Doolin, N. (1994) 'The Luck of the Irish?', *Nursing Standard*, vol. 8, no. 46, 40–1.

Down Recorder (1986) 'End This Ugly Mess', 25 June.

Draft Local Government Order (Northern Ireland) Order 1997 (Belfast: HMSO).

Draft Race Relations (Northern Ireland) Order 1996 (Belfast: HMSO).

Dublin Travellers' Education and Development Group (DTEDG) (1992) *Irish Travellers – New Analysis and New Initiatives* (Dublin: Pavee Point Publications).

Dummett, A. (1994) 'The Starting Line: A proposal for a draft Council Directive concerning the elimination of racial discrimination', *New Community*, vol. 20, 530–8.

Eastern Health and Social Services Board (EHSSB) (1989) *Public Health Matters. Second Annual report of the Director of Public Health* (Belfast: EHSSB).

Eatwell, R. (1994) 'Why are fascism and racism reviving in Western Europe?', *Political Quarterly*, vol. 65, 313–25.

Economic and Social Committee (ESC) (1984) 'Opinion on Migrant Workers', *Official Journal* 1984, C 343/28.

Education Reform (Northern Ireland) Order 1989 (Belfast: HMSO).

Englander, D. (1994) *A Documentary History of Immigrants in Britain 1840–1920* (London: Leicester University Press).

Equal Opportunities Commission for Northern Ireland (EOCNI) (1993) *Response to Consultative Document on Race Relations in Northern Ireland*, April.

Ericson, R.V., Baranek, P.M. and Chan, J.B.L. (1989) *Negotiating Control: A Study of News Sources* (Buckingham: Open University Press).

Erikson, T.H. (1993) *Ethnicity and Nationalism* (London: Pluto Press).

Esmail, A. and Everington, S. (1993) 'Racial Discrimination Against Doctors From Ethnic Minorities', *British Medical Journal*, vol. 305, 691–2.

European Parliament (EP) (1985) *Report of the European Parliament's Committee of Inquiry into the Rise of Fascism and Racism in Europe* (Luxembourg: (OOPEC).

—— (1991) *Report of the European Parliament's Committee of Inquiry on Racism and Xenophobia* (Luxembourg: OOPEC).

European Union (EU) (1997) *European Union's Treaty of Amsterdam* (Luxembourg: OOPEC).

Fitzgerald, G. (1992) *Repulsing Racism: Reflections on Racism and the Irish* (Dublin: Lip).

Fitzgerald, M. (1993) *Ethnic minorities and the criminal justice system*, Royal Commission on Criminal Justice, Research Study no. 20 (London: HMSO).

Foley, C. (1995) *Human Rights, Human Wrongs: The Alternative Report to the UN Human Rights Committee* (London: Rivers Oram Press).

Fong, L.K.W. (1981) *Chinese Children in Liverpool*. Thesis, Diploma in Special Education, University of Liverpool.

Ford, C. (1991) Interview, *Rafferty*, 'Racism in Northern Ireland', BBC Radio Ulster, 20 May.

Foreign and Commonwealth Office (FCO) (1996) *A Partnership of Nations* (London: HMSO).

Fowler, R. (1991) *Language in the News: Discourse and Ideology in the Press* (London: Routledge).

Galtung, J. and M. Ruge (1965) 'The Structure of Foreign News: the Presentation of the Congo, Cuba and Cyprus crises in four foreign newspapers', *Journal of International Peace Research*, vol. 1, 64–91.

Gardner, K. and A. Shukur (1994) '"I'm Bengali, I'm Asian, and I'm living here": The changing identity of British Bengalis', in Ballard, R. (ed.) *Desh Pardesh: The South Asian presence in Britain* (London: C. Hurst).

George, M. (1994a) 'Racism in Nursing', *Nursing Standard*, vol. 8, no. 18, 20–1.

—— (1994b) 'Accepting Differences', *Nursing Standard*, vol. 8, no. 18, 22–3.

Gilbert, G. (1996) 'The Council of Europe and Minority Rights', *Human Rights Quarterly*, vol. 18, 160–89.

Gillespie, R. (1993) 'Multicultural Health Provision', *Health Services Management*, March, 24–5.

Gilroy, P. and Lawrence, E. (1988) 'Two-Tone Britain: White and Black Youth and the Politics of Anti-Racism', in Cohen, P. and Baines, H.S. (eds) *Multi-Racist Britain* (Basingstoke: Macmillan).

Ginnety, P. (1993) *The Health of Travellers. Based on a Research Study with Travellers in Belfast* (Belfast: Eastern Health and Social Services Board).

—— and Ali, R. (1994) 'Health Workshop Report', in *Racism and Poverty Seminar Report* (Belfast: NIAPN).

Glazer, N. (1995) 'Individual Rights against Group Rights', in Kymlicka, W. (ed.) *The Rights of Minority Cultures* (Oxford: Oxford University Press).

—— and Moynihan, D.A. (1963) *Beyond the Melting Pot* (Cambridge, MA: Harvard University Press).

Gmelch, G. and Gmelch, S.B. (1974) 'The Itinerant Settlement Movement – Its Policies and Effects on Irish Travellers', *Studies*, vol. LXIII.

—— (1976) 'The Emergence of an Ethnic Group: The Irish Travellers', *Anthropological Quarterly*, vol. 94, no. 4, October, reprinted December (Washington, DC: The Catholic University America Press).

Gmelch, S. (1986) *Nan: The Life of an Irish Travelling Woman* (London: Souvenir Press).

Goldberg, D.T. (1993) *Racist Culture: Philosophy and the Politics of Meaning* (Oxford: Blackwell).

Gomien, D., Harris, D. and Zwaak, L. (1996) *Law and Practice of the European Convention on Human Rights and the European Social Charter* (Strasbourg: Council of Europe Publishing).

Gordon, M. *et al.* (1991) 'The health of Travellers' children in Northern Ireland', *Public Health* 105, 387–91.

Gordon, P. (1990) *Racial Violence and Harassment* (London: Pluto Press).

Green Party of Northern Ireland (1997) *Green Party Manifesto for the constituency of North Belfast in the Westminster elections* May.

Grimes, A. (1996) 'Under Suspicion', *Frontline*, Social Welfare Law Quarterly, no. 20 (Belfast: Law Centre, Northern Ireland).

Gunaratnam, Y. (1993) *Health and Race Checklist: a Starting Point for Managers* (London: King's Fund Centre).

Hadfield, B. (1984) 'The prevention of incitement of religious hatred – an article of faith', *Northern Ireland Legal Quarterly*, vol. 35, 230–42.

Hainsworth, P. (1996) 'Racism, Anti-Racism and the Extreme Right: the Republic of Ireland and Northern Ireland', *Contemporary European Studies Association of Australia Newsletter*, no. 17, December.

Hall, S. *et al.* (1978) *Policing the Crisis: Mugging, the State and Law and Order* (London: Macmillan).

—— (1992) 'The West and the Rest: Discourse and Power', in Hall, S. and Gieben, B. (eds) *Formations of Modernity* (Cambridge: Polity Press and Open University Press).

Hargreaves, A. (1995) *Immigration, 'race' and ethnicity in contemporary France* (London: Routledge).

Harris, D., O'Boyle, M. and Warbrick, C. (1995) *Law of the European Convention on Human Rights* (London: Butterworths).

Hartmann, P. and Husband, C. (1972) 'The mass media and racial conflict', in McQuail, D. (ed.) *Sociology of Mass Communications* (Harmondsworth: Penguin).

—— and Clark, J. (1974) 'Race as News: A Study in the Handling of Race in the British National Press from 1963 to 1970', in UNESCO, *Race as News* (Paris: UNESCO).

Hartney, M. (1995) 'Some Confusions Concerning Collective Rights', in Kymlicka, W. (ed.) *The Rights of Minority Cultures* (Oxford: Oxford University Press).

Hawes, D. and Perez, P. (1995) *The Gypsy and the State* (Bristol: School for Advanced Urban Studies).

Healey, P. (1996) 'Anger at Tribunal Ruling', *Nursing Standard*, vol. 19, no. 18, 5.

Health and Personal Social Services Management Executive (HPSSME) (1995) *Charter Standards for Community Services* (Belfast: HPSSME).

Hechter, M. (1975) *Internal Colonialism – The Celtic Fringe in British National Development, 1536–1966* (London: Routledge and Kegan Paul).

Hepburn, A.C. (1980) *The Conflict of Nationality in Modern Ireland* (London: Ireland).

Hickman, M. and Walter, B. (1997) *Discrimination and the Irish Community in Britain: A report of research undertaken for the Commission for Racial Equality* (London: CRE).

Home Office (Secretary of State) (1985) *The Government Reply to the Second Paper from the Home Affairs Committee*, Session 1985-5: 'The Chinese Community in Britain' (London: HMSO).

House of Commons (1985) *Education for All*, the Report of the Committee of the Inquiry into the Education of Children from Ethnic Minority Groups (Swann Report) (London: HMSO).

——— (1997) Parliamentary Debates/ Official Report, *Draft Race Relations (Northern Ireland) Order 1997*, Seventh Standing Committee on Delegated Legislation, 6 February.

House of Commons/Home Affairs Committee (HAC) (1985) *Report on the Chinese Community in Britain* (London: HMSO).

——— (1994a) *Racial Attacks and Harassment*, Third Report from the Home Affairs Committee, Session 1993–94, vol. 1 (Report and proceedings) (London: HMSO).

——— (1994b) *The Chinese in Britain*, Third Report from the Home Affairs Committee, Session 1993–1994 (London: HMSO).

House of Lords (1997) *Race Relations (Northern Ireland) Order 1997*, 18 February.

Housing (Northern Ireland) Order 1988 (Belfast: HMSO).

Husband, C. (ed.) (1991) *Race in Britain: Continuity and Change* (London: Hutchinson).

Hutchinson, J. and Smith, A.D. (1996) *Ethnicity* (Oxford: Oxford University Press).

Hutson, N. (1996) *PAFT – a contribution to the debate on mainstreaming equality* (Belfast: SACHR).

Hyman, L. (1972) *The Jews of Ireland* (Dublin: Shannon; London: Israel University Press).

Irish News (1969) 'Jewish Councillor offers services as Ombudsman', 25 August.

——— (1995) 'Alexander won't lose rag over taunts', 2 March.

——— (1995) 'Fascist sings the praises of "white" Belfast', 18 November.

——— (1996) 'Shadow of Drumcree hangs over boy's death', 11 October.

——— (1997) 'West Belfast man hits out at Garda "racism"', 4 November.

Irish Press (1956) 'Unionist call for curb on gypsies', 9 March.

Irwin, G. (1996) *Ethnic Minorities in Northern Ireland* (Coleraine: Centre for the Study of Conflict, University of Ulster).

—— and Dunn, S. (1997) *Ethnic Minorities in Northern Ireland* (Coleraine: Centre for the Study of Conflict, University of Ulster).

Jackson, H. and McHardy, A. (1995) *The Two Irelands: The problem of the double minority* (London: Minority Rights Group).

Jamdagni, L. (1996) 'Race Against Time', *Health Service Journal*, 7 March, 30–1.

Jeffery, P. (1976) *Migrants and refugees: Muslim and Christian Pakistani families in Bristol* (Cambridge: Cambridge University Press).

Joly, D. (1995) *Britannia's crescent: making a place for Muslims in British society* (Aldershot: Avebury Press).

Jones, T. (1997) *The Draft Local Government Order (Northern Ireland) Order 1997 –Paper for the Standing Advisory Commission on Human Rights*, May (Belfast: SACHR).

Joyce, N. (1985) *Traveller: An Autobiography* (Dublin: Gill and Macmillan).

Kapur, N. (1997) *The Indian Community in Northern Ireland* (Belfast: MCRC).

Kenny, M. (1994) 'Final Thoughts: A Case For Celebration', in McCann, M., Ó Síocháin, S. and Ruane, J. (eds) *Irish Travellers: Culture and Ethnicity* (Belfast: Institute of Irish Studies, Queen's University of Belfast).

Kerven, R. (1988) *Festival! Chinese New Year*, Commonwealth Institute (London: Macmillan Education).

Kilfeather, L. (1988) *The path back to Islam*, unpublished BA dissertation, Queen's University Belfast, Department of Social Anthropology.

King's Fund Equal Opportunities Task Force (1990) *Racial Equality: The Nursing Profession* (London: King's Fund Centre).

Klebes, H. (1993) 'Draft Protocol on Minority Rights to the ECHR', *Human Rights Law Journal*, vol. 14, 140–8.

—— (1995) 'The Council of Europe's Framework Convention for the Protection of National Minorities', *Human Rights Law Journal*, vol. 16, 92–115.

Kymlicka, W. (ed.) (1995) *The Rights of Minority Cultures* (Oxford: Oxford University Press).

Lee, S.Y. (1993) *The Way Forward*, speech at celebration of tenth anniversary of the Chinese Chamber of Commerce (NI) (Belfast: CWA).

—— (1996) 'The Chinese Community' in *Speaking Out*, Conference Report on Health and Social Needs of Ethnic Minorities Working Party on Health, Belfast, November (Belfast: CWA).

—— (1997) Chairman of the Chinese Welfare Association, Speech for the launch of the Chinese Interpreting Service, Spires Conference Centre, Belfast, 8 December.

Leeson, P. (1993) 'Towards a Commission for Racial Equality (NI): a Model for Best Practice', *Just News*, vol. 8, no. 10, 7.

Leong, F.C. (1995) *A Literature Review of Ethnic Minority and Social Care Needs* (Belfast: Multi-cultural Resource Centre/ Northern Health and Social Services Board).

—— (1996) *Issues Pertaining to Ethnic Minority Elders in Northern Ireland*, Press Release to BBC Northern Ireland, September.

Lerner, N. (1993) 'The Evolution of Minority Rights in International Law', in Brölmann, C., Lefeber, R., and Zieck, M. (eds) *Peoples and Minorities in International Law* (Dordrecht: Martinus Nijhoff), 77–101.

Lieberman, M. (1989) 'Living in Peace in a Troubled Land', *The Jewish Monthly*, vol. 103, no. 7, 10–19 (Washington, DC: B'nai Brith).

Liégeois, J.P. (1987) *Gypsies and Travellers* (Strasbourg: Council of Europe).

—— (1994) *Roma, Gypsies, Travellers* (Strasbourg: Council of Europe Press).

Littlewood, R. and Lipsedge, M. (1988) 'Psychiatric Illness Among British Afro-Caribbeans', *British Medical Journal*, vol. 296, 950–1.

Local Government (Miscellaneous Provisions) (Northern Ireland) Order 1985 (Belfast: HMSO).

Local Government (NI) Order 1997.

Lomas (1989) *Debates of the European Parliament*, no. 2-374/56, 14 February.

London, M. (1986) 'Mental Illness among Immigrant Minorities in the United Kingdom', *British Journal of Psychiatry*, vol. 149, 265–73.

McAlister, S. (1937) *The Secret Languages of Ireland* (Cambridge: Cambridge University Press).

McAllister, P. (1996) 'Australian Multiculturalism: Lessons for South Africa?', *Indicator SA*, vol. 13, no. 2, 72–8.

McAlpine, Thorpe and Warrier International Management Consultants (1994) *Perceptions of Nursing Care in the UK within Ethnic Minority Communities* (London: McAlpine, Thorpe and Warrier).

McCann, M., Ó Siocháin, S. and Ruane, J. (eds) (1994) *Irish Travellers: Culture and Ethnicity* (Belfast: Institute of Irish Studies, Queen's University of Belfast).

McCart, J. (1985) 'Accommodation for Travelling People in Northern Ireland', unpublished paper.

McCarthy, P. (1994) 'The Sub-Culture of Poverty Re-considered', in McCann, M., Ó Siocháin, S. and Ruane, J. (eds) *Irish Travellers: Culture and Ethnicity* (Belfast: Institute of Irish Studies, Queen's University of Belfast).

McCormack, V. (1998) 'Employment Equality: Government Retreats from SACHR Blueprint for Change', *Just News*, April, vol. 13, no. 4.

McCrudden, C. (1996) *Mainstreaming Fairness? A discussion paper on 'Policy Appraisal and Fair Treatment'* (Belfast: CAJ).

McDonagh, M. *et al.* (1988) *Pride and Prejudice – The Case of the Travellers* (Dublin: Navan Travellers Committee).

—— (1998) *Benchmarks for Change: Mainstreaming Fairness In The Governance of Northern Ireland* (Belfast: CAJ).

McDonagh, M. and McVeigh, R. (1996a) *Minceir Neeja In The Thome Munkra* (Belfast: BTEDG).

—— (1996b) *Irish Travellers in the USA* (Belfast: BTEDG).

MacEwen, M. (1995*) Tackling Racism in Europe: An Examination of Anti-Discrimination Law in Practice* (Oxford and Washington, DC: Berg).

McGill, P. (1996) *Missing the Target: a Critique of Government Policy on Targeting Social Need in Northern Ireland* (Belfast: NICVA).

McGovern, D. and Cope, R.V. (1987) 'First Psychiatric Admission Rates of First and Second Generation Afro-Caribbeans', *Social Psychiatry*, vol. 22, 139–49.

McKnight, E. (1993) 'The 'Special Needs' of Chinese Children and the Proposed Children (NI) Order', *ChildCare News*, vol. 11, no. 3, January–February (Belfast: ChildCare).

—— (1994) *Racism (Northern Ireland)*, Equality in Education Conference Report (Belfast: Co-Operation North).

McVeigh, R. (1990) *Racism and Sectarianism: A Tottenham/West Belfast Comparison*, unpublished PhD. thesis, Department of Social Studies, Queen's University of Belfast.

—— (1992a) 'The Specificity of Irish Racism', *Race and Class*, vol. 33, no. 4.

—— (1992b) *Racism and Travelling People in Northern Ireland* Paper for Standing Advisory Commission on Human Rights, 17th Annual Report (London: HMSO).

—— (1996) *The Radicalization of Irishness: Racism and anti-racism in Ireland*, Pamphlet no. 3 'Ireland: Between Two Worlds' Series (Belfast: CRD).

—— (1997a) 'Ethnic Minorities and the "Numbers Game"', *Just News*, vol. 12, no. 3.

—— (1997b) *Minority Ethnic Groups and Racism*, Centre for Research and Documentation (CRD) north/south factsheet series, series no. 5 (Belfast: CRD).

—— (1997c) 'Theorising Sedentarism: the roots of anti-nomadism', in Acton, T. (ed.) *Gypsy Politics and Traveller Identity* (Hatfield: University Hertfordshire Press).

—— (1998) 'Theorising the Racism/Sectarianism Interface', in Miller, D. (ed.) *Rethinking Northern Ireland: Culture, Ideology and Colonialism* (London: Longman).

Malinverni, G. (1991) 'The draft Convention for the Protection of Minorities/Proposal of the European Commission for Democracy through Law', *Human Rights Law Journal*, vol. 12, 265–73.

Mann-Kler, D. (1997) *Out of the Shadows: An Action Research Report into Families, Racism and Exclusion in Northern Ireland* (Belfast: Barnardos, Belfast Travellers' Education and Development Group, Committee on the Administration of Justice, Chinese Welfare Association, Craigavon Asian Women and Children's Association, Indian Community Centre, Northern Ireland Council for Ethnic Minorities, Save the Children).

Marger, M. (1989) 'Asians in the Northern Ireland Economy', *New Community*, vol. 15, no. 2, 203–10.

Marie, J-B. (1996) 'International instruments relating to human rights/classification and status of ratifications as of 1 January 1996', *Human Rights Law Journal*, vol. 17, 61–77.

Marks, S. (1992) 'The Complaint Procedure of the United Nations Educational, Scientific and Cultural Organization', in Hannum, H. (ed.) *Guide to International Human Rights Practice*, 2nd edition, (Philadelphia: University of Pennsylvania Press) 86–98.

Marmot, M.G. and McDowell, M.E. (1986) 'Mortality Decline and Widening Social Inequalities', *Lancet*, vol. 2, 274–6.

——, Aldestein, A.M. and Bulusu, L. (1984) *Immigrant Mortality in England and Wales 1970–78: Causes of Death by Country of Birth* (London: HMSO).

Mason, C. (1991) 'Working in a Divided Community', *Nursing Standard*, vol. 6, no. 11, 20–3.

Mason, D. (1995) *Race and Ethnicity in Modern Britain* (Oxford: Oxford University Press).

Mayall, D. (1995) *English Gypsies and State Policies* (Hatfield: University of Hertfordshire Press).

Merrill, J. and Owens, J. (1986) 'Ethnic Differences in Self-Poisoning: a Comparison of Asian and White Groups', *British Journal of Psychiatry*, vol. 148, 708–12.

Miles, R. (1986) 'Labour, Migration, Racism, and Capital Accumulation in Western Europe', *Capital and Class*, vol. 28, 49–86.

—— (1989) *Racism* (London: Routledge).

Ministry of Home Affairs (1948) *Report of Committee on Gypsies and Like Itinerants* (Belfast: HMSO).

—— (1955) *Report on 'Itinerant Gypsies'* (Belfast: HMSO).

Modeen, T. (1969) *The International Protection of National Minorities in Europe* (Abo, Finland: Abo Akademi).

Modood, T. (1994) *Racial Equality: Colour, Culture and Justice* (London: IPPR).

——, Beishon, S. and Virdee, S. (1994) *Changing Ethnic Identities* (London: PSI).

Moore, R., Harrisson, S., Mason, C. and Orr, J. (1996) *An Exploration of Inequalities in Health and Assessment of Related Need in Two Northern Ireland Communities* (Belfast: DHSS).

Multi–cultural Resource Centre (MCRC) (1994) *Estimated Ethnic Minority Population in Northern Ireland* (Belfast: MCRC).

—— (1996) *Caring for Children from Ethnic Minorities in Northern Ireland* (Belfast: Bryson House).

Murphy, K. (1990) 'Nurses' Experiences of Caring for Ethnic Minority Clients', unpublished MSc dissertation, King's College, London.

—— and Macleod Clark, J. (1993) 'Nurses' Experiences of Caring for Ethnic Minority Clients', *Journal of Advanced Nursing*, vol. 18, 442–50.

National Health Service Management Executive (NHSME) (1993) *Minority Ethnic Staff in the NHS: A Programme of Action* (Lancashire: NHSME).

—— (1994a) *Ethnic Group Data Collection*, EL(94)77 (London: NHSME).

—— (1994b) *Planning and Policy Guidance 1994/5*, EL(93)54 (London: NHSME).

News Letter (1996) 'Nazi-type symbols at soccer games: Hate gospel targets fans', 6 March.

—— (1997) 'Hatred flag displayed by Linfield fans', 11 March.

Ní Shúinéar, S. (1944) 'Irish Travellers, Ethnicity and the Origins Question', in McCann, M., Ó Síocháin, S. and Ruane, J. (eds) *Irish Travellers: Culture and Ethnicity* (Belfast: Institute of Irish Studies, Queen's University of Belfast).

Noonan, P. (1994) *Travelling People in West Belfast* (ed. Rolston, B.) (Belfast: Save the Children).

Northern Health and Social Services Board (NHSSB) (1995) *First steps – A Survey of the Health and Social Care Needs of the Chinese Population in the Northern Health and Social Services Board* (Ballymena: NHSSB).

Northern Ireland Anti-Poverty Network (NIAPN) (1994) *Racism and Poverty* (Belfast: NIAPN).

Northern Ireland Commissioner for Complaints (1984) *Annual Report for 1983* (Belfast: HMSO).

Northern Ireland Committee (Irish Congress of Trade Unions) (NIC/ICTU) (1993) *Comments on the CCRU's Consultative Paper on Race Relations in Northern Ireland in Northern Ireland*, April.

Northern Ireland Co-Ordinating Committee on Social Problems (1981) *Services for Travelling People in Northern Ireland* (publisher unknown).

Northern Ireland Council for Ethnic Minorities (NICEM) (1996a) *Mission Statement* (Belfast: NICEM).

—— (1996b) Conference on 'Identifying and Addressing the Health and Social Needs of Ethnic Minorities in Northern Ireland', Belfast, November.

Northern Ireland Housing Executive (NIHE) (1995) *Housing Needs of the Chinese Community* (Belfast: NIHE).

Northern Ireland Women's Coalition (NIWC) (1996a) *Manifesto Election Communication* (Forum Election).

—— (1996b) *Community Relations*, NIWC policy paper.

—— (1996c) *Equity*, NIWC policy paper.

—— (1996d) *Health*, NIWC policy paper.

—— (1996e) *Human Rights*, NIWC policy paper.

—— (1996f) *Inclusion and Accommodation*, NIWC policy paper.

Nuffield Foundation (1981) *Teaching Chinese Children, A Teacher's Guide* (Oxford: Nuffield Foundation).

Nursing Standard (1996) 'Nurse wins Claim For Racial Discrimination', vol. 11, no. 7, 8.

Ó Broin, E. (1997) 'Living Between Green and Orange: Ethnic Minorities in the North of Ireland', in Crowley, E. and MacLaughlin, J. (eds) *Under the Belly of the Tiger: Class, Race, Identity and Culture in the Global Ireland* (Dublin: Irish Reporter Publications).

O'Clery, C. (1987) *Phrases Make History Here: Political Quotations on Ireland* (Dublin: O'Brien).

O'Connell, J. (1994a) *Reach Out* (Dublin: Pavee Point Publications).

—— (1994b) 'Ethnicity and Irish Travellers', in McCann, M., Ó Síocháin, S. and Ruane, J. (eds) *Irish Travellers: Culture and Ethnicity* (Belfast: Institute of Irish Studies, Queen's University of Belfast).

O'Leary, R. (1990) *A report on social work education provision in response to the needs of social workers, educationalists and the minority ethnic communities in Northern Ireland* (Belfast: Bryson House).

Office for Public Management (OPM) (1996) *Responding to Diversity. A Study of Commissioning Issues and Good Practice in Purchasing Minority Health* (London: OPM).

Office of Population, Census and Surveys (1995) *Regional Trends 1995* (London: HMSO).

Okely, J. (1983) *The Traveller Gypsies* (Cambridge: Cambridge University Press).

Ó Rian, G. (1995) 'Why Cultural Action?', in Ní Laodhóg, N. (ed.) *A Heritage Ahead – Cultural Action and Travellers* (Dublin: Pavee Point Publications).

Osborne, B. (1996) *A Policy Appraisal and Fair Treatment (PAFT) Appraisal for the Acute Hospitals Reorganisation Project in Relation to 'In Shape For the Future', 'Singular Service' and 'Seeking Balance'* (Jordanstown: University of Ulster).

Osborne, R. *et al.* (1996) 'The implementation of PAFT guidelines in Northern Ireland', in McLaughlin, E. and Quirk, P. (eds) *Policy Aspects of Employment Equality in Northern Ireland* (Belfast: SACHR).

Owen, D. (1994) *South Asian People in Great Britain: Social and Economic Circumstances.* NEMDA 1991 Census Statistical Paper no. 7 (Coventry: Centre for Ethnic Relations, University of Warwick).

Oyediran, J. (1992) 'The UK's Compliance with Article 4 of the International Convention on the Elimination of all Forms of Racial Discrimination', in Coliver, S. (ed.) *Striking the Balance: Hate Speech, Freedom of Expression and Non-Discrimination* (London: Article 19).

Pang, L.C. (1991) *Sociological Study of Chinese Immigrants in Belfast*, unpublished BSc dissertation, University of Ulster, Jordanstown.

Paris, C., Maginn, P. and Gray, P. (1995a) *A Review of Policies Affecting Travellers in Northern Ireland* (Derry: Housing Research Centre, Magee College, University of Ulster).

—— (1995b) *Review of Policies affecting Travellers* (Belfast: DOE).

Payne, D. (1995) 'Unequal Treatment', *Nursing Times*, vol. 91, no. 46, 16–17.

Peach, C. (ed.) (1996) *Ethnicity in the 1991 Census. Volume Two. The ethnic minority populations in Great Britain* (London: HMSO).

Police Authority for Northern Ireland (PANI) (1995) *'Everyone's Police': A Partnership for Change.* A Report on a Community Consultation undertaken by the Police Authority for Northern Ireland in 1995 (Belfast: PANI).

—— (1997) *Listening to the Community: Working with the RUC* (Belfast: PANI).

Policy Planning and Research Unit (PPRU) (1995) *Northern Ireland Annual Abstract of Statistics* (Belfast: PPRU).

Porter, S. (1993) 'Critical Realist Ethnography: the Case of Racism and Professionalism in a Medical Setting', *Sociology*, vol. 27, no. 4, 591–609.

Progressive Unionist Party of Northern Ireland (1997) *Manifesto* (General Election).

Race Relations (Northern Ireland) Order (1996) (Belfast: Department of Economic Development).

Rathwell, T. and Phillips, D. (1986) *Health, Race and Ethnicity* (London: Croom Helm).

Rawlings-Anderson, K. (1992) *Nurses' Experience of Caring For Ethnic Minority Clients*, unpublished MSc dissertation, King's College, London.

Robinson, V. (1996) 'The Indians: onward and upward', in Peach, C. (ed.) *Ethnicity in the 1991 Census. Volume Two. The ethnic minority populations in Great Britain* (London: HMSO).

Rodley, N. (1995) 'Conceptual Problems in the Protection of Minorities: International Legal Developments', *Human Rights Quarterly*, vol. 17, 48–71.

Rolston, B. (1991) 'News Fit to Print: Belfast's Daily Newspapers', in Rolston, B. (ed.) *The Media and Northern Ireland: Covering the Troubles* (Basingstoke: Macmillan).

Rosas, A. (1993) 'The Protection of Minorities in Europe: A General Overview', in Packer, J. and Myntti, K. (eds) *The Protection of Ethnic and Linguistic Minorities in Europe* (Abo, Finland: Abo Akademi).

Ross, H. (1998) 'A Fragment of the Scattered House of Israel', *Causeway*, vol. 5, no. 1, spring, 29–32.

Royal Ulster Constabulary (RUC) (1996) *Chief Constable's Annual Report 1995* (Belfast: RUC).

—— (1997) *Chief Constable's Annual Report 1996* (Belfast: RUC).

Runnymede Trust (1986) *The Chinese Community in Britain* (The Home Affairs Committee Report in Context) (London: Runnymede Trust Research Report).

Ryan, M. (n.d.) *Small world: A handbook on introducing world religions in the primary school* (Belfast: Stranmillis College).

Said, E.W. (1978) *Orientalism: Western Concepts of the Orient* (Harmondsworth: Penguin, 1995).

Sciarra, S. (1995) 'European Social Policy and Labour Law – Challenges and Perspectives', *Collected Courses of the Academy of European Law*, vol. IV, 301–340.

Sciortino, G. (1991) 'Immigration into Europe and public policy: do stops really work?', *New Community*, vol. 18, 89–99.

Scope (1980) 'Travelling People', no. 36, September.

—— (1986) 'Travellers Evicted in Downpatrick', No. 95, July.

Secretary of State for Northern Ireland (1998) *Partnership for Equality: The Government's proposals for future legislation and policies on Employment Equality in Northern Ireland*, Cm 3890 (White Paper), March (London: HMSO).

Shachter, J. (1945) *The Belfast Chevra Gemorra* (Belfast: The Narod Press).

Shanks, M. (1977) *European Social Policy, Today and Tomorrow* (Oxford: Pergamon Press).

Shaw, A. (1988) *A Pakistani community in Britain* (Oxford: Blackwell).

Sharma, S. (1997) Interview, *Hearts and Minds*, BBC TV, 16 October.

Sheldon, T. and Parker, H. (1992) 'The Use of "Ethnicity" and "Race" in Health research: a Cautionary Note', in Ahmad, W. (ed.) *The Politics of 'Race' and Health* (Bradford: Race Relations Research Unit, University of Bradford).

Sibley, D. (1987) 'Racism and settlement policy – the state's response to a semi-nomadic minority', in Jackson, P. (ed.) *Race and Racism: Essays in Social Geography* (London: Allen and Unwin).

Simpson, G.E. and Yinger, J.M. (1972) *Racial and Cultural Minorities: An Analysis of Prejudice and Discrimination* (New York: Harper and Row).

Sinn Féin (1996) *Sinn Féin Policy Document*, August.

Smaje, C. (1995) 'True Colours', *Health Service Journal*, 26 January, 28–9.

Smith, D.J. (1977) *Racial Disadvantage in Britain. The PEP Report* (Harmondsworth: Penguin).

Social Democratic and Labour Party (SDLP) (1997) *Real Leadership Real Peace*, Manifesto: Westminster Parliamentary Election, 1 May.

Sohn, L.B. and Buergenthal, T. (1973) *International Protection of Human Rights* (Indianapolis: Bobbs-Merrill Co. Inc.).

Solomos, J. (1993) *Race and Racism in Britain*, 2nd edition (Basingstoke: Macmillan).

Spencer, M. (1995) *States of Injustice – a guide to human rights and civil liberties in the European Union* (London: Pluto Press).

Standing Advisory Commission on Human Rights (SACHR) (1984) *Report for 1983–84* (London: HMSO).

—— (1987) *Report for 1985–86* (London: HMSO).

—— (1990) *Religious and Political Discrimination and Equality of Opportunity in Northern Ireland* (London: HMSO).

—— (1991) *Report for 1990–91* (London: HMSO).

—— (1992) *Report for 1991–92* (London: HMSO).

—— (1993) *Report for 1992–93* (London: HMSO).

—— (1997a) *Employment Equality: Building for the Future*, Cm 3684, June (London: HMSO).

—— (1997b) *Letter of response to the Department of the Environment concerning the Draft*, 2 May.

Starting Line Group (1996) 'Signatories of the Starting Point' (Brussels: Starting Line Group).

Stephenson, J. (1997) Interview, *Hearts and Minds*, BBC TV, 16 October.

Stringer, P. (1992) *Health Inequalities, Religious Affiliation and Rural–Urban status* (Belfast: DHSS).

Sugar, R. (1990) 'Millisle Farm', *The Jewish Monthly*, October 1990, 26–9 (Washington, DC: B'nai Brith).

Sunday Life (1995) 'Nazis launch anti-Jew hate campaign', 29 January.

Swepston, L. (1992) 'Human Rights Complaint Procedures of the International Labour Organisation' in Hannum, H. (ed.) *Guide to International Human Rights Practice*, 2nd edition, (Philadelphia: University of Pennsylvania Press) 99–116.

Tan, S.P. (1983) *Food Ideology and the Food Habits of the Chinese Immigrants in London and the Growth of Their Young Children. Report of a Survey* (London: School of Hygiene and Tropical Medicine).

Taylor, M.J. (1987) *Chinese pupils in Britain, A review of research into the education of pupils of Chinese origin* (London: Windsor Nfer-Nelson).

The Gypsies Bill (Northern Ireland) 1950.

The Northern Ireland Census 1991 Summary Report (Belfast: HMSO).

Thornberry, P. (1991a) *Minorities and Human Rights Law* (London: Minority Rights Group).

—— (1991b) *International Law and the Rights of Minorities* (Oxford: Clarendon Press).

Townsend, P., Davidson, N. and Whitehead, M. (1992) *Inequalities in Health: the Black Report – the Health Divide* (London: Penguin).

Trident Housing Association (1995) *Annual Report and Accounts* (Birmingham: Trident).

Troyna, Barry (1981) *Public Awareness and the Media: A Story of Reporting on Race* (London: CRE).

Tuchman, G. (1978) *Making News: A Study in the Construction of Reality* (New York: Free Press).

Tung Sing Housing Association (1996) *Annual Report and Accounts* (Manchester: Tung Sing).

Ulster Unionist Party (UUP) (1993) *Race Relations in Northern Ireland*, March.

—— (1997) *Secure the Union, Build your future*, The Ulster Unionist Party: General Election Manifesto, 1 May.

United Nations (1965) *International Convention on the Elimination of All Forms of Racial Discrimination* (Geneva: Anti-Racism Information Service).

—— (1992) *Draft Declaration on the rights of persons belonging to national ethnic, religious, and linguistic minorities* (Geneva: UN).

van Dijk, T.A. (1987) *Communicating Racism: Ethnic Prejudice in Thought and Talk* (Newbury Park, CA: Sage).

—— (1988) *News Analysis: Case Studies of International and National News in the Press* (Hillsdale, NJ: Lawrence Erlbaum Associates).

—— (1991) *Racism and the Press* (London: Routledge).

—— (1993a) *Elite Discourse and Racism* (Newbury Park, CA: Sage).

—— (1993b) 'Analysing Racism through Discourse Analysis: Some Methodological Reflections', in Stanfield, J.H. II and Dennis, R.M. (eds) *Race and Ethnicity in Research Methods* (Newbury Park, CA: Sage).

Vertovec, S. (1996) 'Multiculturalism, culturalism and public incorporation', *Ethnic and Racial Studies*, vol. 19, no. 1, 49–69.

Wallace, R. (1997) *International Human Rights: Text and Materials* (London: Sweet and Maxwell).

Walmsley, D. (1994) 'Ethnic Minorities at the Mercy of Racists', *Belfast Telegraph*, 27 January.

Watson, A. (1989) 'Chinese Children in Northern Ireland', *ChildCare News*, vol. 10 (Belfast: ChildCare).

―― (1993) *The Chinese Community in Northern Ireland*, unpublished CQSW dissertation, University of Ulster, Jordanstown.

―― (1996) 'Barnardos Chinese Health Project', speaking at conference '*Speaking Out*, Identifying and Addressing the Health and Social Needs of Ethnic Minorities in Northern Ireland', Belfast, November.

Watson, H. (1994) 'Women and the veil: personal responses to global process', in Ahmed, A.S. and Donnan, H. (eds) *Islam, globalization and postmodernity* (London: Routledge).

Watt, I.S. (1991) *The Health Needs of the Chinese Community in Kingston-upon-Hull*, MPH dissertation (Hull: Academic Unit of Public Health Medicine).

Webber, F. (1991) 'From ethnocentrism to Euro–racism', *Race and Class*, vol. 32, 11–17.

Wedderburn Tate, C. (1996) 'All Talk and No Action', *Nursing Management*, vol. 3, no. 5, 7.

Werbner, P. (1984) 'Business on trust: Pakistani entrepreneurship in the Manchester garment trade', in Ward, R. and Jenkins, R. (eds), *Ethnic communities in business: Strategies for economic survival* (Cambridge: Cambridge University Press).

―― (1990a) *The migration process: Capital, gifts and offerings among British Pakistanis* (Oxford: Berg).

―― (1990b) 'Manchester Pakistanis: division and unity', in Clarke, C., Peach, C. and Vertovec, S. (eds) *South Asians overseas: migration and ethnicity* (Cambridge: Cambridge University Press).

―― (1991) 'The fiction of unity in ethnic politics: Aspects of representation and the state among British Pakistanis', in Werbner, P. and Anwar, M. (eds) *Black and ethnic leaderships in Britain* (London: Routledge).

White, C. (1997) 'Race Discrimination', in Dickson, B. (ed.) *Civil Liberties in Northern Ireland*, 3rd edition (Belfast: CAJ).

Wilson C.C., II and Gutiérrez, F. (1995) *Race, Multiculturalism, and the Media: From Mass to Class Communication*, 2nd edition (Thousand Oaks, CA: Sage).

Workers Party (1996) *Workers Party Candidates Challenge Racism and Sectarianism*, Election Media Release, 19 May.

World Health Organization (WHO) (1985) *Targets for Health for All: Targets in Support of the European Regional Strategy for Health For All* (Copenhagen: WHO).

Wrench, J. (1996) *Preventing Racism at the Workplace – a report on 16 countries* (Luxembourg: OOPEC).

Wright, J. (1996) 'The OSCE and the Protection of Minority Rights', *Human Rights Law Quarterly*, vol. 18, 190–205.

Yau, H.L. (1996) *A Guide for Chinese Residents in the UK* (Hong Kong: Sing Tao Publications).

Yu, P. (1994) 'From Social Alienation to Social Deprivation – A Response from the Chinese Community', in *Racism and Poverty Seminar Report,* Northern Ireland Anti-Poverty Network (Belfast: Northern Ireland Anti-Poverty Network/Northern Ireland Council for Voluntary Action).

Index

Index by Auriol Griffith-Jones